UNION MERGERS
IN HARD TIMES

For Sally & Reeve, July 1997
my two good friends — and a
great couple.
With love,
Gary

Union Mergers
in Hard Times

The View from Five Countries

Gary N. Chaison

ILR Press AN IMPRINT OF
Cornell University Press
ITHACA AND LONDON

Cornell International Industrial and Labor Relations Report No. 31

First published 1996 by Cornell University Press.

Printed in the United States of America

 This book is printed on Lyons Fall Turin Book, a paper that is acid-free and totally chlorine-free.

Library of Congress Cataloging-in-Publication Data

Chaison, Gary N.
    Union mergers in hard times : the view from five countries / Gary N. Chaison.
        p.   cm.—(Cornell international industrial and labor relations reports ; no. 31)
    Includes bibliographical references and index.
    ISBN 0-8014-3330-4 (cloth : alk. paper).—ISBN 0-8014-8380-8 (paper : alk. paper)
        1. Trade-unions—Mergers—Case studies.   I. Title.   II. Series.
HD6490.C62C43   1996
331.87—dc20   96-28101

To Joanne

Contents

Tables

Figures

Acknowledgments

When I first wrote about union mergers twenty-five years ago, I soon realized how dependent I was on the generosity of others. This is a complex and sometimes perplexing topic. Fortunately, union officers and staff were willing to share details on merger negotiations and outcomes, industrial relations scholars described the economic and historical contexts of mergers, and government officials and reference librarians guided me to vast amounts of printed information. I tried to express appropriate gratitude when I wrote my first book on union mergers, an analysis of the merger causes and outcomes in the United States, published in 1986. Here I examine union mergers not just in the United States but in four other countries as well, and I find that my debt is far greater.

First, I thank the many union officers and staff members who agreed to lengthy interviews and so generously shared their experiences and insights. I cannot name them in the text because it was understood that their comments were not to be presented with attribution. To each, I am most grateful.

In the United States, I benefited tremendously from discussions with Rudy Oswald of the AFL-CIO, Howard Forman of the United Food and Commercial Workers, Pat Thomas of the Service Employees, Phil Ray of the American Federation of State, County and Municipal Employees, and George Kohl of the Communications Workers. In Canada, I was fortunate to meet with Jim Hunter and Kevin Collins of the Canadian Brotherhood of Railway, Transport and General Workers, Derek Fudge of the National Union of Public and General Employees, Larry Katz of the Canadian Union of Public Employees, Joe Hanefin of the Communications, Energy and Paperworkers Union, and Bill Chedord of the Canadian Labour Congress. I learned of the intricacies of some landmark mergers and the important union merger tradition in Britain from Gavin Laird of the Amalgamated Engineering and Electrical Union, Phil Wyatt of the General, Municipal, Boilermakers, Peter Morris of Unison, Joe Irvin and Bernard Harbor of the Transport and General Workers, and Bryan Ward of the Trades Union Congress.

Economic attachés at embassies in Washington agreed to meet with me and discuss the most recent trends in their countries. David Imber of the Australian Embassy and Rob Moore-Jones of the New Zealand Embassy gave expert briefings on two very complicated and quickly changing labor relations systems. My special thanks to John Russell of the British Embassy for a pair of interviews in which he so clearly explained the impact of the recent government policies on the labor movement and labor–management relations.

Several government officials and staff specialists generously shared their research findings and impressions of the union merger scene. My thanks to Lisa Williamson of the United States Bureau of Labor Statistics, and, in Britain, to Ted Whybrew and Bernard Price of the Certification Office for Trade Unions and Employers' Associations, Bill Hawes of the Advisory Conciliation and Arbitration Service, and Andrew Hardman and Bernard Carter of the Industrial Relations Branch of the Employment Department. Emma Waterland, also of the International Relations Branch was extremely considerate and efficient when she arranged my itinerary in Britain.

It has always seemed to me that the considerable contributions of librarians are taken for granted by researchers. Is this because we feel that librarians are only doing their jobs when they help us? Or perhaps we are reluctant to acknowledge publicly how little we could do without them as our guides. Whatever the reason, the very least I can do is to acknowledge that this book could not have been written without the assistance of many skilled and dedicated librarians. It would be impossible to thank each by name, for I am indebted to so many. I offer a warm thank you to the reference librarians at the British Library in London, the National Library of Canada in Ottawa, the libraries of the Bureau of National Affairs and the Canadian Embassy, both in Washington, D.C., the library of Labour

Canada in Hull, Quebec, and the library of the Canada Labour Relations Board in Ottawa. All the librarians at Clark University's Goddard Library were, as always, first-rate, but I am particularly indebted to the two members of the interlibrary loan staff. Ed McDermott patiently processed and often corrected what must have seemed like an endless stream of requests. Sue Wheeler was always kind and always right.

My research on union mergers has benefited from discussions with numerous colleagues over the years. A few must be thanked individually. Joe Rose of McMaster University could always be relied on for information and impressions about the latest happenings in Canada; far more important, through our research collaboration over more than two decades he has set a standard for rigorous analysis and clear writing that I try to follow when I work solo. Raymond Harbridge of Victoria University of Wellington so kindly shared his vast knowledge of the tumultuous labor relations scene in New Zealand. At crucial junctures in my research, I received important information on Australian industrial relations from Len Pullin of Monash University, and Pat Wright of the University of Adelaide. Pradeep Kumar of Queen's University was a fountain of information about the Canadian unions and provided invaluable assistance in arranging interviews. Kathy Gill of the Bureau of National Affairs was a huge help, introducing me to her organization's perceptive and experienced reporters and its excellent library. Finally, special thanks to my Swedish colleagues—Bengt Abrahamsson, Kristina Ahlen, Magnus Sverke, and Arne Eriksson—whose work on union structure convinced me that it was high time to look at union mergers from an international perspective. Of course, all the usual caveats apply; readers are reminded that despite the help from my colleagues, I alone am responsible for any errors in fact or interpretation.

I have also benefited from discussions with participants too numerous to mention at symposia where I presented papers on union mergers. These include those attending the Fourth Annual Meeting of the National Union Administrators' Group (1993) at the AFL-CIO's Meany Center, Silver Springs, Maryland, and the first and the second Symposium on Emerging Union Structures in Worcester, Massachusetts (1992), and Stockholm, Sweden (1995).

I have had many bright and energetic research assistants over the years; my thanks to Glen DeConza, Olie Eichler, Joyce Mongeaux, and Maureen Healy. Lisa Beittel and Pooja Subharwal did some remarkable detective work, tracking down information that was often obscure or inaccurately cited, or both.

Jan Perry of Clark University's Graduate School of Management typed this manuscript with her usual skill and good humor. She never complained, at least not to me, about my cryptic handwriting and my never-ending revisions. My thanks to Diane Adams, also of Clark's School of Management, for responding with great expertise and even greater patience to all of my questions on matters of grammar and style, no matter how basic or arcane.

I am grateful for research grants from the Canadian Studies Faculty Research Program at the Canadian Embassy in Washington, D.C., and the Clark University Academic Development Fund. Clark's Graduate School of Management provided generous supplemental travel funds.

Two anonymous reviewers of the manuscript raised important issues, and I appreciate the careful reading they gave it. I also benefited a great deal from the suggestions of two reviewers who read the proposal for this study.

My thanks to the editorial staff of Cornell University Press for their fine work. Craig Triplett, copyeditor, reviewed the manuscript with exceptional care, and Carol Betsch, senior manuscript editor, so patiently and skillfully guided the manuscript to publication.

People who have worked with my editor, Fran Benson, know that she is one of the best in the business. By her kindness, concern, and expertise, she has shown me why she is such a widely respected and sought-after editor. I thank her for believing that I could and should do this project.

In my 1986 book, I thanked my wife, Joanne Danaher Chaison, for her assistance and support in the preparation of the manuscript and for ''much more.'' Ten years later and with deep appreciation, I can only add another ''much'' to ''much more.'' Page limitations and my limitations as a writer prevent me from fully expressing my debt to Joanne. With great pride and boundless affection, I dedicate this book to her.

G. N. C.

Acronyms

ACTU	Australian Council of Trade Unions
ACTWU	Amalgamated Clothing and Textile Workers Union
AEEU	Amalgamated Engineering and Electrical Union
AEU	Amalgamated Engineering Union
AFL-CIO	American Federation of Labor and Congress of Industrial Organizations
AFSCME	American Federation of State, County and Municipal Employees
AFT	American Federation of Teachers
APEX	Association of Professional, Executive, Clerical and Computer Staffs
ASU	Australian Municipal, Administrative, Clerical and Services Union
ATWU	Amalgamated Textile Workers Union
CAW	Canadian Automobile Workers [officially National Automobile, Aerospace and Agricultural Implement Workers of Canada]
CBC	Canadian Broadcasting Company
CBRT&GW	Canadian Brotherhood of Railway, Transport and General Workers
CEP	Communications, Energy and Paperworkers Union of Canada
CIRA	California Intern and Residents Association

CLC	Canadian Labour Congress
CLRB	Canadian Labour Relations Board
COHSE	Confederation of Health Service Employees
CUPE	Canadian Union of Public Employees
CUPW	Canadian Union of Postal Workers
CWA	Communications Workers of America
DAGWU	Distribution and General Workers Union
EETPU	Electrical, Electronic, Telecommunication and Plumbing Union
FFAW	Fishermen, Food and Allied Workers
FTAT	Furniture, Timber and Allied Trades Union
GCIU	Graphic Communications International Union
GMB	General, Municipal, Boilermakers
IAM	International Association of Machinists
ILGWU	International Ladies Garment Workers Union
ILO	International Labour Organization
IPCS	Institute of Professional Civil Servants
ITU	International Typographical Union
LCUC	Letter Carriers Union of Canada
NALGO	National and Local Government Officers Association
NDP	New Democratic Party
NEA	National Education Association
NLRB	National Labor Relations Board
NUHHCE	National Union of Hospital and Health Care Employees
NUPE	National Union of Public Employees
NZCTU	New Zealand Council of Trade Unions
OECD	Organization for Economic Cooperation and Development
PSAC	Public Service Alliance of Canada
PSU	Public Sector Union
RWDSU	Retail, Wholesale and Department Store Union
SEIU	Service Employees International Union
SFPOA	San Francisco Police Officers Association
TASS	Technical, Administrative and Supervisory Section of the Engineering Amalgamated Union
TGWU	Transport and General Workers Union
TUC	Trades Union Congress
UCATT	Union of Construction, Allied Trades and Technicians
UFCW	United Food and Commercial Workers
UNITE	Union of Needletrades, Industrial and Textile Employees

UNION MERGERS
IN HARD TIMES

CHAPTER 1

Introduction:
The Union Merger Process

The largest unions in one country were formed by mergers; most of the smallest unions in another country disbanded because of mergers; the most militant union in another grew through mergers; and, in still another country, nearly all unions, large and small, merged. All of these events occurred since 1980. Clearly, something important is happening—labor movements are being transformed and the instrument for this transformation is the union merger.

The recent flurry of merger activity and the prominence of many newly merged unions makes me ask: How and why do labor unions merge in hard times? What role do mergers play in the unions' strategies to deal with membership losses, management opposition, and hostile governments? Are there distinctive national profiles of union mergers? What causes merger waves?

I answer these questions by examining merger trends in five countries: the United States, Canada, Great Britain, Australia, and New Zealand. My purpose is not to test a theory of union mergers or to report on the intricacies and intrigues of merger negotiations and postmerger accommodations; I did this in a monograph published in 1986. Rather, I develop national profiles of merger activity and I trace these to changes in economies, legislation, union–management relations, and the evolution of worker representation since 1980.

I try to avoid treating mergers abstractly as simple transactions between organizations, or dwelling on the details of a few selected mergers and assuming that general premises will somehow emerge from lengthy case studies. Instead, I examine the national character of mergers as shaped by the surrounding industrial relations systems, particularly forces affecting union growth and influence. For each of the five countries, I examine the merger record since 1980, discuss some landmark mergers or merger forms to illustrate prominent reasons for mergers and barriers to mergers, and appraise the possibilities of merger waves.

There are several reasons why I compare mergers in the United States, Canada, Great Britain, Australia and New Zealand. First, each country's labor movement is free of domination by the government or political parties (Martin 1989). Labor unions function primarily as worker representatives by negotiating collective agreements, then administering and enforcing them at workplaces. Consequently, union officers can freely select merger partners, initiate merger negotiations, jointly decide on merger terms. Ultimately, union members are asked to accept or reject their officers' merger proposals. Government officials and party functionaries cannot compel union mergers; there are no arranged marriages between unions. As I explain in later chapters, this feature—the voluntary nature of mergers—affects merger frequency, the compromises reached in merger negotiations, and the ability of mergers to reform union structure in desired directions.

Second, since the early 1980s, unions in the five countries have seen hard times, in other words, the move from stable to turbulent labor relations. This change is most evident in the symptoms of union decline—sustained membership losses, meager organizing gains, and diminished influence in bargaining and politics.

During the major recessions of the early 1980s and 1990s, and in the years after, unemployment was high and real wages fell. As a result unions in the five countries had to moderate their wage and benefit demands, and modify work rules. Unionized employers competed with low-cost foreign and domestic producers who often operated without unions. In their effort to compete by increasing productivity and lowering labor costs, employers sought both to weaken the existing unions and to keep them from organizing nonunion facilities.

With the decline in manufacturing and growth of the service sector, employment shifted from heavily unionized to lesser unionized industries. Most unions were not equal to the new organizing task, lacking the techniques, resources, or the determination for massive membership recruitment in expanding areas. Organizing was becoming more difficult because, compared with their blue-collar predecessors, the new entrants to the workforce tended to be better educated, had less psychological attachment to their places of employment, and more often worked part-time or in temporary positions. To these workers, the unions' traditional call to collective action for better wages and benefits had less appeal (Griffin, McCammon, and Botsko 1990; Clarke and Niland 1991; Blanchflower and Freeman 1992). Although changes in the levels of union membership varied in each of the five countries, most unions recognized that significant growth was improbable in the near future. In the absence of organizing drives of heroic proportions, unions could not offset the membership lost through declining employment.

At the same time, new technologies increased the efficiency of small-scale production facilities. This, combined with management's intense pursuit of greater productivity, led to the decentralization of collective bargaining. Negotiations shifted from multi-employer or industrywide levels to the level of the single employer, or from the multiplant to single-plant units. Effective union representation demanded greater skill and participation from local officers and staff (Katz 1993; Niland 1994). Persons whose job once was to enforce and interpret collective agreements or national wage settlements now found they had to negotiate them. New staffing and training requirements drained union resources, and national officers became heavily involved in coordinating lower-level negotiations.

Finally, during the recent hard times, the union movements of each of the five countries were highly fragmented, that is, composed of many small unions (table 1). We should keep in mind that only gross comparisons can be made across countries because of differences in record keeping (Chaison and Rose 1991b). Also, the figures for the United States and Canada exclude small regional and single-company unions because data is unavailable, but such unions are included in the tabulations for Great Britain, Australia, and New Zealand. Nonetheless, table 1 gives a general view of the extensive union fragmentation in 1980, the starting point for this study. The proportion of unions with less than 50,000 members ranged from 80 percent in the United States to 99 percent in New Zealand; the proportion with less than 10,000 members ranged from 57 percent to 95 percent in those two countries. The number of unions of all sizes varied from 208 in Canada to 438 in Great Britain.

We should not assume that small unions are ineffective. On the contrary, some may negotiate only a few collective agreements. Others may repre-

Table 1. Union fragmentation in the United States, Canada, Great Britain, Australia, and New Zealand, 1980

	Union membership (thousands)	Number of unions	Percentage of unions with fewer than	
			50,000 members	10,000 members
United States	22,556	304	80%	57%
Canada	3,274	208	92	67
Great Britain	12,947	438	91	80
Australia	2,944	316	96	80
New Zealand	516	265	99	95

Sources: United States: Troy and Sheflin 1985; Canada: Labour Canada 1980; Great Britain: "Membership of Trade Unions in 1980" 1982. Australia: Cameron 1980. New Zealand: New Zealand Department of Labour 1981.

sent workers in narrow geographic areas or serve small, specialized groups such as school superintendents, food inspectors, airline pilots, or engravers. A few, such as unions of performing artists, may even be powerful enough to control the supply of qualified labor to entire industries.

But most small unions have a host of problems. They often cannot achieve economies of scale in operations. Income from membership dues is insufficient to maintain specialized departments and staff needed for lobbying, public relations, and ensuring workplace safety. They find it difficult to provide adequate representation in negotiations and grievance handling, particularly if the membership is geographically dispersed. They also lack the staff and resources for the major recruiting campaigns (Shabecoff 1980; Conant 1984; Strauss 1993; Chaison 1995).

I return to the links between union size and effectiveness in later chapters, and in the conclusion I argue that merger proponents may actually overstate the case against small unions. At this point, it should be made clear that this is not a treatise on union size or a test of the popular premise that bigger unions are better unions. Rather, I discuss mergers as the quickest way to reduce the number of small unions and increase the size of the largest ones. We will see that important features of the context of union mergers are the presence of many small unions, and the governments' and labor federations' belief that the key to structural reform is the creation of larger ones.

Before I examine merger trends in the five countries, it would be best to review the basics of how and why unions merge.

The Union Merger Process

National unions merge with each other in two ways—through amalgamations or through absorptions.[1] An amalgamation joins two or more unions of roughly equal size to form a new union. An absorption (called a "transfer of engagements" in Britain) merges a small union into a larger one; in the process, the small union loses its separate identity and legal status (Chaison 1986). Amalgamations usually join two unions, although there are some multiple or composite amalgamations that join three or more unions. Absorptions are always between two unions—the smaller, absorbed union and the larger, absorbing union. Some unions absorb several others in a short time (e.g., the British GMB absorbed 10 unions in 1986), but each absorption is a separate merger that is individually negotiated and approved by officers and members.

Janus (1978), Stratton-Devine (1990), and McClendon, Kriesky and Eaton (1995) identify a third type of merger, an affiliation, in which a national union absorbs a union that operates on a single plant, single company, or regional basis.[2] These smaller unions are usually called "local independent unions" or "unaffiliated local unions" because they are not part of a nationally-based union or they are not affiliated with a labor federation.

At the earliest stage of the merger process, union officers contact each other for informal discussions to assess the potential gains and losses of merger. These meetings are usually kept secret so that they will not be labeled failures if officers are unable to proceed to formal merger negotiations. If and when the officers believe that a merger is worth serious consideration, merger discussions are publicized in union newspapers and at union conventions. Committees for negotiating merger terms are then created through resolutions passed at the unions' conventions or the meetings of their governing boards. Unions that are particularly active in mergers have permanent committees with the authority to explore any and all possible mergers.

Merger committees, composed of top officers and staff, meet regularly, sometimes over several years, to negotiate the merger documents—the *merger agreement* and the *merger implementation agreement* (these are called the "merger instrument" in Great Britain and the "scheme of merger" in Australia). The merger agreement describes the principles and conditions of the merger, including the composition and powers of governing bodies, the frequency of conventions and the selection of convention delegates, the location of the merged union's headquarters, and the activities of any special union divisions or sections. In amalgamations, the merger agreement usually creates the constitution of the new unions. The merger agreements for absorption and affiliation, on the other hand, only amend the constitution of the larger union by defining the status or structures for absorbed or affiliating unions' members (e.g., modified dues, new officer positions, industrial divisions).

Merger implementation agreements carry out mergers; they legally combine the staffs' pension and health care plans and the strike funds, continue the employment of or retire union officers and staff, and create interim governing bodies until the membership elects officers at the first convention of the merged unions. Implementation agreements often appear as appendixes to the merger agreement.

When merger negotiations are successful and committee members agree on merger terms, they sign the merger documents and present them to the unions' governing bodies for approval. Once endorsed by the officers, merger agreements are distributed to the unions' members, usually along with descriptive pamphlets and special editions of the unions' newspapers. Campaign literature includes the officers' endorsements of the merger and descriptions of the history, structures, leaders and members of the merging unions. The literature also provides responses to members' typical questions: Who will be the new unions' officers? Will my dues increase? Will my local have to merge? Will my local retain control over bargaining?

At the conclusion of the campaign, resolutions approving the merger agreement are presented to the unions' members or delegates at special merger conventions. The legal requirements for the approval of mergers vary from country to country as we will see in later chapters, but they usually include secret ballot elections. Quite often, the members or delegates of the larger unions in absorptions and affiliations are not required by law or by their unions' constitutions to vote on mergers.

The union merger process has pre- and postmerger stages that are separated by the approval of the merger documents. Elsewhere (Chaison 1986), I have described the linkages between premerger conditions (e.g., officers' concerns about losing their jobs) and postmerger arrangements (e.g., the size of the merged union's governing body). In brief, the countervailing forces of the motivation to merge and the barriers to merger affect the conduct and substance of merger negotiations, and these negotiations determine the structure and government of the merged union.

Accordingly, the force of the motivation to merge is best seen in relation to the barriers that must be overcome. Alone, the apparent benefits of a merger are insufficient for successful merger negotiations. Negotiations at impasse will remain so until barriers become less important (e.g., the officers who oppose merger decide to retire), or until the motivation to merge increases (e.g., membership suddenly declines because of a new production technology). As L. Adams (1984, 21) described the countervailing relationship: "Merger is a difficult process requiring delicate negotiations, patience, and sensitivity to personal and institutional sensibilities. Although mergers may be good for the labor movement in general, they usually occur when the economic and institutional problems that create the need to merge outweigh the problems of satisfying that need." Only by examining the relative forces of both the merger motivation and barriers can we understand why a merger did or did not occur and why certain structures or processes were agreed to in negotiations.

The Motivation to Merge

Studies of union mergers usually conclude that the principal motivating factors are declining membership or financial hardship (e.g., Fortin 1973; Chitayat 1979; Undy et al. 1981; Stratton-Devine 1992; Chaison 1986; Aston 1987; Waddington 1995). The two are clearly interrelated. Membership losses reduce dues income and force unions to devote fewer resources and staff to organizing. Consequently, the number of new members is insufficient to offset attrition caused by retirements and job losses. Membership continues to fall and dues income is reduced further (Rose and Chaison 1996). This cycle of decline can be stopped by a surge in organizing or by merger. The former is highly unlikely for resource-starved unions in countries such as Great Britain and the United States where organizing is time consuming and expensive.

Not all merging unions have been declining. For instance, in the United States from 1900 to 1978, membership actually increased during the five years prior to merger for more than a third of amalgamating and national unions, and nearly three-quarters of absorbing unions (Chaison 1981). Most likely, the amalgamating and absorbed unions merged because their officers felt they were too small to operate effectively and saw little possibility of substantial growth. Absorbing unions, on the other hand, used mergers to establish footholds in expanding, lesser-unionized industries, most notably in health care, retailing and the public sector. Absorbing unions also gained the services of experienced officers and staff to exploit their new organizing possibilities.

When we look beyond membership losses, financial hardship or enhanced organizing potential, we find additional reasons for unions to merge: New production processes threaten the employment of the union's members and raise the possibility of costly rivalry with other unions in the industry (e.g., mergers among the printers' unions in the United States and Britain were in reaction to new methods of computerized typesetting); narrow union jurisdictions greatly reduce the chances of future growth (e.g., several British unions confined to the declining textile and clothing industries merged with each other or into large unions with diverse memberships); small unions lack the economies of scale needed to provide basic services for their members (e.g., provincial and citywide unions of public employees in Canada merged into national unions because they could not afford full-time lobbyists and research staff); employer reorganization or diversification places unions at a significant disadvantage in negotiations (e.g., British unions merged when large employers repeatedly shifted production from plants represented by one union to those of another); frequent organizing raids, that is, attempts to win the rights to represent workers who are already unionized, are costly, but merger with an affiliate of a labor federation brings with it the immediate protection of a no-raid agreement; new government regulations impose a minimum size for unions to retain their legal status (e.g., the minimum size for federally registered unions in New Zealand was raised from 15 to 1,000 members in 1987) and this compels small unions to merge if quick growth is impossible and the loss of representational status is to be avoided.

More commonly, unions merge to avoid the high costs and low yields of traditional organizing. Recruiting new members by gaining representation rights at individual workplaces can be extremely time consuming and expensive. Successful organizers must make personal contact with workers and convince them first, that unionism is beneficial in general and second, that the union would be a fair and effective representative. Employers resist organizing campaigns with tactics that range from appeals to workers' loyalty to the discriminatory discharge of union supporters. Organizing in a climate of intense employer resistance, as in the United States, or in the absence of a legal framework for demonstrating the workers' preference, the case in Britain, is a severe drain on union funds and staff time. It is much faster and cheaper to absorb small national unions or affiliate local unions. During these merger campaigns, workers are asked to change unions or have their union become part of another, rather than to select or reject unionism. There is seldom strong employer opposition because the defeat of a merger campaign does not result in a return to nonunion status.[3]

THE BARRIERS TO MERGER

All attempts to merge face some opposition from within the unions themselves. The earliest resistance comes from officers who reject merger overtures because of differences in ideologies (e.g., disagreement about ties with political parties) or union structures and practices (e.g., the role that union locals play in negotiations). Officers oppose mergers that would reduce their status, power, salaries, or benefits by forcing their retirement or moving them to lower positions in merged unions. Older leaders resist mergers if they still feel the bitterness of past rivalries or believe the merger will end their union's traditions (e.g., the frequency of conventions, the publication of the union's newspaper). They may see little to gain from a merger in terms of higher salaries or positions of greater status. Merger might weaken the system of political patronage that enabled them to consolidate and retain power. Opposition can also come from younger officers who feel that they must first establish their own status and record of accomplishment before leaving office through a merger or sharing power in a merged union (Chitayat 1979; Chaison 1986). Druker (1988, 26) observed:

> Trade union leaders are likely to be cautious on organizational matters. The pace of change on mergers, as on many other things, is slow and at times rather unsteady. Much talking is done before anyone gets down to brass tacks and, when serious business is done, it is often because a general secretary [a top union officer in Britain] can see retirement in sight. It is perhaps not surprising that union general secretaries do not rush their unions into amalgamations immediately after they are elected to the top job. But three or four years before retirement they are more likely to regard amalgamation as a serious option.

Obviously, mergers cannot be separated from union politics. Merger proposals provide ammunition for opposition candidates who claim that a vote for the incumbent is a vote to dismantle the union. Officer elections between merger advocates and opponents become de facto referendums over the merger terms and votes of confidence in those who negotiated them. Well aware of this, only the most secure union officers are willing to risk presenting merger proposals to the membership; others will oppose a merger openly, even if they personally believe that it will benefit the union and its members (Chaison 1978; 1986).

Officers also reject mergers for purely financial reasons. An absorption or affiliation may be prohibitively expensive if the smaller union cannot generate sufficient dues income to pay the salaries of the officers and staff who insist on continued employment after the merger. Financial and membership records are always exchanged and audited during merger negotiations and short- and long-term dues revenues are estimated. A merger partner is rejected if it looks like it will become a financial burden (Chaison 1986).

Opposition from top officers can be fatal to a merger attempt because it occurs at the earliest stages, frequently before the merger is publicized. If merger is rejected during informal discussions, a proposal will never be prepared for the scrutiny of lower-level officers and members (Brooks and Gamm 1976).

Union membership forms the second line of merger opposition and typically occurs after officers endorse merger documents. Members resist mergers that they believe will submerge their interests in larger unions. When members form a small minority in the merged union, they are understandably concerned about influencing officers or convention delegates in matters that directly affect them, such as the impact of new technologies or the need to protect pensioners' benefits. Members also oppose mergers that will force their locals to combine with those of another union or that will reduce local control over negotiations. Resistance occurs in two principal forms: antimerger committees that campaign against merger resolutions at local meetings and conventions, and legal challenges in the courts or before government agencies that monitor the merger process. Both are illustrated in later chapters.

Although merger opposition usually comes from within unions, there is occasionally external opposition. For example, labor federations in the United States blocked mergers between their affiliates and unions that were expelled for communist domination or leadership corruption in the 1940s and 1950s. The federations' policy was that expelled unions should not be able to reaffiliate before eliminating the cause of expulsion, for example, by rejecting the incumbent leadership (Chaison 1973). Unions have also tried to block proposed mergers that they thought would impede their own plans for merger or membership expansion. Unions can block a merger by requesting that a labor federation not officially recognize it or by launching a rival organizing campaign to discourage the unions contemplating merger. For example, the Teamsters intervened in the merger negotiations between the Brewery Workers and the Amalgamated Meat Cutters and Butcher Workmen in 1971 by threatening rival organizing campaigns against the latter union if a merger was agreed upon. The Teamsters planned to expand its membership in breweries and sought to absorb the Brewery to create a base for future organizing. The Meat Cutters ended the merger negotiations to avoid antagonizing the Teamsters, and the Brewery Workers, with a declining membership and without other merger options, agreed to be absorbed by the Teamsters in 1973 (Chaison 1986).

Even in the absence of significant internal or external opposition, there may be insurmountable merger barriers when unions try to reconcile differences in their practices and traditions. During negotiations for amalgamations, absorptions, and affiliations, unions have to settle such issues as: the procedure for electing officers, selecting staff, and setting their compensation; the transfer and consolidation of union properties and assets, including local union facilities and strike funds; the combining of officers', staffs', and members' pension and benefit plans; the merger of union departments, and regional and local governing bodies; the membership dues and fees of the new union, and the division of the dues receipts between its national headquarters and locals; the title, editorship, and frequency of publication of the union's newspaper; the degree of autonomy that local unions can exercise in determining bargaining issues and priorities, conducting negotiations, ratifying contracts, calling strikes, and controlling their own financial affairs.

In addition to the above, negotiators for amalgamations must decide on the new union's name, the location of its headquarters, the members' access to the combined strike fund, and the frequency of its conventions and selection of convention delegates (DeCenzo 1981; Chaison 1986).

It can be extremely difficult for merger negotiators to resolve differences in union structures and administration. As I mentioned earlier, union members reject mergers that they believe will submerge their interests and leave them without adequate influence in union decision making. As a result, members are often wary of merger proposals that retain too many of the other union's governing practices or structures. Furthermore, officers oppose arrangements that threaten their status and compensation and may only agree to a merger that expands governing structures to continue the employment of all presidents, secretary-treasurers, and vice-presidents.

After a review of members' and officers' opposition to mergers, I concluded:

> In many unsuccessful merger negotiations, failure stems not from the negotiating committees' inability to devise compromise solutions to the problems of institutional differences, but rather from a belief that any compromise that could be reached by the negotiating teams would arouse strong opposition from officers and members. In the final analysis, the resolution of institutional differences has to be within the boundaries of what is acceptable and capable of winning approval at executive board meetings, conventions, and membership referendums. The joining of union structures may be more of a political than a technical problem and we must consider this dimension when trying to understand why merger negotiating committees are not more flexible or innovative in resolving institutional differences. (Chaison 1986, 85)

COUNTERVAILING FORCES AND POSTMERGER INTEGRATION

I have argued elsewhere (Chaison 1978; 1982a) that the motivation to merge and merger barriers must be compared to each other if we are to understand fully why merger negotiations failed or succeeded, or why particular merger terms were agreed upon. We only ignore the dynamics of the merger process when we focus solely on the reasons for merger. Some merger discussions continue for years without progress until the motivation to merge increases for one or both of the unions (e.g., new production technologies sharply reduce employment in the core jurisdiction), or merger barriers are reduced (e.g., the officers opposed to the merger retire or are defeated in elections). Mergers that seem beneficial to all have been blocked because of disagreement over largely symbolic issues (e.g., the name of the new union or the titles of officers). But as the motivation to merge increases, officers devise compromise solutions.

The structures of merged unions are shaped during merger negotiations by the relative strengths of the merger barriers and the motivation to merge. The various degrees of union integration after mergers are shown in figure 1. Amalgamations range from complete fusions of unions to federated structures (Chaison 1982b). In the complete fusion, a rare arrangement, the new union's singular identity is affirmed in its constitution and there are no references to the structures and practices of the predecessor unions (e.g., officer positions are *not* allocated on the basis of their previ-

Figure 1. Degrees of integration of union structures after amalgamations, absorptions, and affiliations

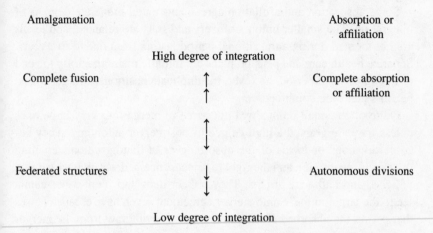

ous union's membership). Most often, amalgamations call for moderate degrees of integration; temporary positions are created for the continued employment of officers and staff, locals are not required to merge (at least for a few years), and initial officer positions are allocated on the basis of prior affiliation (e.g., the president from one union, the secretary treasurer from the other). Representation on governing bodies is proportionate to the membership of the merging unions—a union contributing 40 percent of the new union's members gets 40 percent of the seats on the executive council. This arrangement is phased out after the union's first or second convention.

Unions occasionally amalgamate without any plans for eventual integration. They form federated structures and become autonomous divisions with their own full-time officers and staff. Special conferences are held prior to the merged union's convention. Separate newspapers may even be published. Such continuing federated structures have been used extensively in British amalgamations to join unions of different crafts and occupations, and the new unions have become centers of additional merger activity because they can guarantee a high degree of postmerger autonomy (Chaison 1986).

Integration is also possible after absorptions and affiliations. At one extreme, an absorbed or affiliated union becomes an indistinguishable part of the larger union; its properties and funds are transferred, locals are merged or rechartered, and officers pensioned off or given positions as consultants in the new union. Such complete and immediate integration is highly unusual.

Some absorption and affiliation agreements entail moderate degrees of integration. The smaller union's officers and staff are retained, and locals are not merged during a transitional period lasting from one to five years. Separate health care and pension plans are initially maintained. By the end of the transitional period, however, the duplicate positions, structures, and benefits plans are combined.

Quite often, small unions will not agree to merge into very large ones unless they are granted a high degree of postmerger autonomy. They become divisions or locals of the absorbing or affiliating union, retaining their own constitution and the right to select officers, determine bargaining policies, and authorize strikes. They collect dues and remit a per capita fee to the larger union. Some merger agreements even have escape clauses that permit the absorbed or affiliated unions to withdraw from the merger by a vote of its members or officers during a specified period.

The degree of postmerger integration is determined by the relative strength of merger barriers and motivation. For instance, if merger motivation is not particularly strong and many officers oppose a merger that entails any loss of their status and influence, an acceptable merger plan must have low degrees of integration and expanded governing structures. If members are extremely concerned about the submergence of their interests, local autonomy must be granted or divisions created for the locals in the members' industry or occupation. On the other hand, if the motivation to merge is strong, as it would be following precipitous membership losses and severe financial hardship, officers and members will agree to more complete integration despite their concerns about the submergence of their interests.

MERGER OUTCOMES

Union mergers are highly touted as ways to rescue dying unions, breath new life into stagnant ones, and create streamlined, effective labor movements. Many observers, among them legislators, union officers, and employers, see mergers as the surest and fastest way to build stronger, more stable unions. But the impact of mergers is not that simple or certain. Mergers can be evaluated in terms of bargaining power, organizing ability, protection against raids, officer compensation, membership participation in union governance, and economies of scale in union operations (Brooks and Gamm 1976; Chitayat 1979; Chaison 1986). While it is tempting to compare a newly merged union to some abstract standard of union effectiveness, a realistic and comprehensive appraisal should consider not only what happened when a union merged but what might have happened if it had not. In my earlier book (Chaison 1986), I examined alternative ways of evaluating merger outcomes in the United States, Canada, and Great Britain and reached several conclusions.

First, the impact of a merger is seldom equally felt by the involved unions. There may be little change when an absorbing or affiliating union takes in a very small union. The former's members usually do not have to approve the merger and many may not even be aware of it. But the officers and members of the small absorbed or affiliating union do experience the merger outcomes, whether they are economies of scale in operations, higher officer compensation, or greater bargaining power. In contrast, when two unions amalgamate, they are more evenly affected by the merger outcomes because they are roughly the same size and a new union is created while the old ones are dissolved.

Second, most merger outcomes are affected by the extent of postmerger integration. Integration, as we have seen, results from compromises in merger negotiations and the relative strength of the merger motivation and barriers. Consequently, when we appraise merger outcomes, we should consider the positions of the parties in merger negotiations. For instance, if the merger barriers are high relative to the force of the motivating factors, and the primary barrier is the members' fear of the submergence of their interests, we should expect that merger negotiations will succeed only if the parties agree to low postmerger integration. This might entail permanent, autonomous divisions. Criticism of the merged union's unwieldy governing structures and high operating costs must be tempered with an understanding that without these features the merger would not have been possible. At the other extreme, if the merger's objective is to protect a union against organizing raids by linking it with another that is covered by a federation no-raid agreement, the desired merger outcome can be immediately and fully realized, regardless of the integration of the unions after merger. In this case, we can quickly and directly appraise the merger's success.

Third, with the exception of protection against raids, merger outcomes are seldom apparent at the time of the merger. Almost all mergers go through transitional stages during which officer positions are duplicated, neighboring locals are not forced to merge, premerger dues and fees are still paid, and separate headquarters or regional offices are maintained. If there is significant opposition to merger or if the motivation to merge is weak, there are long transitional periods when temporary rules and structures are in force. It would be premature to evaluate a merger in terms of cost effectiveness or economies of scale until the transition period has ended and the merged union settles into its final state.

This brief introduction to the terminology and dynamics of union mergers serves as a foundation for the review of merger trends in five countries. Each of the next five chapters begins with a brief introduction to the context of mergers in terms of the significant, recent changes in that county's industrial relations system. We will see how adverse economic conditions, increased nonunion competition, employer opposition to unionism and, at times, openly hostile governments and assertive labor federations have prodded unions into merger negotiations or at least the active consideration of merger options. In some countries, labor laws also influenced mergers: they induced or encouraged mergers, or were effective weapons in the hands of merger opponents.

After discussion of the context of its mergers, the country's merger record since 1980 is briefly reviewed, followed by discussions of landmark mergers, prominent merger forms, special conditions affecting mergers, and actual or possible merger waves. From this discussion will emerge the country's profile of union mergers. The concluding chapter reviews merger trends, compares the national profiles of union mergers, and describes the common features of mergers in the five countries.

CHAPTER 2

The United States:
Merging for Growth and Survival

It would be difficult to exaggerate the severity of the problems faced by American unions. Since the early 1980s, labor relations have been shaped by the pressures of an expanding nonunion sector. Facing intense competition, unionized employers sought to reverse the unions' past bargaining gains and halt future organizing. And nonunion employers resisted organizing campaigns with a fervor that had not been seen since the 1920s.

Union membership fell sharply as new members were far too few to offset job losses at unionized firms. The labor movement seemed discouraged and in disarray, with neither an effective response to the employers' bargaining offensive nor a plan to stem its membership losses. By the end of the 1980s, it was clear that the unions were in crisis and that any resurgence in size and influence was highly unlikely, at least in the near future.

Dewey (1971) observed how the pace of union mergers quickened from 1956 to 1971 as once rival unions combined after the merger in 1955 of the two federations, the American Federation of Labor and the Congress of Industrial Organizations. Janus (1978) and Chaison (1980) found that merger activity remained fairly stable through the 1970s. But L. Adams (1984, 27) predicted that "the process of labor organizations striving to adapt, survive, and prosper within the changing configuration of the U.S. economy is likely to keep merger activity fast-paced and highly competitive."

In this chapter, I show how severe membership losses and the unlikelihood of membership gains have made mergers more attractive. American mergers involved large unions searching for quick, inexpensive growth and a broader membership base, and small unions confined to declining industries and incapable of reversing membership losses. A few unions also aggressively pursued affiliations—absorptions of local and regional unions—as a primary growth strategy. But what seems most impressive about recent American mergers is not their number or form, but the sheer difficulty of completing them. The recent merger record must be viewed against the backdrop of the labor federation's neutrality and labor laws that do little to simplify or standardize how national union mergers are approved.

The Context

DECLINING UNION MEMBERSHIP

Two prime indicators of recent union decline are membership losses and the collapse of union organizing. From 1980 to 1993, American unions lost 3.5 million members; union density, the proportion of employed wage and salary workers who are union members, fell from 23 to 16 percent (see table 2).[1] This completely reversed the membership gains of the previous 25 years and halved the union density rate from its high of 33 percent in the mid-1950s (Chaison and Rose 1991b; Rose and Chaison 1996).

The disaggregated figures show public sector membership increasing by almost 1.3 million members since 1980, but this was only slightly above the expanding employment in that sector; consequently, union density rose only 2 percent, from 36 to 38 percent. In private employment, the unions were nearly decimated; 4.8 million members were lost and density dropped from 20 to 11 percent. Private sector density is now at its lowest point since the early 1930s, before the mass organizing campaigns that followed the passage of protective labor legislation (Rose and Chaison 1996).

Membership loses have been widespread; down 182,000 members in mining, 442,000 in construction, 630,000 in transportation, communications, and public utilities, and 379,000 in wholesale and retail trade. Unions gained only 71,000 new members in the expanding service sector, while union density fell from 9 percent to 6 percent. Although membership did rise in 1993, the first time in 14 years, the disaggregated data showed

Table 2. Union membership and density by industry in the United States, 1980, 1993

Industry	Members (thousands)			Density[a]		
	1980	1993	Change	1980	1993	Change
Private sector[b]	14,283	9,556	−4,727	20.1%	11.2%	−8.9%
Mining	285	103	−182	32.0	16.0	−16.0
Construction	1,371	929	−442	30.9	20.0	−10.9
Manufacturing	6,726	3,592	−3,134	32.3	19.2	−13.1
Transportation, communications, and public utilities	2,554	1,924	−630	48.4	30.5	−17.9
Wholesale and retail trade	1,746	1,367	−379	10.1	6.3	−3.8
Finance, insurance, and real estate	162	131	−31	3.2	1.9	−1.3
Services	1,439	1,510	+71	8.9	5.8	−3.1
Government	5,764	7,018	+1,254	35.9	37.7	+1.8
Total	20,047	16,574	−3,473	23.0	15.8	−7.2

Sources: 1980: United States Department of Labor 1981; 1993: Behrmann 1994.
[a]The percentage of employed wage and salary workers who are union members.
[b]Excludes agriculture.

continued decline in the traditional core of union membership. The net gain of about 200,000 members was due to 370,000 new public sector members offsetting losses in other sectors, including 160,000 fewer members in manufacturing (Behrmann 1994).

The decline in membership is due to exceptionally low levels of organizing—essentially the collapse of the union recruitment process. The primary means for recruiting new union members in private employment are the secret-ballot certification elections conducted by the National Labor Relations Board (NLRB). Union members gained through these elections as a proportion of nonagricultural employment fell from 0.23 percent in 1980 to 0.09 percent in 1986 and 0.07 percent in 1992 (Freeman and Rebick 1989; "Union Membership, 1992" 1993; Rose and Chaison 1996). Workers in newly certified bargaining units dropped from 152,000 in 1980 to 70,000 in 1982, and never returned to the previous level throughout the 1980s and early 1990s. Unions have been able to maintain fairly stable success rates, between 40 and 50 percent, but only by proceeding to elections where there were good chances of victory. As a result, the average number of certification elections per year fell from 3,431 for 1975–1981 to 1,594 for 1982–1992—a 54 percent decrease (Chaison and Dhavale 1990; Rose and Chaison 1996).[2]

Even when unions were certified, the employers' resistance in bargaining and their replacement of strikers when bargaining collapsed prevented unions from transforming election victories into stable bargaining relationships. Less than half the unions certified in 1987 had collective bargaining agreements five years later (Pavy 1994).

The decline in organizing activity and membership gains has been traced to intense employer opposition to unionism.[3] Meyer and Cooke's (1993) index of employer opposition supports that conclusion. The index indicates the annual number of cases of discrimination against union supporters during organizing campaigns relative to the number of certification elections and first contracts after certification victories. In 1977 the index was 0.6, but rose in 1979 to 1.4 and in 1981 to 2.7. In 1983 it reached 3.5 and remained above 3.0 through the decade.

Kochan and Weinstein (1994) observed that the frequency of illegal firing during organizing campaigns increased from 1 in every 25 elections and 1 of every 600 union supporters in the early 1950s to 1 in every 4 elections and 1 in every 48 supporters by the end of the 1980s. Such discharges delay the processing of election petitions, discourage workers from supporting unions, increase the unions' costs of organizing, and reduce the number of campaigns that unions can take to the election stage.

The rising opposition to unionism both before and after organizing campaigns is commonly attributed to the employers' exposure to foreign and domestic nonunion competition, and their belief that they would be at a serious disadvantage if their flexibility was restricted and labor costs increased by collective bargaining (Kochan, Katz, and McKersie 1986; Farber 1990). In such a climate, it is highly unlikely that American unions can organize sufficient new members to reverse declining membership and density. For example, Chaison and Dhavale (1990) found that unions were able to use certification elections to gain only one-sixth of the new members needed to offset job losses in unionized firms. Consequently, for union density to stay at just its present level, unions would have to expand greatly organizing activity, organize at larger facilities, and increase their victory rate. Simply winning more elections is not enough. The expense of this new organizing would be prohibitive. It now costs unions about $1,000 for each new worker organized; unions would have to spend about $300 million on organizing each year to increase net membership. This is well beyond the resources of the union movement (Kochan and Wever 1991).

In the midst of the overall membership decline, there are some unions devoting impressive energy, imagination and resources to organizing.[4] The Service Employees International Union (SEIU), for example, has had impressive organizing gains from public demonstrations and consumer boycotts that pressure employers to recognize it as bargaining agent. It also devotes about a quarter of its budget to organizing while most unions allocate 5 to 10 percent. The SEIU's membership has increased by 80 percent since 1980 (Shostak 1994; Ybarra 1994; Bureau of National Affairs 1995g). The United Food and Commercial Workers also assigns a high priority to organizing and has developed an extensive program for volunteer organizers. Its organizing gains constitute about half those of all AFL-CIO unions since 1980 (Nulty 1994). The United Steelworkers of America also selects and trains volunteer organizers from among its members. Field training is provided through quick "blitz" campaigns focusing on nonunion companies, ranging from foundries to health care facilities, in selected cities (Bureau of National Affairs 1995n).

There are also reports of unions "organizing smarter" by using more sophisticated appeals to workers, hiring young, well-trained and enthusiastic organizers, allocating greater funds to organizing (Bureau of National Affairs 1995b; Hurd 1995). But despite some impressive gains, the increment to total membership falls far short of the numbers needed to stem membership loses. For example, in 1990 it was reported that AFL-CIO affiliates organized 250,000 workers, but still suffered a *net* loss of 15,000 members ("Labor Letter" 1991). Expanding unions are now the exception—only 16 of 80 AFL-CIO affiliates recorded any growth from 1985 to 1993 (Bureau of National Affairs 1993a).

Even when the economy improves and employment grows, membership losses continue because union members are concentrated in the slowest growth industries, in older firms and facilities in these industries, and in occupations that are shrinking because of technological change (Kochan 1989; Kochan and Verma 1992). Moreover, if unionized firms do expand, unions can no longer count on automatic membership gains. American employers are responding to economic uncertainty and rising foreign and domestic competition by subcontracting work, using temporary and part-time workers, and shifting work to nonunion domestic or overseas facilities (Kilborn 1992; Lohr 1993; Meyer and Cooke 1993; Uchitelle 1994).

If the present levels of organizing and job losses continue, union density in the private sector could fall to 5 percent by the end of the century (Freeman and Rogers 1993).[5] We might then see the "islands of unionism" described by Mitchell (1989); unions will remain fairly strong in some sectors (e.g., public employment, automobile manufacturing, the railroads) and in a few specialties (e.g., performing arts, professional athletics), but they will be surrounded by a vast sea of nonunion employment. In the absence of legislation that empowers unions (highly unlikely at present), the innovations in employee relations, work processes, and compensation and benefits will come from the nonunion sector, and the protection of workers' rights will be largely through labor laws rather than unionism and collective bargaining (Heckscher 1988).

In light of such a serious decline in union membership and influence, it was not surprising that in 1995 both the AFL-CIO president, Thomas R. Donohue, and the challenger for his office, John J. Sweeney, president of the SEIU, vowed to commit substantial funds for organizing. When Sweeney won, he stated: "We are going to put resources into organizing at a pace and scale that is unprecedented" (Greenhouse 1995, A28). It was reported that there would be a fivefold increase in funds for training organizers (Kilborn 1995a; Greenhouse 1996a). Many observers believe, however, that despite the new focus on organizing, the problems of the unions will remain in terms of a hostile political environment and an indifferent public. Economic restructuring and foreign competition will continue to shrink union employment (Bureau of National Affairs 1995c, g; Greenhouse 1995). The membership gains through intensive new organizing might, at least in the near future, be sufficient only to offset attrition (Bureau of National Affairs 1995c, g).

The Dominant Nonunion Sector

Union–management relations in the United States are presently shaped by the influence of the expanding nonunion sector. About 4 of every 5 workers in manufacturing and construction are employed in nonunion firms. The service sector is nearly nonunion, with only 1 in 20 workers at unionized workplaces. Even in the most heavily unionized sectors—transportation, communications and public utilities—there are two nonunion workers for every union member (table 2).

I emphasized earlier that the primary cause of the membership losses is the employers' intense opposition to unionism. Since the early 1980s, nonunion employers have resorted to tactics ranging from legal procedural delays to the illegal discharge of union supporters to thwart organizing drives. One survey conducted in the mid-1980s showed that 95 percent of private-sector employers actively resisted unionism; about three-quarters hired consultants to develop anti-union campaigns (AFL-CIO 1985).

Employer opposition has not been limited to organizing. Employers have been assertive in collective bargaining, seeking control of the negotiating agenda and reversing past union gains. In response to employers' threats of mass layoffs and plant closings, unions often agreed to cuts or freezes in wages and benefits, and the elimination of work rules that restricted productivity (Mitchell 1982; Rubenfeld 1983; Bell 1989). Such concession bargaining was widespread during and soon after the severe economic recession of the early 1980s, particularly in industries with reduced consumer demand (e.g., construction), significant foreign and domestic nonunion competition (e.g., automobiles, steel, and other basic manufacturing), or deregulation (airlines, communications, and trucking) (Mitchell 1985). Although concession bargaining subsided in the late 1980s (Mitchell 1990), its initial intensity and its continuation beyond the early stages of the economic recovery reveal the widespread decline in bargaining power (Bell 1989).

Most American unions now negotiate defensively, concentrating first on protecting past bargaining gains, particularly health-care benefits, then promoting job security by restricting employer subcontracting of work performed by union members, and finally negotiating plans for retraining to buffer the impact of new work processes. Negotiated wage increases have been moderate and are usually lower than previously negotiated increases (Sleemi 1995). One bargaining review concluded that "negotiators are in an unenviable position as they wrestle with continuing foreign competition, rising health care costs, pressures to reduce labor costs, and maintaining workers' standards of living" (Williamson 1993, 77).

Decreasing union density weakens the unions' bargaining power, which, in turn, often discourages new membership. Low union density weakens the unions' bargaining position because employers resist demands more resolutely when they face serious nonunion competition. And fewer union gains at the bargaining table make nonunion workers doubt the value of unionism, so organizing becomes even more difficult (Mitchell 1989; Rose and Chaison 1996).

The persistence of concession bargaining and the intensity of employers' opposition to unionism in both nonunion and unionized facilities may signal the end of a fifty-year period of union–management coexistence and toleration. American employers seem to be retreating from their commitment to collective bargaining and moving toward a nonunion model of labor relations in which workers participate in decision making as individuals rather than as union members. The traditional employer strategy of containing union influence through negotiations is often replaced by one of aggressively avoiding unions at nonunion operations and displacing them at unionized ones (Edwards and Podgursky 1986; Adams 1989b).

American unions are now extremely vulnerable. Investment and production by businesses abroad, certain to appeal to more unionized companies after trade liberalization under the 1993 North American Free Trade Agreement, perpetuates the decline in union jobs in the private sector (Robinson 1994). Intensive and widespread nonunion competition, either foreign or domestic, prevents unions from achieving their traditional objective of taking wages out of competition; higher wages and benefits can no longer be negotiated without major job losses. In the public sector, budgetary constraints will stop and may even reverse membership gains. Since 1980, there have been numerous proposals for labor law reforms that expedite the union certification process and strengthen workers' rights to select union representation in the private sector, but such reforms became less likely after the 1994 elections, when the Republicans took control of Congress. Finally, American employers are increasingly turning to a low wage strategy, seeking to compete on world markets by relying on relatively inexpensive labor. Union avoidance is critical to this approach. Under such disheartening circumstances, I expect to see the merger option selected by many unions, for some as an alternative path to sustained growth and for others as the only way to ensure continued survival as bargaining agents.

The Merger Record

Table 3 shows the form and frequency of national union mergers by period after the founding of the AFL-CIO in 1955. Mergers since 1980 are also tabulated by year in table 4 and listed in Appendix 1.

Between 1980 and 1994, the average yearly merger rate rose by 41 percent—about one merger per year—compared to the average during the preceding decades. The 1980-to-1994 period shows the first substantial increase in the merger rate since 1956. Although the year-to-year changes were erratic between 1980 and 1990, the merger rate was high from 1991 to 1995. It would be premature to characterize the 21 mergers since 1991

Table 3. Mergers among national unions in the United States, 1956–1994

Period	Amalgamations	Absorptions	Total	Average number of mergers per year	Absorptions as a percent of total mergers
1956–1959	3	6	9	2.3	67%
1960–1969	5	19	24	2.4	79
1970–1979	6	21	27	2.7	78
1980–1994	5	52	57	3.8	91
Total	19	98	117	3.0	84

Sources: Dewey 1971; Janus 1978; Adams 1984; Williamson 1995.

Table 4. Mergers among national unions in the United States, 1980–1994

Year	Amalgamations	Absorptions	Total
1980	0	5	5
1981	1	2	3
1982	1	4	5
1983	1	3	4
1984	0	1	1
1985	0	3	3
1986	0	3	3
1987	1	4	5
1988	1	2	3
1989	0	4	4
1990	0	0	0
1991	0	5	5
1992	0	5	5
1993	0	6	6
1994	0	5	5
Total	5	52	57

Source: Appendix 1.

as the start of a merger wave, but it does indicate a heightened interest in mergers.

Absorptions are the far more popular merger form, outnumbering amalgamations by ten to one. This trend can be explained by the relative ease of negotiating the inclusion of a small union into a much larger one, compared to the more difficult task of creating a new union by amalgamating two or more unions of roughly equal size (Chaison 1986). The relative frequency of absorptions increased in recent years, however, most likely because more small unions have recognized the inevitability of their decline and have turned to merger for survival. Between 1980 and 1994, 91 percent of national-union mergers were absorptions, compared to 78 percent during the seventies and 79 percent during the sixties (table 3).

Since 1980, merging unions have been primarily small, declining unions seeking economies of scale in operations, and both large and small unions searching for alternatives to traditional membership recruitment. Typical is the case of the Glass, Pottery and Plastic Workers, a union which lost one-quarter of its members because of plant closures in the six years prior to its 1988 amalgamation with the Molders and Allied Workers. It merged in order to achieve adequate levels of staffing and membership services. Without merger, it could not have afforded to hold its next convention without a dues increase (Hatfield 1988). Similarly, when the National Union of Packinghouse and Industrial Workers merged into the United Food and Commercial Workers (UFCW) in 1989, it had 3,500 members— less than 10 percent of its peak membership. Had it not merged, membership services would have been sharply curtailed (Bureau of National Affairs 1989f). A UFCW officer claimed that the merger would "greatly amplify their [the Packinghouse Workers'] power at the bargaining table and provide much needed resources and expertise for organizing additional members" ("Packing Union Joins UFCW" 1989, 5).

In the six years before its absorption by the Machinists in 1988, the Marine and Shipbuilding Workers lost half of its members because of the decline in shipbuilding (Bureau of National Affairs 1988b). Environmental issues and automation caused the loss of nearly two-thirds of the Woodworkers' members in the 20 years before it merged into the Machinists in 1994. Aside from benefiting from the 500,000-member Machinists' research and organizing departments, the 20,000-member Woodworkers hoped that the larger union's lobbying organization in Washington, D.C., would help in environmental battles over federal timberlands in the West (Bureau of National Affairs 1994d). In the same year and industry, the 15,000-member Association of Western Pulp and Paper Workers merged into the 500,000-member United Brotherhood of Carpenters. Greater economies of scale, and bargaining and lobbying power were cited as the reasons for the merger (Bureau of National Affairs, 1994b; e).

After having discussed merger with several unions over the years, the Rubber Workers merged into the United Steelworkers in 1995. In its last year, the Rubber Workers had 98,000 members, down from 180,000 in 1980. It had been weakened by an unsuccessful ten-month strike at Bridgestone/Firestone that began in 1994. This action depleted its strike fund and forced it to borrow $3 million and raise dues. Absorption into the Steelworkers gave the Rubber Workers access to a strike fund of over $160 million. The absorbed union became the Rubber/Plastics Industry Conference of the Steelworkers (Bureau of National Affairs 1995l; Narisetti 1995; "Rubber Workers Ends Strike" 1995).

The 1995 merger of two clothing unions is a classic example of the reasons for amalgamations.[6] The International Ladies Garment Workers (ILGWU) and the Amalgamated Clothing and Textile Workers (ACTWU) had their core memberships in an industry where jobs were lost because of the surge in low-priced foreign imports. The ACTWU's membership fell to about 175,000 from a 1976 peak of 400,000, while the ILGWU's fell to 125,000 from 457,000 in 1968. Both unions had much in common, including their political activism, campaigns against sweatshops, and lobbying for protective labor legislation. The ILGWU's members were primarily employed in women's apparel businesses in the Northeast. The ACTWU's membership were more diverse occupationally and geographically, with many in manufacturing in the South and Southwest.

Merger talks between the ILGWU and the ACTWU had been on and off for fifty years; the successful round lasted three years. The unions settled finally because both had suffered serious membership losses and had little hope for recruiting new members in an industry with so many small, nonunion companies and such intense foreign competition. The officers of the new union, UNITE (Union of Needletrades, Industrial and Textile Employees), announced their intent to organize aggressively despite the difficulties by launching a $10 million organizing campaign. Jay Mazur, president of the ILGWU and the first president of UNITE, commented on the primary objectives of the merger: "Part of coming together was an attempt to stabilize membership losses. It will give us increased presence—if you want to call it power I will accept that—in the legislative arena, the political arena, with the industry. And above all, it will give us some additional power in organizing the unorganized" (Szekely 1995, 1–2).

Over a twelve-year transition period, the dues of the two unions will be equalized, each will have its own international vice-president and Canadian vice-president, and votes will be weighted so that the two unions have equal power in balloting. Either union can opt out of the merger within six years if it believes there has been a serious breach of the merger agreement (Bureau of National Affairs 1995j).

UNITE is being created by two unions in roughly similar jurisdictions, but the mergers listed in appendix 1 clearly show how far union jurisdiction has declined in importance in the United States. Mergers often joined unions with dissimilar memberships: the Leather Workers into the Office and Professional Employees, the Upholsterers into the Steelworkers, the Tile, Marble, and Granite Workers into the Carpenters, the Furniture Workers into the Electrical Workers, and the Writers into the Auto Workers. This diversity is not unexpected. Most large unions already have exceptionally heterogeneous memberships because since the early 1980s they have been recruiting practically any interested workers (Chaison and Dhavale 1991; Chaison 1995). Officers of small unions agree to absorptions not because of matches in memberships but because favorable merger terms were offered; for example, proposals called for high degrees of postmerger autonomy or continued employment of officers (Chaison 1986). Alongside mergers creating greater membership diversity, however, were mergers between unions with similar or overlapping jurisdictions. The appendix shows unions combining within such industries as glass and pottery, communications, airlines, printing, retail and wholesale, and clothing and textiles.

A few unions have become centers of merger activity, diversifying their jurisdictions and expanding quickly through absorptions. The UFCW absorbed 8 unions between 1980 and 1994, including those of barbers and beauticians, retail workers, insurance workers, packinghouse workers, and garment workers. The Service Employees absorbed 5 unions, ranging from jewelry workers to locomotive firemen and oilers. The Machinists also absorbed 5 unions with members as diverse as woodworkers and pattern makers. The Communications Workers took in unions of typographers, telegraphers, and broadcast technicians.

What the tables and appendix 1 cannot show is the inherent difficultly of merging unions because of the need for agreement on governing structures and practices that allay officers' and members' fears of the submergence of their interests. For instance, the absorption of the Retail, Wholesale and Department Store Union (RWDSU) into the UFCW in 1993 came at the end of 13 years of intermittent negotiations. The 100,000-member RWDSU became a district council of the 1.3 million–member UFCW. A merger settlement was reached only after the RWDSU was promised a high degree of autonomy and the right to terminate the merger during its first four years (Bureau of National Affairs 1993d,e; Byrne 1993). The merger discussions between the National Education Association (NEA) and the American Federation of Teachers were less successful. The talks had been on and off for thirty years when an agreement finally seemed near in 1994. But negotiations broke down at the end of the year over the issues of leadership, federation affiliation, regional autonomy, and the composition of governing bodies (Lieberman 1993; Richardson 1993; Bureau of National Affairs 1995k).[7] In July 1995, however, there was new hope for a possible merger. Delegates to the NEA's convention voted to have their officers revive the merger discussions with the NEA by focusing on the need to eliminate jurisdictional disputes, coordinate legislative activities, and confront common educational and political problems (Bureau of National Affairs 1995h).

In this review of merger activity, we should keep in mind that merger proponents must often guide their settlements through officer and member approval without the aid of federation or legislative policy. The rising trend in union mergers since 1980 seems remarkable when we consider the barriers that had to be overcome.

The Underlying Trends

THE LEGAL FRAMEWORK

Labor laws in the United States do not promote national union mergers or reduce merger barriers. They do not prescribe procedures for drafting absorption or amalgamation documents, informing union members about merger terms, or balloting for merger approval. Merger agreements are not approved and deposited with government agencies. Merged unions are not registered. There are, however, some legal requirements for affiliations because these mergers can change the identities of bargaining agents selected by workers and can raise questions about whether employers must continue to honor their bargaining obligations.[8]

The National Labor Relations Board evaluates affiliations by asking, first, if the merger vote had been conducted with due process, and second, if the merged union is essentially the same organization that was certified to represent the bargaining unit. The due process requirement means that members must be notified about the merger, merger terms must be fully disclosed, there must be sufficient opportunity to discuss the proposal, and secret ballot elections must be held to determine the members' preference. When the board investigates the continuity of the bargaining relationship, it compares pre- and postmerger conditions, for example, the composition and powers of governing boards, and the members' rights to ratify collective agreements, nominate candidates, run for union office, and approve strikes. If the merger significantly alters the union, the employer could refuse to recognize it as bargaining agent. The union might then have to undergo a new organizing campaign and win a certification election to regain its bargaining status.

These standards apply only to affiliations, not national union amalgamations or absorptions. In the latter, change normally extends beyond the scope of bargaining units (the basis on which the representative was selected), and the board does not have to examine whether the workers' choice of bargaining agent has been negated by merger. Mergers of national union are generally treated as internal union affairs, but the courts may review how a merger was approved if members or officers argue that there were improper amendments to the unions' constitutions, members were inadequately or deceptively informed about merger terms, or there was insufficient opportunity for casting merger ballots. Merger opponents may also claim that merger negotiations and approval deviated from the union's constitutional procedures for modifying governing structures or conducting membership referendums (Chaison 1986). In later sections, we will see how such legal challenges can be powerful weapons in the hands of merger opponents.

FEDERATION POLICY

The AFL-CIO's role in its affiliates' mergers is one of restrained encouragement and neutral assistance as an "honest broker." When the American Federation of Labor and the Congress of Industrial Organizations merged in 1955, affiliates were assured that their jurisdictions would remain intact. Mergers would not be forced even though the two federations sometimes chartered rival unions in the same industries and occupations. The AFL-CIO's constitution proclaimed the objective of encouraging "the elimination of conflicting and duplicating organizations and jurisdictions through the process of voluntary agreements and voluntary merger"(Goldberg 1956, 237).

Since the merger, AFL-CIO officers have initiated merger contacts between union officers, mediated at impasses in affiliates' merger negotiations, and consistently declared the benefits of mergers. In the words of its recently retired president, Lane Kirkland, the federation's role was to "do our very best to be helpful to the parties and to cajole and to persuade and to give technical assistance as they pursue their mergers" ("Kirkland Discusses Issues" 1985, 2).

For a while, it seemed that the federation might be more active in affiliates' mergers. In 1981, the AFL-CIO executive council created a merger committee to promote mergers among unions in roughly similar jurisdictions and to assure clear and coherent jurisdictions among the remaining unions. The council believed it could reduce the number of affiliates by as much as two-thirds through mergers. Plans were made to survey affiliates to determine the level of merger interest. Retired union officers would be enlisted as merger advisors and mediators (AFL-CIO Merger Committee 1981, 1983). A merger program was briefly discussed but then abandoned in the later 1980s, and the merger committee has since been dissolved. Apparently, the federation was concerned about intruding into affiliates' affairs and believed that officers' attention would be more appropriately focussed on pressing political and organizing problems.

It has also been proposed that the federation examine the jurisdictions of merging affiliates and withhold recognition if they seemed to be mismatched. In 1985, an AFL-CIO strategy committee, the Committee on the Evolution of Work, released its report suggesting ways to revitalize the labor movement. Among its recommendations was that there be more union mergers. But the Committee observed that "mergers are difficult to effectuate and, if poorly conceived, can cause a union to lose that identity which helps bind the members and the organization. . . . Accordingly, both active AFL-CIO encouragement of mergers and guidelines as to appropriate and inappropriate mergers deserve a high priority. . . . Mergers are more likely to be effective if partners share a community of interest" (AFL-CIO 1985, 30).

The committee suggested that the AFL-CIO review affiliates' mergers and approve them when unions share communities of interest, which was defined as substantial overlap in the industries in which their members work. This would ensure that mergers "represent the optimum, beneficial combination" (AFL-CIO 1985, 33). A formula was devised for determining when merging unions have a presumptive community of interest.[9] The committee's recommendations, however, were never formally adopted by the AFL-CIO executive council and have had little if any bearing on the affiliates' choice of merger partner (McDonald 1993).

There is one way in which the federation is presently empowered to evaluate mergers. The AFL-CIO is concerned that affiliates might establish superficial alliances solely to extend coverage of the federation's no-raid agreement to unaffiliated unions. Under such arrangements, the unaffiliated unions receive charters as locals or divisions and pay per capita fees to the affiliated union, thereby gaining protection against raids through its association. Such mergers are in name only and discouraged by the federation. Since 1984, the federation has established and revised guidelines for determining when an acceptable degree of postmerger integration occurs; for example, the absorbed union must be granted a regular charter as a local or section, and its members must have the right to full membership and pay regular dues no later than four years after the merger. Unless such conditions are met, the protection of the no-raid agreement will not be extended to the unaffiliated union (AFL-CIO 1989).

THE INHERENT DIFFICULTY OF MERGING NATIONAL UNIONS

In the absence of a legal framework facilitating mergers and pro-active federation policies, American unions feel the full force of merger barriers, whether internally or externally generated. Merger opponents can block the process in several ways. They can turn officer elections into de facto merger votes by matching pro- and antimerger candidates against each other. They can postpone merger votes with lawsuits charging that union constitutions were violated. The two cases described below—the mergers of the International Typographical Union and the National Union of Hospital and Health Care Employees—illustrate the difficulty of consummating mergers in the United States.

The Merger Attempts of the International Typographical Union. The International Typographical Union (ITU) was chartered in 1852 and was the oldest American union in existence when it merged in 1987. The ITU was widely known as a model of union democracy because of its two-party political system (Lipset, Trow, and Coleman 1956), although in recent years decision making has become centralized and members' influence has declined (Stratton 1989).

Since 1970, new technologies have blurred the boundaries of traditional printing crafts, which has cost some printers their jobs. (L. Adams 1984; Wallace 1985). In 1977, the ITU began to explore a merger with the Newspaper Guild, a union of reporters, editors, and clerical workers.[10] Computerization had transformed much of typesetters' and printers' jobs; work that was once within the ITU's jurisdiction now originated at computer terminals in newsrooms. The new technology also strengthened the employers' bargaining position because strikes were easier to defeat when work could be performed outside of the printers' bargaining unit (Eisen 1986). In 1986, one industry observer commented that "the ITU is presiding over a dying craft and they are desperately looking for a safe harbor . . . merger is not going to change the fact that they are going to continue to dwindle in number" ("A Dying Craft" 1986, A26).

Informal merger talks between the 75,000-member ITU and the 32,000-member Guild broke off in 1981, because the unions disagreed over dues and local autonomy, and the Guild members' feared that their interests would be submerged in the larger ITU. Despite these difficulties, however, both unions' officers still believed there might be some value in merging and meetings were resumed in early 1982. In September, the two unions announced that they had agreed to amalgamate, forming the Media Employees International Union. Merger proposals were scheduled for presentation and approval at special conventions, with membership referendums to be held in 1983.

External forces, however, soon derailed the ITU–Guild merger. The proposed amalgamation conflicted with the plans of the International Brotherhood of Teamsters to absorb the ITU along with other printing unions and gain a foothold for future organizing in the printing industry. In August 1983, Jackie Presser, the Teamsters' president, addressed the ITU convention in San Francisco, and urged delegates to reject the Guild merger and to join with the Teamsters instead. The delegates responded by rejecting the Guild agreement, but they then authorized the ITU officers to explore mergers possibilities with another major printing union, the 175,000-member Graphic Communications International Union (GCIU).[11] The ITU president, Joe Bingel, opposed this resolution, arguing that talks with the GCIU should wait until meetings were held with the Teamsters.

The ITU found itself caught between the Teamsters' plans for expansion and the AFL-CIO's campaign to create a single printing union through mergers of affiliated unions. The Teamsters had been expelled from the AFL-CIO in 1957 for leadership corruption. The ITU, GCIU, and the Guild were AFL-CIO affiliates.

A week before the AFL-CIO's convention in October 1983, Bingel announced that substantial progress had been made in merger negotiations with the Teamsters. Lane Kirkland, AFL-CIO president, attempted to divert the merger and met with Bingel and officers of the Guild and the GCIU during the federation's convention. The meetings were described as exploratory and the parties agreed to confer again although no date was set. Kirkland believed that a merger of the three printing affiliates was "the best solution to the needs of the workers in its industry which has been so dramatically impacted by new technology and automation" (Bureau of National Affairs 1983c, A10).

In November 1983, Robert S. McMichen, the ITU's first vice-president and a major opponent of the proposed merger with the Teamsters, defeated Bingel in the election for the union presidency by a vote of 26,855 to 21,935. But Bingel challenged the election results, claiming that several ITU locals had improperly used dues to assist McMichen's campaign. These charges were upheld by the ITU's canvassing board and the election was set aside. McMichen then filed objections to this decision with the Department of Labor. The ITU's canvassing board recommended that a repeat election be held, but Bingel and other officers asked that it be postponed until the Department of Labor had ruled on McMichen's objections. If the objections were upheld, the Department of Labor would supervise the rerun election.

With his election challenged and set aside, McMichen was dismissed as an ITU officer, but was then hired by the AFL-CIO to chair a committee promoting mergers of printing unions. The results of the ITU's officer election remained contested for the next few months. Merger negotiations with the GCIU continued but broke down in March 1984. The ITU claimed that the GCIU refused to put their merger proposal in writing, while the GCIU accused the ITU's leaders of inciting a bidding war between the Teamsters and GCIU over merger terms. The ITU's merger committee then resumed talks with the Teamsters.

In April 1984, the ITU and Teamsters announced that they had agreed on merger terms that would make the ITU an autonomous trade division headed by a director appointed by the Teamster president. The agreement would continue the employment of the ITU's officers, preserve its current dues, and permit it to maintain its own headquarters.

The AFL-CIO leadership strongly opposed the ITU–Teamster merger, contending that the settlement was premature and that ITU's members should be given the opportunity to choose between the Teamsters and the GCIU. McMichen formed a committee within the ITU to campaign against the Teamsters and promote the GCIU as an amalgamation partner. Calling itself the "Committee for One Big Union in the Printing Industry," McMichen's group published a newsletter and distributed posters with the slogan "Labor Strength Plus Respect," an obvious reference to the Teamsters' poor public image. It also distributed sections of the Teamsters' constitution that they claimed were undemocratic and in conflict with the ITU's constitution. The campaign newsletter emphasized that joining with the GCIU "would pay off not only at the bargaining table, but in the legislative arena, in organizing efforts and, when push comes to shove, on the picket line" (Bureau of National Affairs 1984a, 313). ITU members were also reminded that a merger with the Teamsters, a union expelled from the AFL-CIO, could result in their union's expulsion and leave it vulnerable to organizing raids from affiliates. The AFL-CIO assisted the campaign against the Teamsters by hiring a public-relations consultant and financing court challenges.

The pro-Teamster forces held regional meetings with ITU members to discuss merger terms. They maintained that the merger would greatly enhance the ITU's bargaining power because the Teamsters represented newspaper drivers in many cities, important allies during strikes, and had sufficient resources to organize nonunion firms. As the campaign progressed, the great symbolic and practical importance of its outcome became apparent. A vote for the merger would be a victory for Jackie Presser who was trying to rehabilitate the Teamsters' poor image by absorbing a union widely known for its democratic governance. The Teamsters would also be getting an important base for its future expansion in the printing industry. A merger with the Teamsters would be a major defeat for Lane Kirkland and other proponents of building a new unified printing union from affiliates. It would also demonstrate the futility of trying to isolate the expelled Teamsters from the mainstream of the union movement.

The referendum on the ITU–Teamsters merger, scheduled for May 16, 1984, was blocked by a court order obtained by McMichen and his supporters. The dispute over ITU officer elections would first have to be resolved. In June, the Department of Labor nullified the earlier election after finding that both sides had campaigned illegally, mostly by promoting their candidates in publications supported by union dues. In a repeat election supervised by the government, McMichen defeated Bingel by a vote of 28,167 to 15,276. McMichen's slate of officers was also victorious, gaining a majority of the seats on the union's five-member executive board. McMichen interpreted this outcome as the members' rejection of a Teamsters merger and their willingness to explore merger possibilities with the GCIU. Bingel petitioned the Department of Labor to set the election aside, claiming that McMichen received illegal assistance and compensation from the AFL-CIO. This charge was dismissed and the new officers were sworn in.

By now, both sides were adept at legal maneuvering to block each others' merger proposals. Despite the election of their opponents to the ITU's governing board, the supporters of the Teamster merger remained active. They argued that the petition for a vote on the Teamster merger had been signed by officers of 178 ITU locals, a sufficient number under the union's constitution for a membership referendum. Seeing a new chance for a vote, Teamster leader Presser expressed his determination to pursue the merger and "not walk away from our friends and commitments" (Bureau of National Affairs 1985f, A6).

As they sought to reconcile the opposing merger campaigns, delegates at the ITU's September 1984 convention decided to force the issue to a conclusion. A deadline of ninety days was set for the negotiation of a merger with the GCIU. If McMichen and the other officers could not reach a settlement with the GCIU, a membership referendum on the Teamsters' merger proposal would be held.

In December 1984, with the deadline less than a month away, the ITU's and GCIU's merger committees announced their agreement on merger terms. The merger plan would be submitted for approval by the unions' executive boards in January 1985 and, if passed, membership referendums would be held in April. Believing that its own merger campaign was finally blocked, the Teamsters condemned the ITU–GCIU settlement as a sell-out reached by union officers through secret meetings and side deals.

The Teamster's disappointment proved to be premature. The GCIU's officers met in March and rejected the merger proposal because of the financial projections based on the ITU's membership. They felt that if the ITU's membership continued to decline, dues income would not be sufficient to cover the salaries of the numerous ITU staff members and officers who were guaranteed jobs under the merger agreement. The membership referendum was canceled.

With the collapse of the ITU–GCIU merger, the Teamsters restarted its campaign. Under the resolution passed by the ITU's convention, the ITU–Teamster merger proposal would finally be presented to the membership. An intensive campaign followed, with a referendum held in April 1985. When the ballots were counted, the Teamsters was rejected by a 2-to-1 margin of the ITU's membership; 17,547 members were in favor of the merger and 34,234 against. McMichen declared, "We're confident this strong vote will put the Teamster affair well behind us," and, with an obvious allusion to the Teamsters status and reputation, claimed that the deciding factors in the election were the ITU's "traditions of democratic

unionism and involvement with the mainstream of organized labor''
(''Printers Union Rejects a Teamster Merger'' 1985, A21). The Teamsters
blamed their loss on strong anti-Teamster sentiments among retired members (30,000 of the ITU's 75,000 members) and the ITU officers' campaign against the merger.

With both the GCIU's and the Teamsters' merger proposals rejected
and membership continuing to decline, the ITU officers began to explore
new merger possibilities. On July 3, 1986, officers from the Communications Workers of America (CWA) visited the ITU's headquarters and presented their merger plan. Two weeks later, merger terms were offered by
officers of the International Association of Machinists.

The CWA merger proposal was endorsed by ITU officers: ''We are very
much in tune in terms of our jurisdictions, and the merger agreement has
the added plus of allowing us to lower our members' international union
dues by two-thirds, while still retaining our identity, democratic procedures and control over our own affairs'' (''ITU Schedules Referendum''
1986, 2). The Machinists' proposal was rejected by the ITU's leadership
and never presented to convention delegates or the membership. In August
1986, only a year after the rejection of the Teamsters, the ITU's convention
endorsed the merger with the CWA by a narrow margin—14,266 in favor
and 14,042 against.[12]

The ITU's officers predicted that merger with CWA would lead to the
creation of ''one huge printing and electronics communications union''
(McMichen, Austin, and Boarman 1986, 2). They claimed that the CWA
and ITU negotiated with many of the same employers because major
newspaper companies had diversified into cable television and telecommunications. But Allan Heritage, the ITU's first vice-president and a sup-
porter of the ITU–Teamsters merger, argued that the merger terms were
accepted because the ''present majority leadership felt they couldn't go to
the convention without a merger document. So the CWA merger agreement was hastily negotiated, resulting in numerous flaws'' (Heritage
1986b, 5). He claimed that greater autonomy and separate ITU headquarters and staff were stipulated in the rejected Teamsters' proposal.

In a referendum held in October and November, 80 percent of the ITU's
members voted for the merger (29,740 members in favor and 7,625
against). The merger documents were signed in February 1987, creating a
semi-autonomous Printing, Publishing and Media Workers Sector within
the CWA. Although it was initially reluctant to create an industry division
because that might lead to factionalism, the CWA offered this arrangement

because it anticipated extensive organizing in the electronic and print media. It also knew that it had to match the level of autonomy stipulated in earlier merger proposals considered by the ITU.

In officer elections held at the time of the merger referendum, Mc-Michen was elected to a three-year term as president of the new sector and as a vice-president of the CWA. Mergers of local unions within the sector were encouraged but not compelled. The sector held an annual conference prior to the annual CWA convention. Membership and benefits were continued for the ITU's retirees.

The twists and turns of the ITU's merger campaigns show the force and complexity of the barriers to mergers in the absence of a uniform, legally enforceable process for approving them as well as a clear federation role in affiliates' mergers. Merger plans were devised and/or examined by officers of the ITU, the Guild, the GCIU, Teamsters, the CWA, the Machinists, and the AFL-CIO. External merger opponents openly supported and encouraged internal opponents. Campaigns to reject merger proposals were intertwined with officer elections. The fight against mergers was carried to the courts and the Department of Labor. Legal maneuvering stalled members' votes on merger terms.

The inseparability of union politics and the merger approval process is also vividly illustrated in a case nearly as complex but certainly as contentious as the ITU's—the dual absorption of the National Union of Hospital and Health Care Employees.

The Merger of the National Union of Hospital and Health Care Employees. The predecessor of the National Union of Hospital and Health Care Employees was a local formed in the 1930s among pharmacists in New York City (Local 1199 of the Retail, Wholesale and Department Store Employees (RWDSU)). Over the years, bargaining units of health-care workers were added throughout the United States and also given the 1199 designation. In 1981, the health-care section within the RWDSU composed of locals designated 1199 attempted to split off and merge with the SEIU, but it was blocked by its parent union (Chaison 1986).

During the next three years, relations deteriorated between the RWDSU and its health-care section. The RWDSU wanted a larger share of the section's dues (it received less than a quarter), tried to divide the section into locals, and sought control over health care organizing. The section, now operating under the name National Union of Hospital and Health Care Employees (NUHHCE), fought to retain its autonomy and insisted on controlling its own organizing staff. When it appeared that these differences could not be resolved, 14 locals of health-care workers left the RWDSU and were charted by the AFL-CIO as the NUHHCE. Locals carrying the 1199 designation in New York City remained with the RWDSU.[13]

Delegates to the NUHHCE's 1987 convention approved a resolution to explore merger possibilities with other health care unions. The merger search was motivated by the need to gain access to greater organizing funds and staff and to intensify recruiting efforts in its largely nonunion jurisdiction. Only one-tenth of the 6 million health care workers in the United States were unionized. The numerous small associations of health care workers seemed incapable of mass recruitment and of countering intense and sophisticated employer opposition. An NUHHCE merger committee soon received proposals from the Service Employees International Union (SEIU) and the American Federation of State, County and Municipal Employees (AFSCME). AFSCME's proposal was selected by a vote of 4 to 2 committee members.[14]

In September 1988, however, members of NUHHCE's executive board, led by Secretary-Treasurer Jerry Brown, rejected the AFSCME proposal and voted to merge with SEIU. The NUHHCE's president, Henry Nicholas, challenged this move as illegal because approval was not given by a majority of the union's 26-member executive board. Nicholas and his supporters had left the executive-board meeting to prevent a vote, but a majority of those remaining voted for the SEIU merger. The pro-SEIU merger faction claimed that each executive-board member could vote the number of members that he or she represented, and that the merger was approved by a margin of 41,000 to 28,000. After the balloting, the board recessed, reconvened again without the pro-AFSCME faction present, and reaffirmed its earlier decision to merge with the SEIU. It claimed that it was embarking on a historic combination of the two major unions of health-care workers, 70,000 in NUHHCE and 370,000 in SEIU, and that this would lead to the surge of organizing in the industry.

The dispute moved to the courts. Brown and the other supporters of the SEIU merger filed a suit to compel the NUHHCE's officers to proceed to a membership vote on the merger. Then, seeing an irreparable split in the union's governing body, 13 NUHHCE members asked in a separate suit that a referendum be conducted with both the SEIU and AFSCME on the ballot and without an executive-board recommendation. The judge responded by issuing a restraining order preventing campaigns or referendums for merger with the SEIU or AFSCME separately.

The conflict became personal and racial. At court hearings, Nicholas charged that the SEIU's president, John J. Sweeney, was trying to take control of the NUHHCE by improperly negotiating a merger agreement with a dissident group: "It is an unparalleled development in the labor movement for the head of one AFL-CIO affiliate to try stealing the members of a strong union with one of America's most respected union leaders, who happens to be black. The profound agony of the whole situation is the act of one international president [Sweeney of the SEIU]—and the rest of the labor movement must be troubled by this—to steal members away from another union president" (Bureau of National Affairs 1989k, A3).

The Brown and Nicholas factions accused each other of undemocratic practices to keep the merger proposal from the membership. They debated the composition of a quorum of the NUHHCE's executive board and the formula for weighing votes. The Brown faction was accused of circulating leaflets falsely telling the membership that the full executive board had approved the merger agreement with the SEIU. The legal contest remained an internal struggle; neither the SEIU nor AFSCME were parties to the lawsuits.

Despite the bitter conflict and the rhetoric of the officers, the two merger proposals were actually quite similar. Both created health-care divisions and contributed about $30 million for organizing health-care workers. Under AFSCME's proposal, the new division had jurisdiction over health-care workers with the exception of those already represented by AFSCME. The NUHHCE could also dissolve the merger after two years by a majority vote of its executive board and members. The SEIU proposal allowed NUHHCE to retain bargaining rights for the health-care workers that it already represented; new units could be organized with the approval of the SEIU. The NUHHCE could withdraw from a merger with SEIU after three years by a majority vote of its members.

The AFL-CIO's officers, concerned about a possibly widening conflict between two major affiliates, mediated the dispute and announced a compromise settlement in February 1989. AFSCME, SEIU and the two NUHHCE factions agreed to a referendum to be conducted by the American Arbitration Association on May 1, 1989. The ballot asked first, whether the NUHHCE members wanted their union to merge and second, which union should be a party to the merger. Ballots were tabulated at district levels; this all but assured a split in NUHHCE, with districts going to different unions. One observer commented that the agreement for balloting was a "peaceful settlement of the dispute based on the realization that the split within the union was so severe that members weren't going to peacefully go in one direction" (Bureau of National Affairs 1989b, A10).

When the referendum proposal was accepted, the NUHHCE's factions dropped their lawsuits, and the judge ended the restraining order that had blocked the union from acting on the competing merger proposals. The balloting was completed on May 27, 1989. Majorities in all NUHHCE districts voted to merge. Districts with 51,430 members joined the SEIU and those with 25,230 members went to AFSCME.

The merger campaigns of the NUHHCE and the ITU might seem inordinately complicated and contentious, but I have selected them to illustrate the full force and complexity of the opposition to mergers in the United States. Merger opponents proceed to the courts and government agencies, and the merger question is quickly entangled in officer elections. The law is used to block rather than facilitate merger, often with the intent of keeping competing proposals from the membership. Mergers are exceedingly difficult to complete if they are opposed by significant officer or membership factions.

The ITU's merger campaigns are admittedly atypical in regard to the federation's role. The AFL-CIO's support of a competing merger proposal, a rare intrusion in affiliates' affairs, can be explained by the fact that much more was at stake than the single merger of a medium-sized union. The choice of merger options became a test of the federation's ability to isolate expelled unions and to promote and coordinate mergers among the many unions within a single, declining industry. The NUHHCE merger shows the AFL-CIO in its customary role; officers served as neutral, "honest brokers" of merger terms and as mediators at merger negotiations.

Affiliations, or Organizing the Organized

Affiliations have become an important merger form in the United States, though one that is seldom recognized in studies of merger trends. Major studies by Brooks and Gamm (1976), Chitayat (1979), and Chaison (1986) deal entirely with national-union mergers. Chronicles of merger activity by L. Adams (1984) and Williamson (1995) list only affiliations of state-wide public-employee associations into national unions, not those of local and regional unions. Although the evidence is fragmentary, it now appears that many large national unions are entering into affiliations and that a few are using them as the primary means for growth and diversification.

AFSCME uses affiliations to establish its presence in geographic areas where there is organizing potential, for example, among groups of public employees who recently received the legal right to join unions and engage in collective bargaining. The CWA weighs location heavily in its selection of affiliation partners, merging only with those unions whose members can be served by nearby staff and that will increase the CWA's regional bargaining or political power. For instance, the CWA affiliated with the 12,000-member Combined Law Enforcement Association of Texas because it was already a major union in that state, and it anticipated even greater political power after the merger. After the merger, the CWA became the largest union in Texas with 50,000 members ("Independent Joins CWA" 1992).

The UFCW generally affiliates with unions that are not geographically isolated and whose members can be serviced cost effectively. It has little concern for the unions' industries or occupations—affiliated unions have included leather workers in New York City and baseball players in Puerto Rico (United Food and Commercial Workers 1993).

Small unions usually weigh their affiliation options after major events jeopardize their ability to grow and represent workers. Such events include changes in once accommodative and predictable relationships with major employers, the introduction of privatization in the public sector, severe membership losses following raids, and new production technologies that threaten union jobs. For example, when a 3,500-member union of nurses and other health-care professionals in New Jersey and Delaware affiliated with the Operating Engineers, it was seeking shelter from raids. After losing a bargaining unit to an AFL-CIO affiliate, the union solicited affiliation proposals from several AFL-CIO unions. It joined with the Operating Engineers in 1992 because it was offered complete autonomy as a new district (Bureau of National Affairs 1992). When the *Boston Globe* was acquired by the New York Times Company in 1993, the members of the Boston Globe Employees Association voted to affiliate with the Newspaper Guild. Their objective was to become stronger in negotiations and counter the power of their new, larger employer (Bureau of National Affairs 1994a). The transformation of the publishing industry from many small companies to a few large ones was one of the reasons for the affiliation of the 3,000-member National Writers Union with the Auto Workers ("Writers' Bloc" 1991).

Large unions approach affiliation targets as they would non-union workplaces. They gather information on the smaller union's internal politics, financial condition and relations with employers. Frequently, the national union's officers contact officers from the local or regional union, visits are made to each union's headquarters and, if interest continues, formal merger committees are established to explore options and draft merger documents. On occasion, initial contacts are made by dissident members of the smaller union who are dissatisfied with their union's policies or leadership. If the dissidents enjoy substantial membership support, the national union will encourage them to run for office on a pro-affiliation platform. Officer elections will then become de facto referendums on affiliation.

The affiliation campaign is directed at achieving majority support of the smaller union's membership. This is usually evidenced by a secret ballot election conducted by a neutral agency such as the American Arbitration Association. Elections must satisfy the due-process standards of the National Labor Relations Board. The board itself does not conduct affiliation votes.

The SEIU assigns affiliation campaigns to a special group within its organizing department, while AFSCME and CWA use their regular organizing staff. Typical campaign literature familiarizes members and officers with the history and practices of the national union and the benefits of merger. For example, the SEIU published a sixteen-page brochure describing its finances, membership growth and diversity, relationship with federations, and governing structures. Affiliating unions were assured that they will retain their own constitutions and by-laws and hire their own staffs, control assets, and negotiate collective agreements. A small union could merge into a neighboring SEIU local without compulsion or interference from SEIU headquarters. A larger one could become an SEIU local with "the right to its own identity, continuing its name, traditions, practices" (Service Employees International Union n.d.(a), 14).

A brochure designed for the SEIU's 1992 campaign with the San Francisco Police Officers Association (SFPOA) emphasized postmerger autonomy:

New affiliates such as SFPOA have a valuable additional guarantee [aside from the SEIU's decentralized structure] because autonomy and independence are guaranteed in writing as part of a written affiliation agreement. Specifically, SFPOA will retain the right to set its own Constitution and By-laws, elect its own officers, hire its own staff, negotiate and sign its own contracts, decide what issues should be taken to grievance and arbitration, decide its own dues structure and control its assets and budget. (Service Employees International Union n.d. (b), 2).

National unions often compete over affiliations, particularly those involving larger unions and those providing entry into major unorganized jurisdictions (e.g., health-care and local-government services). Bidding wars can start. For example, the California Intern and Residents Association (CIRA), representing about 2,000 physicians-in-training, discussed affiliation with eight unions over five years before joining SEIU in 1990. The SEIU was accepted because it allowed the CIRA's officers and members to retain control and promised resources and support to organize the nonunion interns and residents in California. It also promised to lobby for state legislation limiting hours of work for interns and residents (Bureau of National Affairs 1990c).[15]

The SEIU has become the major affiliating union through its aggressive "reach out" program (Adams 1984, 2). From 1980 to 1993, it affiliated 57 unions. More than a third of these were in state employee associations in California (79,000 members), Oregon (12,000), Maine (11,000), New Hampshire (5,000), Wyoming (2,600), and Georgia (1,600). The SEIU also affiliated 47 regional and local unions. These included such diverse organizations as the Chicago Crossing Guards Association (1,200 members), the Anaheim (California) Municipal Employees Association (750), the Madison (Connecticut) School Secretaries (80), the San Diego County Employees Association (5,000), and the Nevada Corrections Association (400) (Service Employees International Union 1993). From 1980 to 1993, the SEIU's membership increased by 360,000 (Gifford 1982; Bureau of National Affairs 1993a); half of these new members joined through affiliations and about 30 percent were in three absorbed national unions.

Critics argue that affiliations have become inadequate substitutes for traditional organizing; although they may resolve growth problems for a few unions in the short term, they do not increase total union membership or extend the frontiers of unionism. Officers and staff of unions active in affiliations, however, liken them to organizing—the smaller unions' members and officers gain a new awareness of and appreciation for unionism when they join with a larger, more militant union. Affiliations bring union members into the mainstream of the labor movement and provide them with more effective representation. Advocates argue that affiliations can increase total union membership when they lead to greater organizing in lesser unionized industries. Left to their own resources, smaller local or regional unions could not take full advantage of organizing opportunities. Finally, they argue that affiliations are not entered into indiscriminately and solely for the sake of quick membership gains; national unions reject affiliation partners that are geographically isolated and difficult to service.

For a small number of American unions, including the SEIU, AFSCME, and CWA, affiliations are becoming critical for growth and diversification. As I noted in chapter 1, affiliations are fast, inexpensive and high-yield alternatives to traditional membership recruitment at workplaces. The workers are already union members and affiliation votes can be carried out without jeopardizing bargaining status. There may be opposition from employers who would rather not deal with larger, more militant or effective unions, but "vote-no" campaigns would be less intense than those directed against the establishment of a bargaining relationship. Far less is at stake.

Those unions most successful in attracting affiliating unions have decentralized structures that accommodate the smaller unions' officers and members while allowing them their autonomy and their industrial or occupational identity. It has yet to be determined whether these union are evolving into quasi-federations that successfully accommodate a diverse membership in autonomous locals and divisions, or if officers will become preoccupied with containing conflicts among the diverse membership factions, and between locals organized at workplaces and those more autonomous ones created through affiliations (Chaison 1995). Also, despite the officers' and staff members' claims, the impact of affiliations on organizing is unclear. Do affiliations discourage traditional organizing by providing a convenient alternative, or do they encourage it by shifting staff and resources to unions and areas where they were not previously available? In all likelihood, the impact of affiliations is mixed, varying from merger to merger and from union to union. Some may have opened the door to new organizing and the first effective representation for groups of workers; others may be little more than the granting of a local charter, basically a change in the union's stationery, in return for the payment of a per capita fee.

A NEW SUPER-UNION?: THE PROPOSED MERGER OF THE AUTO WORKERS,
THE STEELWORKERS, AND THE MACHINISTS

At a press conference held on July 27, 1995 in Washington, D.C., Stephen Yokich, George Kourpias and George Becker, the presidents of the United Automobile Workers, the United Steelworkers and the International Association of Machinists, respectively, announced their unions' intention to amalgamate. This surprised not only close observers of the labor movement but nearly all of the unions' members, staff, and local officers. The secrecy of the merger talks was even more remarkable in light of its objective; the creation of an American super-union with nearly two-million members, a strike fund of more than $1 billion, an unlimited jurisdiction, and the undisputed position as the principal union in manufacturing (Bureau of National Affairs 1995a,e; Kilborn 1995b; Swoboda 1995).

The merger announcement led to widespread speculation about the power and policies of the new union and the possibility that the merger would revitalize the American labor movement. One commentator suggested that the merger was ''an historic development that could serve as a catalyst for other union mergers'' (Bureau of National Affairs 1995a, AA2). Another believed it was ''a move that could change the shape of the American labor movement [and] a major shift toward a Western European style of union organization [that brings together workers from several industries and occupations]'' (Swoboda 1995, C2). Still another saw the merger creating a union ''with the strength to start setting standards in wages and benefits'', thus leading to a ''turnaround in the downward trend in the standard of living in America'' (Bureau of National Affairs 1995e, AA2). But on a less optimistic note, other commentators warned that the new union might be so large that it would have a more bureaucratic leadership and less camaraderie among the members than it predecessors (Bureau of National Affairs 1995a; Feder 1995). One editorialist saw the merger adding little to the unions' power, aside from a larger strike fund, and believed the merger was a sign of the labor movement's declining fortunes rather than its revival—''Like corporations in trouble, unions grab at mergers for survival'' (Weinstein 1995:A12).

Despite the various opinions about the merger's probable impact, there was little doubt why the three unions planned to merge. Stiff competition from foreign and domestic nonunion producers and the long-term decline in manufacturing employment due to new technologies and work processes caused a loss of 1.4 million members for the three unions since the mid-1970s. Since then, the Auto Workers has lost half of its members, while the membership of the Steelworkers and Machinists fell by 30 percent and 40 percent, respectively (Weinstein 1995). The unions' leaders believed that Republican election victories and their control of Congress in 1994 ended any chances of new legislation that might renew union growth by making organizing easier, faster, and less expensive. (Swoboda 1995).

Aside from its motivating forces, there was little else about the proposed merger that was conventional. The unions' presidents announced their intention to merge before the merger terms had been settled. The document they signed, the Unity Declaration, shows only agreement on the need to merge; merger details are unspecified and left for future negotiation. The declaration begins with a statement that the three unions "hereby agree to combine our individual strength" to form a "new, two-million member strong, union by the year 2000" (Bureau of National Affairs 1995d, E1). The benefits of merger are described broadly in terms of more effective organizing, bargaining, and political action. The officers conclude, "our enduring vision of a world of dignity, security and prosperity for the many—not just the few—requires nothing less than that we create a new union for a new era. We intend to answer that call" (Bureau of National Affairs 1995d, E1).

Formal negotiations between merger committees had not even begun when the declaration was signed. According to a published report, the three union presidents met for dinner at a downtown Washington steak house on July 19th and, after only about five minutes of discussion, decided that the time was right to act on a merger. After three hours, the officers were convinced that a merger was not only desirable but feasible, and they soon returned to their unions' headquarters to brief their executive boards on their plan. A week later, the executive boards met in Washington and unanimously approved the Unity Declaration (Swoboda 1995).

The tone of the merger announcement is highly optimistic. The unions will soon initiate a program of joint political action and take advantage of opportunities for coordinated bargaining and organizing. Merger committees will be formed to resolve issues of structure and governance (Bureau of National Affairs 1995e). What the announcement does not mention, however, is the complexity of the negotiations required to combine three unions of roughly equal size. For example, a common barrier to merger, deciding who will serve as the new union's first president, is believed to be overcome in this case because the three incumbents are required by their union's constitutions to retire from office before the merger is completed in the year 2000 (Swoboda 1995). But the leadership issue might still be divisive. First, the merged union will have to be led by an officer from one of the three unions, even if there are also "associate president" positions. The choice of the new leader might be seen by the unions' members as a contest for dominance of the new union. Second, the limitations on the current officers' terms are specified only under the present unions' constitutions, which could be modified when the new union's first constitution is drafted. Third, it is unclear whether the new union's officers will be selected by direct membership vote or by delegates at a convention. In either case, a formula will have to be devised to give the unions an equal voice in the first officer elections at the very least (Moody 1995).

Prolonged negotiations for merger can be fraught with political and technical difficulties, and decisions may not completely satisfy the three unions' members. For example, there are differences among the unions in the voting power given to retirees in officer elections. This is not a minor issue—the new union will have about 1.2 million retired members (Bureau of National Affairs 1995e). Also, some procedure will be needed for settling claims to the combined strike fund; about four-fifths of the fund will come from the Auto Workers and the union would certainly not agree to the fund's unrestricted use by the others (Rose, Christian, and Nomani 1995).

Each of the three unions has a caucus of activists promoting democratic leadership and greater membership participation. During merger negotiations, we can expect the caucuses to coordinate their campaigns for such changes as increased local autonomy, direct officer elections, and greater representation of women and minorities on governing bodies. They will actively oppose any merger proposal that appears to continue or introduce autocratic, highly centralized leadership (Moody 1996).

Finally, other unions may ask to join the merger talks, or they may be invited to do so, and this could change the initial vision of the structure and governance of the new union. When the merger was announced, President Kourpias of the Machinists said: "I think 80 unions within the AFL-CIO are too many. This is why we keep this door open for those who would like to join us in this endeavor" (Bureau of National Affairs 1995a, AA2). One newspaper columnist suggested that the United Mine Workers and the newly formed Union of Needletrades, Industrial and Textile Employees might join the merger negotiations at later stages (Swoboda 1995).

Despite the numerous uncertainties and unresolved issues, observers that I have spoken to give the merger a better than even chance of being successfully negotiated and approved. The early announcement and commitment to the merger might add momentum to negotiations and stiffen the officers' resolve to devise satisfactory terms. Most of the unions' members are probably convinced that some sort of merger is inevitable and that their unions acting alone have little chance of ever regaining their previous size and power.

If merger is completed, we can expect to see the features common to amalgamations: the initial duplication of officers' positions, headquarters, newspapers, and benefit and pension plans; guarantees of continued employment for union staff; and the creation of industrial and occupational divisions to allay the fears of members that their interests will be submerged in a huge, diverse union (Chaison 1986). But it is also possible that the political and technical obstacles cannot be overcome. If this happens, some documents will be signed to fulfill the promise of the Unity Declaration, but these will create an alliance rather than a merger. There will be a sharing of facilities and staff (e.g., joint offices for lobbying and research), and close coordination of organizing campaigns and negotiations with the same employers or those in the same industries. The three unions, however, will retain full autonomy.

Whichever does occur—a merger or an alliance—the labor movement will follow the unions' negotiations closely. The possibility of a merged super union or a powerful new alliance may suggest the inevitability of merger. Union officers will take a closer look at the available options and partners, and some will return to ongoing merger negotiations with new resolve to reach a settlement.

Does the proposed merger signal the dawning of the age of the super-union in the United States—the evolution of a labor movement dominated by a few huge unions created by amalgamations, growing through additional mergers, and representing workers in jurisdictions without limits? Presently, there is not enough evidence to support the case for this structural change. Other large unions, for example the United Food and Commercial Workers, the Communications Workers, and the Service Employees, seem content to confine their merger activity to absorptions and affiliations rather than amalgamations and, as we saw earlier, are using these mergers as principal growth strategies. Even if the American Federation of Teachers and the National Education Association revive merger talks and successfully negotiate to form the largest union in the United States, the new union's membership would be confined to education and there would be limited potential for growth and diversification through additional mergers. Although no other super-unions may evolve, we can expect that a merged (or allied) Auto Workers, Steelworkers and Machinists will form a new center for merger activity, attracting other unions into affiliations and absorptions because of its high priority on organizing and its financial strength and economies of scale.

The motivation to merge appears to have increased significantly since 1980. Most American union officers and members are pessimistic, seeing little chance of reversing membership losses or regaining lost economic or political influence, at least in the near future. Merger barriers are always substantial, but they are formidable in the United States in the absence of a proactive federation policy toward mergers or legislation that simplifies the merger process and resolves merger opposition quickly and to finality. This point will become clearer when I contrast the American situation with that in other countries, particularly the merger waves initiated and guided by the labor federation in Australia and the numerous, complex union mergers made possible in Britain by merger-friendly legislation. At this point, we should keep in mind that recent increased merger activity has occurred despite the sheer difficulty of merging unions in the United States.

We also saw signs of numerous union affiliations and these may portend the state of union organizing in the United States. National unions are resorting to mergers with local or regional unions as an inexpensive and expedient growth strategy. It remains to be seen if affiliations, basically organizing the already organized, will detract attention and resources from traditional organizing.

It would be premature to predict a major wave of national union mergers in the United States despite the new interest in mergers that will almost certainly be generated by an amalgamation (or alliance) of the Auto Workers, Steelworkers, and Machinists. The evidence does show, however, that during the recent hard times unions have relied increasingly on the merger option for growth and survival. I attribute the heightened interest in mergers to the limited possibilities of growth through organizing, the precipitous decline in private sector unionized employment and union membership, and the intense employer opposition to unionism.

CHAPTER 3

Canada: New Pressures
and Possibilities

Since the early 1980s, Canadian unions have operated in an environment
marked by severe recessions, rising foreign competition, declining employment in heavily unionized industries, and pressures for labor force
reduction in the public sector. Most observers would agree that organized
labor has been remarkably resilient; union membership expanded after
1980, employers' attempts to reduce or freeze wages and benefits were
widely rejected, and unions remained active in politics and coalition activities (Kumar 1993; Chaison and Rose 1991a). But a realistic appraisal of
the state of the unions would also have to conclude that the hard times are
far from over, significant membership growth will be difficult to sustain,
and bargaining and political relationships will be severely strained as Canadian unions move into the next century.

The "tribulations and modest triumphs" of the 1980s (List 1990, B1)
and the difficulties that lie ahead are causing Canadian unions to explore
merger options with a new sense of urgency. Fundamental changes in
merger activity are already under way. Merger options are being appraised,
often for the first time, by both small and large unions. The decline of
international unions, the increased potential for forced mergers, and the
recent formation of a general union have placed the Canadian labor movement at the threshold of an important merger wave.

The Context

THE UNSTEADY GROWTH OF THE CANADIAN LABOR UNIONS

The recession of 1981–1982 was the worst economic downturn since the 1930s; the gross domestic product fell by 3.2 percent in real terms in 1982, the number of persons employed declined by 3 percent, and output was down sharply in the resource industries, a crucial sector of the Canadian economy (Thompson 1991). The recession was followed by an uneven recovery and unemployment remained persistently high, generally above 8 percent, through the decade (Chaykowski and Verma 1992a). The 1990–1991 recession brought even greater job losses in manufacturing, with a stronger impact on the manufacturing base in Ontario, followed by a slow and uncertain recovery (Kumar and Coates 1991; Thompson 1994). Consumer confidence remained low because of concerns about job insecurity and possible tax increases. One observer commented: "In the wake of the 1981–82 recession, consumer spending was a major engine of growth because jobs and incomes grew rapidly and householders used up their savings to finance new purchases. The fact that those ingredients are missing this time is one reason for the sluggishness of the economy's recovery from the recession of the early 1990s" (Little 1994, B4).

Despite adverse economic conditions and heavy job losses at unionized facilities, unions gained almost 700,000 members after 1980 (see table 5). Union density fluctuated within a range of less than 3 percentage points and was near its 1980 level in 1994—about 38 percent. Unions were able to offset attrition, recruiting 4 new members in services and public administration for each 1 lost in manufacturing (Statistics Canada various years). (Compare this to the dismal record of American unions after 1980 described in the preceding chapter—a net loss of more than 3.5 million members and a decline in density from 23 to 16 percent.[1])

The membership gains of Canadian unions have been attributed to the importance they assign to organizing and the presence of supportive federal and provincial labor laws. Union officers and members are generally willing to devote staff and financial resources to organizing, believing that the fulfillment of the labor movement's mission must include the extension of the benefits and protection of collective bargaining to nonunion workers (Robinson 1992). Canadian labor laws facilitate organizing by enabling workers to choose union representation through membership-card counts or expedited elections, thus avoiding protracted anti-union campaigns by management, so common, as we saw earlier, in the United States. Some

Table 5. Union membership and density in Canada, 1980–1994

Year	Union membership (thousands)	Union density[a]
1980	3,397	37.0%
1981	3,487	36.7
1982	3,617	37.0
1983	3,563	37.9
1984	3,651	38.8
1985	3,666	38.1
1986	3,730	37.7
1987	3,782	37.0
1988	3,841	36.5
1989	3,944	36.2
1990	4,031	36.2
1991	4,068	36.3
1992	4,089	37.4
1993	4,071	37.6
1994	4,078	37.5

Source: Canada Bureau of Labour Information 1995.

[a]Union membership as a percentage of nonagricultural paid workers.

provincial labor laws increase the likelihood that newly certified unions will establish bargaining relationships by having arbitrators decide the content of first collective agreements if impasses are reached in negotiations. Bans on the use of striker replacements have prevented employers from forcing newly certified unions into strikes, replacing strikers, and then petitioning for decertification (Rose and Chaison 1990b; Chaison and Rose 1993).

Although membership gains in Canadian unions may be impressive, particularly when compared to the near collapse of organizing in the United States (see, e.g., Rose and Chaison 1990a, b; Lipset 1995), some recent trends show the limits of union growth. First, the rate of union expansion has slowed dramatically. Union membership increased by 49 percent in the 1960s and by 56 percent in the 1970s, but by only 19 percent in the 1980s. The growth rate from 1990 to 1994 was about 1 percent—an increase of only 47 thousand members over 4 years (Labour Canada various years; Canada Bureau of Labour Information 1995).

Second, we can no longer assume that the public and para-public (e.g., health-care and education) work forces will continue as the primary source of new members. Union density is near the saturation point in public administration (81 percent in 1990), educational services (77 percent) and health and social services (51 percent) (Statistics Canada 1992). Financial constraints and efforts to reduce budget deficits have frozen or cut jobs in federal and provincial employment. Without the nearly automatic membership increases that followed expanding public-sector employment, unions must offset attrition by successfully organizing large private sector bargaining units (Thompson 1994). That will be extremely difficult—many larger firms are already unionized and those that are not, primarily in financial and retail services, are proving adept at defeating organizing campaigns. In the absence of a substantial rebound in organizing gains through private-sector organizing, union growth will be moderated and union-density rates will stabilize through the 1990s.

Collective Bargaining

Collective bargaining was transformed during the 1980s. The collective bargaining system that developed in Canada during the 1950s relied on a growing domestic market and tariff protection against imports. The unions' strategy was fairly straightforward—take wages and benefits out of competition on the industry level by organizing major employers. Negotiated wage and benefit increases were only indirectly related to changes in productivity. But, by the 1980s, the Canadian economy was responding to a global marketplace; wages and benefits could no longer be taken out of competition, nor could their costs be passed on to consumers (Chaykowski and Verma 1992a, b).

The Canadian economy is highly sensitive to international trade—about 44 percent of the gross domestic product was derived from imports in 1987, with the United States as the major trading partner (Chaykowski and Verma 1992a). The Free Trade Agreement of 1989 further exposed unionized firms to extensive nonunion competition by reducing and eventually eliminating tariffs between Canada and the United States. The North American Free Trade Agreement of 1993 extends the market to Mexico.[2]

Bargaining power was also reduced in the public sector because of expanding competition as the government subcontracted work or sold physical assets and the accompanying right to conduct business to private, often nonunion firms. For example, the federal government sold Crown corporations such as Canadair and Air Canada and the province of Saskatchewan sold public enterprises in the energy sector. Municipalities often relied on private contractors for waste removal, snow removal, and the maintenance of public buildings and streets (Thompson 1992). At a convention of the National Union of Public and General Employees, delegates were told of negotiating difficulties and membership losses because weather stations were being turned over to private operators, and airports and halfway houses were run by businesses (Slotnick 1988c).

Through the 1980s, Canadian unions were generally able to resist employers' demands for concessions in the forms of modified work rules, wage and benefit freezes or reductions, lump-sum wage payments, and two-tiered wage plans that assign lower wages to newly hired workers (Rose and Chaison 1992). When concessions were granted, unions usually saw them as temporary setbacks in response to severe economic conditions and individual firms' financial difficulties rather than as fundamental shifts in bargaining power (Kumar 1993). In the early 1990s, however, the unions' bargaining performance worsened. With increased frequency, public- and private-sector unions signed "social contract" agreements that reduced payrolls and modified work rules to avoid wage freezes and mass layoffs (Labour Canada 1993). According to Canada's Bureau of Labour Information, "In the public and para-public sector, the driving force has been the severe wage restraint—sometimes legislated—in response to rising budget deficits. In the private sector, the recession and sluggish economic recovery, and the urgent need to enhance productivity and competitiveness have resulted in changed priorities in bargaining" (Bureau of Labour Information 1993, 1).

Wage increases for all major collective agreements declined from 5.6 percent in 1990 to 3.6 percent in 1991 and 2.2 percent in 1992. Private sector increases were at 2.5 percent in 1992, a record low, and public-sector increases dropped to 2.0 percent (Bureau of Labour Information 1993).

POLITICAL ACTIVITY AND SOCIAL UNIONISM

The long-term growth and continued influence of the Canadian unions might not have been possible without their extensive participation in federal and provincial politics. The Canadian Labour Congress (CLC), the principal labor federation in Canada, was a cofounder of the New Democratic Party (NDP) in 1961 and played a central role in the NDP's precursor, the Cooperative Commonwealth Federation, a socialist, farm, and labor party formed in 1932. The unions and the CLC have remained influential in formulating the social-democratic policies of the NDP.

Political activism has benefitted organized labor in several ways. First, laws that directly affect unions and their members were passed in provinces with NDP governments; for instance, NDP-controlled legislatures in Ontario and British Columbia imposed limitations on employers' use of striker replacements and strengthened the unions' ability to organize and achieve first contracts (Chaison and Rose 1993; Scotland 1995). Second, under the Canadian parliamentary system, the Liberals and Conservatives (the parties in power in the federal Parliament and most provincial legislatures) vie with each other and the NDP for workers' support by favoring pro-union legislation (e.g., expedited procedures for certifying unions as bargaining agents) as well as policies of concern to the broader work force (e.g., health-care, pension, and pay equity programs) (Bruce 1989). Third, labor often pursues its political objectives by working through coalitions with other progressive groups such as the women's movement, social-justice organizations and environmentalists. As a result, unions can credibly promote themselves as the voice of working men and women, and deflect charges of being a special interest group that only deals with the concerns of unionized workers (Schenk and Bernard 1992).

Union officers and, to a lesser degree, union members devote energies and resources to politics because of their implicit acceptance of the values inherent in social unionism—the ideology guiding the labor movement's mission, which is the advancement of the social and political interests of all Canadians, the empowerment of workers, and the creation of a more equitable society (R. Adams 1989a; Robinson 1992, 1994; Schenk and Bernard 1992). Expressions of social unionism include carrying out independent political action through formal affiliations with a social-democratic party; assigning a high priority to organizing; lobbying for social legislation; forming alliances with community groups to promote social and economic issues; and cooperating with employers on the national and industry levels to deal with issues of mutual concern, such as productivity and industry restructuring (Thompson and Blum 1983; Robinson 1992; Kumar 1993).

The effectiveness of political activities has been the subject of recent debate within the labor movement. Union activists in provinces with NDP governments have felt betrayed by the public employers' threats of job cuts and wage freezes, and they question the need to maintain formal political ties. NDP governments have been accused of courting the business community (Zwolinski 1993). At the federal level, the NDP lost three-quarters of its seats in Parliament after the 1993 elections. In Ontario, the most populous province, an NDP government lost office to the Conservatives in 1995 after satisfying neither the union movement nor the public at large, yet being attacked as too strongly favoring unions. Recent defeats and disappointments are causing a reevaluation of political strategies, but the questions that are being asked deal primarily with tactics and formal political ties. The basic principles of social unionism are deeply embedded, which makes the emergence of an apolitical labor movement highly unlikely.

Legislation highly favorable to unions has been rescinded as provincial governments have changed. In Canada's most populous province, Ontario, the new Conservative government passed legislation in 1995 that replaced certification based on membership cards with a requirement for expedited elections, and it substantially relaxed bans on the employers' use of striker replacements. The unions' reaction was a call for mass demonstrations against the provincial government and its policies (Rusk 1995).[3] Despite the changes brought on by new legislation, there is little possibility of an unraveling of the fundemental rights to join unions and engage in collective bargaining.

The Merger Record

A recent increase in merger activity is shown in table 6. The average number of mergers per year rose from 1.5 in the 1960s to 2.6 in the 1970s, to 2.9 in the 1980s, and then rose sharply to 4.8 in the early 1990s. The initial cases were almost equally divided between amalgamations and absorptions. Amalgamation activity was high in the 1960s and 1970s because rival unions in similar industries entered into merger negotiations in the aftermath of the mergers of labor federations—the 1955 merger of the American Federation of Labor and the Congress of Industrial Organizations in the United States, and the 1956 merger the Trades and Labor Congress and the Canadian Congress of Labour in Canada (Chaison 1980). The potential for these amalgamations was soon exhausted and absorptions became the primary merger form.

The figures in table 6 and the list of recent mergers in appendix 2 show that Canadian national unions (i.e., unions headquartered in Canada) are using absorptions as a growth strategy. The number of absorptions exclusively among national unions rose from 2 in the 1960s to 6 in the 1970s and 24 in the 1980s and early 1990s. The most active absorbing union was the Canadian Auto Workers (CAW) with 9 absorptions, followed by the Canadian Union of Public Employees (CUPE) with 4 absorptions. CAW

Table 6. Union mergers in Canada, 1960–1993

Type of merger	Number of mergers			
	1960s	1970s	1980s	1990–93
Mergers among Canadian national unions				
Amalgamations: National with national	5	0	2	1
Absorptions: National into national	2	6	13	11
	7	6	15	12
Mergers among international unions				
Amalgamations: International with international	2	5	2	0
Absorptions: International into international	5	13	6	2
	7	18	8	2
Mergers between Canadian national unions and international unions				
Amalgamations: National with international	0	0	0	0
Absorptions: National into international	1	0	3	2
Absorptions: International into national	0	0	0	0
	1	0	3	2
Mergers between Canadian sections of international unions				
Amalgamations: Canadian section with Canadian section	0	0	1	0
Absorption: Canadian section into Canadian section	0	0	0	0
	0	1	2	1
Mergers between Canadian sections of international unions and national unions				
Amalgamation: Canadian section with international	0	0	1	0
Absorption: Canadian section into national	0	1	0	2
Absorption: National into Canadian section	0	0	0	0
	0	1	1	2
Total mergers	15	26	29	19
Mergers per year	1.5	2.6	2.9	4.8
Percentage of total mergers that were absorptions	53%	81%	79%	95%

Sources: Chaison 1979; Labour Canada various years; Labour Canada 1994.

and CUPE accounted for about half of the absorptions during the 1990s. After 1980, absorbed unions included some of the smallest unions in Canada (e.g., the Canadian Union of Industrial Employees and the Canadian Association of Passenger Agents, each with about 250 members), larger unions that were unable to grow because of foreign competition (e.g., the United Electrical Workers with 9,400 members), and five unions caught in the downsizing and tumultuous bargaining after the airline industry was deregulated.

Table 6 shows a sharp rise in merger activity. Canadian unions are merging in increasing numbers in reaction to the continuing hard times and new economic and political uncertainties. Significant and sustained economic growth is unlikely, forcing large Canadian unions (e.g., CAW, CUPE) to turn to absorptions as alternatives to traditional organizing, while small ones merge to avoid stagnation and decline. The new complexity and higher stakes of bargaining, particularly the need to evaluate and counter employers' proposals for wage moderation, downsizing and work rule modifications, have made small unions feel overwhelmed and in need of the staff and expertise of the larger ones. Finally, although labor's approach to politics may be in flux, a large, expanding and nation-wide membership resulting from merger still provides political clout and a dominant role in coalitions (Chaison 1986; Chaison and Rose 1989; Mawhinney 1989; Ewer and Yates 1995).

The Underlying Trends

THE FIGHT FOR CANADIAN-SECTION AUTONOMY: THE ABSORPTION OF THE FFAW INTO THE CAW

International unionism was once a dominant feature of the Canadian industrial relations system. The earliest Canadian unions were primarily regional and citywide bodies, while the stronger American-based unions (international unions) organized workers on both sides of the border. At the turn of this century, 95 percent of Canadian union members belonged to international unions (see table 7). The proportion gradually declined to 57 percent in 1934 as national unions organized extensively in the transportation and communications industries. The internationals rebounded when they won bargaining rights in mass production industries such as automobiles and steel. The share of Canadian union members in international unions stabilized through the 1950s and early 1960s, but then began

Table 7. Percentage of Canadian
union membership in international
unions, selected years, 1902–1994

Year	Percentage of union membership in international unions
1902	95%
1911	90
1921	73
1929	72
1934	57
1939	60
1944	65
1949	71
1954	72
1959	73
1964	71
1969	65
1977	49
1980	46
1985	39
1990	32
1991	31
1992	31
1993	30
1994	30

Sources: Chaison and Rose 1989;
Labour Canada various years; Canada
Bureau of Labour Information 1995.

to fall as national unions recruited public and professional workers, and as civil service associations gained bargaining rights and reconstituted themselves as national unions (Dawes 1987; Chaison and Rose 1989).

In 1977, national unions could finally claim the majority of Canadian union members. International unions have since continued their decline, falling in number from 80 to 59 and losing nearly 400,000 members. In 1994, international unions accounted for only 30 percent of union members in Canada (Labour Canada various years; Canada Bureau of Labour Information 1995).

The Canadian sections of international unions (also called divisions, regions or conferences) enjoy various degrees of autonomy. At one extreme, Canadian members directly elect officers who control section administration and finances; at the other extreme, Canadian officers are appointed by international headquarters and must seek its approval for major bargaining and administrative decisions. Since the 1970s, pro-autonomy movements within most Canadian sections have been largely successful. International unions often voluntarily relinquished control over Canadian sections because they recognized the symbolic and practical importance of autonomy to Canadian members, wished to avoid provocations that could lead to secession, and were preoccupied with the task of reversing declining size and bargaining power at home (Thompson and Blum 1983; Dawes 1987; Chaison and Rose 1989). The drive for autonomy gained impetus during the 1970 and 1974 Canadian Labour Congress conventions, which passed resolutions calling for minimum standards of self-governance for locals and sections of international unions. These included the right of Canadian members to select their own officers and the right of these officers to determine policies and speak for their unions in Canada (Chaison 1986).

It is important to recognize how international unionism affects the form and frequency of union mergers in Canada. When autonomy is restricted, Canadian sections must participate in their parent unions' mergers negotiated in the United States and are unable to pursue their own mergers in Canada. On the other hand, a high degree of autonomy usually includes the Canadian sections' right to refrain from participating in the parent unions' mergers as well as the ability to negotiate mergers with other Canadian sections or national unions. This is exceptional freedom. Independently negotiated mergers or rejections of international union mergers have the effect of severing ties between the Canadian sections and international unions (Chaison 1979).

High degrees of Canadian section autonomy were apparent in some recent mergers. In 1992, the Canadian section of the National Association of Broadcast Employees and Technicians rejected its parent union's merger with the Communications Workers in the United States and negotiated an absorption into a new national union, the Communications, Energy and Paperworkers Union in 1994 (Crawley 1994). When the Retail, Wholesale and Department Store Union (RWDSU) joined the United Food and Commercial Workers (UFCW) in 1993, the merger agreement referred to the "separate identity and status" of the RWDSU's Canadian sections and the "sovereignty of Canada and the fundamental right of Canadian labor bodies to govern their affairs" (Bureau of National Affairs 1993b, A3). About 80 percent of the RWDSU's Canadian membership rejected the merger and voted to combine with the United Steelworkers of

America (Bureau of National Affairs 1993c; Gouldson 1993). The problems that arise when merger attempts are frustrated because of the lack of autonomy are illustrated in the following case—the Canadian Auto Workers' (CAW) campaign to absorb a large Canadian local of the United Food and Commercial Workers (UFCW).[4]

The UFCW was formed in 1979 by the amalgamation of two international unions, the Retail Clerks International Union and the Amalgamated Meat Cutters and Butcher Workmen of America. The unions' Canadian sections—Region 18 from the Meat Cutters and Region 19 from the Retail Clerks—did not merge, primarily because of ideological differences among officers. Region 18's officers were more militant and advocates of social unionism, while Region 19's officers were relatively conservative. When Frank Benn, the director of Region 18, announced his retirement in August 1986, UFCW president William Wynn proposed merging the two regions. Officers of Region 18 protested, believing that control over the merged Canadian section would go to Clifford Evans, the director of Region 19. Wynn withdrew the merger proposal but then antagonized the Canadians further when he appointed William Hanley as head of Region 18 without consulting the region's officers or members.

In January 1987, the UFCW imposed a trusteeship—a suspension of local self-governance for disciplinary reasons—on a large pro-autonomy local in British Columbia that was engaged in an organizing dispute with a neighboring UFCW local. Although the international officers claimed to have acted within their constitutional authority, they soon ended the trusteeship to avoid a deepening dispute. However, the trusteeship and the earlier appointment of Region 18's director galvanized the autonomy movement in the UFCW's Canadian locals. Five-hundred local officers met in Toronto and endorsed a proposal authorizing Canadian officers to set union policy, employ their own staff, and impose trusteeships. The UFCW's president rejected the proposal, declaring that Canadian sections had sufficient autonomy and their officers would continue to be appointed.

The dispute over autonomy within the UFCW soon led to a confrontation with the CAW that nearly split the Canadian union movement along national and international union lines. The CAW (officially known as the National Automobile, Aerospace and Agricultural Implement Workers of Canada) was formed by the Canadian section of the United Automobile Workers after it seceded in a dispute over autonomy in collective bargaining. Canadian officers had deviated from the 1984 pattern of wage and work rule concessions negotiated with General Motors in the United

States. Led by an outspoken and charismatic president, Bob White, the CAW became the focal point of nationalism for the Canadian labor movement and the principal opponent of the emerging "corporate agenda" of free-trade initiatives, mass layoffs and plant closings (Holusha 1984; Ewer and Yates 1995).

In March 1987, Richard Cashin, a president of the UFCW's Local 1252, negotiated an agreement with Bob White for the local's absorption into the CAW. The 23,000-member local represented inshore and deep-sea fishermen, and fish plant and supermarket workers mostly in the province of Newfoundland.[5] Cashin conceded that he had neglected to follow the UFCW's procedure for disaffiliation, which included a membership vote and arbitration of disputes over the dissolution of the local assets. He claimed that his impatience was justified because of the UFCW's earlier rejection of demands for greater autonomy, and the strong possibility that UFCW headquarters would place the local in trusteeship even if the appropriate procedures were followed.

Local 1252 changed its name to Fishermen, Food and Allied Workers Union (FFAW) and was charted as Local 465 by the CAW. The UFCW's officers condemned the merger and protested to the Canadian Labour Congress (CLC) that they had been raided by the CAW. Both unions were affiliates of the federation. CLC officers rebuked White for violating basic principles of union solidarity. One officer commented: "You don't respond with cannibalistic fervor when you see another union having internal problems" (Slotnick 1987c, A1). White responded: "This is a unique case. It is not an attempt to expand an attack on international unions or pick off locals one at a time. I didn't seek this group out, but I'm not going to turn my back on them" (Slotnick 1987f, A12). He added that the CLC should create a safety net for breakaway groups rather than ostracize them. He also argued that the positive aspects of the merger were not being recognized—the fishermen's local, freely deciding to leave the UFCW, would remain in the mainstream of the labor movement by joining the CAW, and it would continue to play a vital role in Newfoundland society. The greater threat to the federation was the authoritarian control of Canadian sections by international unions, not raiding among affiliates. Finally, White proposed that the CLC amend its constitution to permit Canadian sections to leave their parent unions and merge with other unions.

The CLC referred the UFCW–CAW dispute to a neutral referee to determine if there had been a raid and if sanctions should be applied (e.g., the denial of access to CLC services). At the same time, the UFCW challenged the merger in the courts. It claimed that the merger agreement had been quickly negotiated between Cashin and White rather than between duly constituted merger committees, that the merger proposal was never submitted to the local's membership or its executive board for their approval, and that the UFCW's procedure for disaffiliation had been circumvented.

The UFCW–CAW dispute could have split the Canadian labor movement. With 160,000 members, the UFCW was the second-largest international union and the fifth-largest CLC affiliate. If the merger were not stopped, the UFCW might leave the CLC and the balance of power within the federation would shift further away from the international unions and toward the national, public sector unions. But if sanctions were applied against the CAW, there would be a confrontation between the federation and a militant national union with 140,000 members, led by a popular president who was widely considered the rising star of the labor movement.

A wider conflict was avoided when the CLC's referee ruled that the UFCW was precluded from filing charges of raiding because it had also proceeded to the courts to stop the CAW. This eliminated the possibility of CLC sanctions against the CAW. The UFCW could only denounce its opponent at a special meeting of the CLC officers. The UFCW continued with its court case, however, and challenged the FFAW's bargaining status before labor boards.

In April 1987, the UFCW obtained a court injunction blocking the FFAW secession and imposed a trusteeship on the breakaway local. The local's officers responded by resigning and creating a new union. Three hundred delegates met at a founding convention in May, reconstituted the FFAW as an independent union, selected Cashin as president, and ratified a merger agreement with the CAW. They then filed petitions with provincial labor boards for certification elections to displace the UFCW as bargaining agent. Over the next year, elections were conducted in bargaining units of inland fishermen, trawlermen and plant workers. The FFAW was victorious and completed its absorption into the CAW soon after its certification as bargaining agent. The merger is now considered by all involved parties to be a fait accompli; the UFCW's only legal challenge is over the dissolution of the local's assets.

The issues of raiding and Canadian-section autonomy were raised at the CLC's convention in May 1988. After heated debate, delegates passed compromise resolutions. Under a new internal disputes plan, stricter sanctions, for example, the denial of CLC services and the removal of officers from CLC governing bodies, would be imposed against raiding affiliates. This plan was balanced by the inclusion of the Code of Union Democracy and Standards of Canadian Autonomy in the federation's constitution. If violations did occur, affiliates could complain to the CLC's executive council and the ultimate sanction would be expulsion from the federation (Estok 1988; Slotnick 1988b; "Unions Agree" 1988).[6]

The absorption of the FFAW into the CAW followed a circuitous route— attempted merger, secession, certification, and then merger—because of the strenuous opposition of the parent international union. The UFCW was late to recognize the importance of autonomy to its Canadian members and the role of mergers in the demonstration of such autonomy. Undoubtedly, after witnessing the bitter dispute between the CAW and UFCW, few international unions will try to upset the merger plans of Canadian sections or locals, or impose mergers negotiated in the United States. Federation sanctions could be applied if it is shown that officers of Canadian sections are prevented from signing a merger agreement supported by the Canadian membership. Moreover, Canadian sections will always have the option to circumvent their parent unions' authority by following the example of the FFAW, that is, forming a new national union and challenging the international union in certification elections.

The declining influence of international unions and the expanding autonomy of Canadian sections changes the dynamics of union mergers in Canada. The CAW, with ambitious growth plans but declining employment in its core manufacturing jurisdiction, is already testing the limits of Canadian-section autonomy. In 1990, the CAW absorbed the Brotherhood of Railway Carmen with 7,000 members, despite the protests of the international unions. Bob White was elected president of the CLC in June 1992 and left his CAW post; but his CAW successor, Buzz Hargrove, declared that he was also committed to encouraging union mergers (List 1992) and that "mergers are the way of the future" (Papp 1992b, A17). The CAW will remain a major center of merger activity, perhaps continuing as "the undisputed king of mergers" (Ray 1993, 5), because small unions are attracted to its reputation for militancy in bargaining, its national status and secessionist origins, and its willingness to create semi-autonomous locals or divisions to accommodate absorbed unions. The CAW has attracted larger unions as well; in 1994 it absorbed the 33,000-member Canadian Brotherhood of Railway, Transport and General Workers (CBRT& GW) (Crawley 1994). This merger was a major coup for the CAW, not only making it Canada's largest private-sector union but establishing a dominant presence in the railroads. It also reinforced its position as the leading, nationalistic union: As Art Moses points out, "The inclusion of the CBRT&GW within the ranks of the self-consciously nationalistic CAW has intense historical significance, because for many years it was the CBRT&GW that upheld the vision of an independent Canadian trade union movement at a time when Canadian labour was dominated by U.S. based international unions" (Moses 1994, 3).

Ten years after leaving the United Auto Workers, the CAW had an exceptionally diverse membership; more than three-quarters worked outside the automobile industry and only 35 percent were former members of the United Auto Workers. More than two-thirds of its new members came through mergers, with the remainder joining in organizing campaigns (Eaton 1995). Drawing inspiration from the 1995 proposed merger of the auto workers, steelworkers and machinists unions in the United States, the CAW leadership has called for the creation of a huge metal workers union to be formed by mergers around the CAW (Van Alphen 1995), and it has indicated an intent to move into the public sector, starting merger discussions with the postal union (Galt 1994).

A newly formed union, the Communications, Energy and Paperworkers, described in a later section of this chapter, has also declared a policy of growth through mergers and will rival the CAW as Canadian sections play one potential absorption partner against another. This competition will make absorptions of Canadian sections into national unions a principle form of merger and will ensure the continued decline of international unions.

THE IMPACT OF FORCED MERGERS: THE ABSORPTION OF THE LETTER CARRIERS INTO THE POSTAL WORKERS

A basic premise of union merger theories is that mergers are voluntary and that officers and members are free to reject mergers that they believe are unsatisfactory (Chitayat 1979; Chaison 1986; Conant 1993). Labor federations cannot force affiliates to merge, and we have seen that in North America anything beyond a federation's encouragement and assistance would be considered an inexcusable intrusion into internal union affairs. Labor laws neither compel nor encourage mergers but rather protect the rights of union members to make free and informed decisions about merger terms.

Canadian labor boards are empowered to inquire as to whether successor unions (amalgamated unions or absorbing unions) should acquire the bargaining rights of their predecessors.[7] In *International Brotherhood of Electrical Workers et al.* (1991, 8), the Canada Labour Relations Board (the federal labor board) stated: "It seems to us that Parliament intentionally left the matter of mergers . . . among trade unions as private contract considerations between the parties involved. These are internal union matters in which the Board cannot and in our respectful opinion ought not to interfere."

Provincial labor boards have similar policies but reserve the right to make inquiries and hold merger votes to ensure the proper continuity of collective-bargaining representation. It is important to note, however, that labor boards also have the authority to consolidate bargaining units that they believe to be ineffective. A merger follows when the unions for the combined units do not represent workers elsewhere. The dispute between two postal unions in 1988 and 1989 suggests the potential importance of these forced mergers.[8]

The two principal unions in the Canadian postal system, the Letter Carriers Union of Canada (LCUC) and the Canadian Union of Postal Workers (CUPW) formed the Council of Postal Unions in 1967 to negotiate jointly for the operational workers in the Canada Post. The LCUC represented outdoor postal workers, primarily mail carriers, while CUPW's members were indoor workers, mostly mail sorters. In 1974, the LCUC petitioned the Public Service Staff Relations Board for the revocation of the Council's bargaining certificate, claiming that the joint body was no longer capable of fulfilling its bargaining responsibilities. Certification was revoked and the two unions applied for and were granted the right to represent separate operational units.

The post office ceased to function as a government department in 1982. Mail service became the responsibility of the Canada Post Corporation, a crown corporation (i.e., a regulated, private organization). The bargaining units determined under the public-sector law were no longer appropriate when jurisdiction was transferred to the private sector. In the public sector, greater emphasis was placed on occupational categories when defining bargaining units. The postal units were not changed, however, because the Canada Labour Relations Board (CLRB) believed that a review would be a "monumental undertaking" calling for more time and resources than was available at the time (*Canada Post Corporation et al.* 1988, 12).

In 1985, Canada Post petitioned the CLRB to review the appropriateness of all bargaining units in the postal system. Canada Post employees were divided into 26 bargaining units and represented by 8 unions. The board agreed to a review in two stages; first, it would determine the number of units and broadly define their boundaries and, second, it would specify the exact boundaries of the units, determine which employees would be excluded and identify the unions to represent the units. The first phase was completed after 50 days of hearings held between May 1985 and December 1987.

The board decided that Canada Post employees should be represented in four units: one unit for postmasters and assistants, a second for white-collar administrative employees, a third unit of supervisors that cut across all prior bargaining units, and a fourth operational unit. In reaching its decision, the Board stated that its objective was

> to ensure that the configuration of bargaining units . . . provide for employees the greatest benefit while employed in the corporation, to alleviate to the extent possible their considerable fears with regard to job security, and to permit the greatest amount of flexibility to employees in furthering their careers within the organization without being artificially restricted. [We] adhere to the philosophy that favors the formation of large bargaining units and looks with disfavor on the notion of the artificial fragmentation of bargaining units. Maintenance of that philosophy was an additional objective. (*Canada Post Corporation* 1988, 34)

The board emphasized that the case before it was comparable to one of initial certification because it had not previously examined the bargaining unit configuration, and its criteria for determining the scope of bargaining units differed from those in the federal public sector where units were defined by legislation. While the board was concerned with the employees' wishes, it nevertheless believed that

> [e]mployees normally are cocooned within their own bargaining unit. They do not have the advantages of the larger picture and they are therefore not aware of all the facts that are required to determine appropriate bargaining units. . . . We would add, of course, that the wishes of the employees are not forgotten and that it will be those wishes that will ultimately determine the bargaining agent that is to represent them on the basis of the units as configured by the Board. (*Canada Post Corporation* 1988, 37)

The consolidation of the operational units had the secondary effect of forcing a union merger because the units were the only ones represented by the LCUC and CUPW. The two unions could either voluntarily negotiate a merger or face each other in an election in which the winner would absorb the loser by gaining the right to represent its members.

The board based its decision on the premise that there was substantial interaction between letter carriers and mail sorters, and that workers in a single operational unit would be able to apply for vacant positions in the broader unit and thus have greater job security. It also assumed that operating costs would be reduced and the postal system would become more efficient. Optimistically, the Board concluded:

We are satisfied that the overall aspirations and needs of the employee can best be served by combining them into a single bargaining unit. It is hoped that, by having only one bargaining agent instead of two, the internal rivalries that developed during the CPU [Council of Postal Unions] years will be avoided as employees, who in fact have so much in common, combine their collective wills. (*Canada Post Corporation* 1988, 42)

Critics of the board's decision pointed to the differences in the structures and ideologies of the two unions and predicted that a peaceful merger was highly unlikely. The LCUC had several small locals while CUPW had large ones covering wide geographic areas. Compared to the CUPW, the LCUC had few full-time officers. The CUPW was widely considered to be one of Canada's most militant unions while the LCUC was one of the least. One observer asked how the board could order the merger of "two very distinct, ideologically opposite unions" and concluded that the board was far more interested in representational efficiency than the needs and desires of the unions' members (Brunt 1988, 8).

At first it appeared that predictions of a CUPW–LCUC dispute would be disproved. By the end of March 1988, only a few weeks after the board's decision, the two unions announced that they would seek an amicable merger. The LCUC membership voted 83 percent in favor of initiating merger negotiations with the CUPW. The officers of CUPW had the authority under their union's constitution to proceed with merger negotiations. The Public Service Alliance of Canada (PSAC), representing 1500 members in the new bargaining unit, agreed to participate in merger negotiations. The CLC was prepared to mediate if there was an impasse.

On September 3, 1988, the LCUC and CUPW announced that a merger agreement had been reached. Under its terms, a leadership referendum would be held between the LCUC and CUPW presidents, with the winner becoming president of the new union and the loser serving as vice-president. A founding convention would be held in 1990; until that time the union would be administered by a national executive council of 11 officers—5 from CUPW, 5 from LCUC and 1 from PSAC. Local unions would merge over time. The merger committee informed the board of their settlement and asked that the election order be set aside.

The merger agreement was soon repudiated by the LCUC's officers. Published reports implied that the LCUC's officers were upset by false information about their union published in the CUPW newspaper ("Pact Merging" 1988). Observers that I interviewed suggested two other reasons for this reversal. First, the LCUC officers were encouraged by the presence of a large dissident local in the CUPW and believed that its members would support the LCUC in an election. This might be sufficient to tilt the election in favor of the LCUC whose membership comprised less than a majority of the combined unit (about 21,000 of the 44,000 bargaining-unit members). Second, the LCUC business agents (full-time local union officers) did not support the merger agreement because they believed that it would be too difficult to sell to the membership. Sensing an election victory, the LCUC's leaders decided to side with the business agents even though this meant rejecting the efforts of their own merger committee.

The board scheduled an election by mail ballot from mid-November 1988 to mid-January 1989, and the LCUC and CUPW began their campaigns for the winner-take-all contest. The CUPW was attacked for poorly representing part-time workers and having a large backlog of unsettled grievances. The LCUC was criticized for its high officer salaries. The CUPW claimed that it was more effective in negotiations and national politics, and was a stronger advocate for the rights of women members. The LCUC stressed its policy of local control and portrayed itself as one of the most democratic unions in Canada. The PSAC, which decided not to participate in the election, refrained from endorsing either the LCUC or CUPW.

The mail ballot asked, "Which one of the two unions listed hereunder do you wish to have represent you as your bargaining agent in collective bargaining with your employer?" CUPW, the winner of a coin toss, was listed first.

On January 18, 1989 the final tally showed CUPW as the winner with

20,281 votes or 51.1 percent of the returned ballots. Jean-Claude Parrot, CUPW president, denied that the new union was deeply divided by the merger and claimed that it would be more effective because it now represented a broader bargaining unit. Robert McGarry, LCUC president, acknowledged that there could be no role for him in the merged union because of the hostile campaign.

The absorption of the LCUC into the CUPW, mandated by the Board decision and the election results, did not go smoothly. On February 1, 1989, the CUPW became the certified bargaining agent for the operational unit. But the LCUC held a convention, refused to disband, and asked the board to review the merger and unit consolidation. The LCUC tried to regain its bargaining status by gathering 17,000 signatures on a petition for certification. It failed to obtain a majority, however, and its petition was rejected by the board in early 1990.[9]

CUPW officers responded to the challenge by branding the LCUC as a rival union and warning former LCUC members on CUPW governing bodies that they must sever all ties or face either suspension or discharge from office. The CUPW tried to discipline some LCUC supporters, but had to back off when the board decided that it was infringing on the members' freedom of association (*Paul Horsley et al.* 1991).

Five hundred letter carriers jeered delegates entering the hall at CUPW's 1990 convention. Ex-officers of the LCUC formed an organization called "Power Base," launched a legal campaign to reverse the merger, and supported an unsuccessful raid against the CUPW by the International Brotherhood of Electrical Workers. The antimerger forces finally lost support after failing to reverse the CUPW's victory through court and board challenges.

In February 1995, the LCUC failed for the fourth time in as many years to petition the labor board to regain its bargaining position at Canada Post. The newspaper account of this last attempt characterized the LCUC as a "homeless union" ("Letter Carriers Union Fails" 1995, D3).

It should be understood that forced mergers do not always follow bargaining-unit consolidations. In 1992, for example, the board consolidated a unit of shop craft (nonoperating) employees of Canadian Pacific Railway and Canadian National Railway, creating a single bargaining unit from those represented by seven unions. One union, the Railway Carmen, had been absorbed by the CAW and, believing it enjoyed widespread employee support because of its national union link, sought to have the new unit's representative determined by an election. The other unions, all internationals, formed a bargaining council and requested certification, but their request was rejected by the Canada Labour Relations Board. The Carmen/ CAW won an election in 1994 and was certified as the bargaining agent. The losing international unions, however, were not forced to dissolve or merge because they represented employees in units elsewhere.[10]

In 1993 the board consolidated bargaining units in the Canadian Broadcasting Company (CBC) and conducted an election among the 3,500 employees involved in the preparation and presentation of radio and television programs. The ballot listed the Canadian Broadcast Employees Union (a section of the Canadian Union of Public Employees), the Canadian Wire Service Guild (a local of the Newspaper Guild, an international union), and the Media Guild (a section of the Alliance of Canadian Cinema, Television and Radio Artists). The election was won by the Wire Service Guild. The two losing unions terminated their CBC locals but were not forced to merge because they represented workers in other bargaining units.[11]

Despite the railway and broadcasting cases, the LCUC–CUPW merger has far-ranging implications because it serves as a warning to highly specialized unions about the perils of bargaining unit consolidations. Employers do not hesitate to petition labor boards to combine units for greater flexibility, increased productivity, and reduced interunion competition in negotiations. Unions that do not represent workers beyond single bargaining units (e.g., most of the 39 health care and 28 education unions (Labour Canada 1992)) will see the possibility of forced mergers and will voluntarily merge to preempt adverse board decisions and avoid acrimonious merger campaigns. The forced merger of the LCUC into CUPW, one of the most widely publicized industrial relations events of the 1980s, increases merger motivation by making small unions aware of the costs of not merging of their own volition.

Building a General Union: The Communications, Energy and Paperworkers

In 1992, the Communications Workers of Canada, the Energy and Chemical Workers Union, and the Canadian Paperworkers Union amalgamated to form the Communications, Energy and Paperworkers Union of Canada (CEP). All at once, there was a new, major national union. Prior to the merger, the Paperworkers with 70,000 members was the eleventh largest union in Canada, while the Communications Workers with 40,000 members was twenty-fifth, and the Energy and Chemical Workers with 35,000 members was thirtieth. After the merger, the new union ranked seventh among all unions and fourth among private sector unions (Labour Canada 1992). It had 645 locals throughout Canada, general funds of $29 million, and a strike fund of $22 million (Communications, Energy and Paperworkers Union of Canada 1992b,c). "Virtually overnight, CEP . . . vaulted into labour's big leagues" (Papp 1992a, A3).

The CEP amalgamation was the culmination of several movements for Canadian-section autonomy. Figure 2 indicates the schisms and mergers among the three amalgamating unions between 1972 and 1992. The Communications Workers of Canada was formed by the 1984 merger of unions that were once Canadian sections of international unions. The Paperworkers was a Canadian section that left an international union formed by amalgamation. The Energy and Chemical Workers was created by the merger of the Canadian section of Oil, Chemical and Atomic Workers and a national union formed from a breakaway Canadian section of the Chemical Workers.

The amalgamation was also an explicit rejection of the basic tenets of union jurisdiction, that is, the premise that unions should confine their membership to specific industries and occupations, and that these territorial claims, as stated in union constitutions, should be respected by other unions and federations (Chaison and Dhavale 1990). An exceptionally diverse membership was a primary object rather than an unavoidable consequence of the CEP amalgamation. The officers of the three merging unions believed that their organizations were financially unstable and in a weakened bargaining position because their membership was homogeneous. For example, when half the Communications Workers' membership was involved in a strike against Northern Telecom, it was forced to borrow from other unions to pay strike benefits. The Paperworkers felt that their ability to strike was curtailed because they negotiated simultaneously with major employers in the pulp and paper industry (Papp 1992a). Diversification was also a hedge against the risks of the sudden, destabilizing membership losses that may accompany new production technologies and increased competition in product markets. At the time of the amalgamation, CEP officers proudly proclaimed their union as "one of the most diverse organizations in the Canadian labour movement, cutting across the resource and service sectors of the national economy and spanning several major industries—paper, forestry, communications, natural gas, oil, man-

Figure 2. Evolution of the unions amalgamating to form the Communications, Energy and Paperworkers

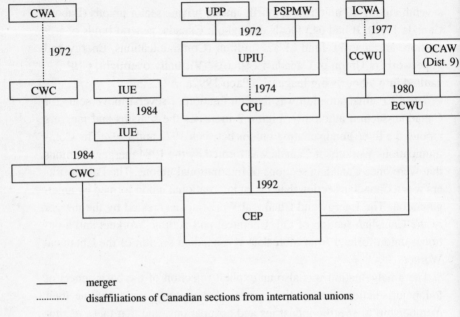

———— merger

·········· disaffiliations of Canadian sections from international unions

CWA	Communications Workers of America
CWC	Communications Workers of Canada
CWC	Communications, Electronic, Electrical, Technical and Salaried Workers of Canada (changed name to Communications and Electrical Workers of Canada in 1986)
IUE	International Union of Electrical, Radio and Machine Workers
CPU	Canadian Paperworkers Union
UPP	United Papermakers and Paper Workers
PSPMW	Pulp, Sulphite and Paper Mill Workers
UPIU	United Paperworkers International Union
ECWU	Energy and Chemical Workers Union
ICWU	International Chemical Workers Union
CCWU	Canadian Chemical Workers Union
OCAW	Oil, Chemical, and Atomic Workers International Union (Labour Canada various years)

ufacturing, mining and transportation, electronics and chemical'' (Communications, Energy and Paperworkers Union of Canada 1992a, 16).

Diversity reduced rather than created merger barriers. Members were not concerned that the new union would be dominated by a single industrial or occupational group. Divisions did not have to be created to allay fears of the submergence of members' interests. Merger negotiators did not have to deal with local union mergers, usually a contentious issue, because neighboring locals represented workers in different industries. Finally, the officers recognized that diversity held the promise of future growth by making the CEP attractive to potential absorption partners who would be reluctant to be enveloped in a homogeneous union.

I observed in chapter 1 that amalgamations are infrequent because of the difficulties of combining unions of equal size. Participants must resolve such issues as local union autonomy, the selection of convention delegates, and the location of union headquarters. Absorption negotiations are far less complicated because only the absorbed union undergoes significant change. The success of the CEP's negotiations for amalgamation can be traced to the close personal relationships between the three unions' presidents. Although a proposed merger of the Energy and Chemical Workers and the Paperworkers was narrowly defeated by the latter's members in 1983 (Gibbens 1983), the unions' officers remained convinced of the benefits of merger. Nine years later, the two presidents, Don Holder of the Paperworkers and Reg Basken of the Energy and Chemical Workers, revived merger discussions during informal meetings with Fred Pomeroy, president of the Communications Workers. The three were close friends and had worked together on Canadian Labour Congress and New Democratic Party committees. Recognizing the strength of a larger union with a diverse membership, the presidents presented resolutions to their unions' executive boards authorizing a merger committee. Negotiations were then initiated by a sixteen-member committee chaired on a rotating basis by the three presidents. First, it was decided that a prerequisite for an eventual merger would have to be the retention of all full-time officers and the creation of geographic divisions. Divisions based on prior union affiliation were rejected because it was felt that they would affirm premerger identities, impede the integration of union governing structures, and eventually lead to factionalism. The merger committee then dealt with technical matters—the new union's constitution, financial practices, and strike funds. When these were resolved, the merger agreement (*Final*

Merger Report 1992) was tentatively approved and distributed to the locals for presentation, debate and ratification.

The merger was endorsed by a vote of 96 percent of the Energy and Chemical Workers, 91 percent of the Communications Workers, and 83 percent of the Paperworkers. At the CEP's first convention, Holder of the Paperworkers, the larger of the three unions, became president, and Basken and Pomeroy became at-large vice-presidents. The remaining officer positions were allocated on the basis of the premerger affiliation. Open elections were scheduled for later years (Communications, Energy and Paperworkers Union of Canada 1992b,c).

The CEP amalgamation is unique in terms of the high degree of cooperation and trust between the unions' officers, the speed of negotiations (less than a year), and the willingness of the unions' members to form a new organization without industrial sections. Nonetheless, the CEP merger is a watershed event because it challenges conventional union jurisdictions in Canada and could generate numerous future mergers. First, the CEP is predicated on the belief that a diverse membership is a source of institutional stability and bargaining power. Although it was initially criticized for combining unions whose members seemed to have little in common, if the CEP merger is successful in bargaining and organizing and remains free of factionalism, other unions will resort to mergers to expand beyond their traditional jurisdictions.[12] The CEP is the first North American union comparable to the British general unions (e.g., the General, Municipal, Boilermakers and the Transport and General Workers Union) which were formed by amalgamations, grew through absorptions, and represent all workers in all industries. (Among the CEP's recent new members are clerical workers in municipal offices and nursing-home workers (Scotland 1995)). A major difference, as we will see later, is that the British general unions are built on a foundation of craft or industry sections.

Second, the CEP is attractive to small unions exploring merger options because it is large, national, and not dominated by any industrial or occupational group. In September 1994, the 3,000-member Southern Ontario Guild left its parent international union, the Newspaper Guild, and negotiated a merger into the CEP. Also, in that year, the 9,000-member National Association of Broadcast Employees and Technicians and 10 Canadian locals of the Communications Workers of America with 1,200 members joined CEP ("News Union Gets OK" 1994; Bureau of National Affairs 1994c). In the future CEP will compete against the CAW and some Canadian sections of international unions (e.g. the Steelworkers) which are using absorptions as a primary growth strategy (List 1992; Papp 1992a). The inevitable result will be a substantial increase in overall merger activity.

Despite their resiliency during recent hard times, Canadian unions now find themselves in a difficult position. Although unions continue to assign a high priority to organizing and operate within a supportive legal framework, significant growth is unlikely. For many unions, job losses in unionized work places in the public and private sector may be too great to be offset by new organizing. At the same time, negotiations have become more complex and contentious; management's vigorous pursuit of flexibility and lower labor costs have forced unions to agree to moderated wages and benefits, and revisions in work rules. Finally, although social unionism remains a source of vitality for Canadian unions, the benefits of political involvement and coalition activities are now being widely debated.

Canadian labor laws neither encourage unions to merge nor simplify the merger process by standardizing procedures for negotiation and approval. Labor federations may promote mergers in a general sense but may not threaten their affiliates' autonomy by pressuring for specific mergers. This is quite similar to the situation in the United States. Yet, as Papp (1992a, A2) observed, "major unions in virtually every sector . . . are shopping for merger partners."

The uncertain economic and political environment, and the limited possibility of significant growth are causing Canadian unions to examine merger options more closely.[13] The three landmark mergers discussed in this chapter illustrate trends which will transform the heightened interest in the merger option into an important merger wave. First, greater Canadian-section autonomy eliminates an important merger barrier—the international unions' prohibitions against their Canadian section mergers—while increasing the number of potential merger participants. Union mergers in Canada are no longer dominated by arrangements negotiated in the United States. Twenty-two percent of mergers from 1980 to 1993 were among international unions, compared to 60 percent for 1960 to 1979 (table 6). Second, the merger of the two operating unions in the postal system, the worst-case scenario of a forced merger, will alert unions confined to single, narrow bargaining units to the consequences of unit consolidations and encourage them to merge and preempt adverse labor-board decisions. Third, the CEP will be a test case of the benefits of membership diversity, while also raising the level of competition between unions seek-

ing to attract absorption partners. If the CEP amalgamation proves successful, it will be difficult for any union to dismiss a potential merger
partner solely on the basis of membership differences.

The merger wave of the next decade could reshape the Canadian labor
movement. Union fragmentation, the presence of many small unions, will
be greatly reduced. Newly autonomous Canadian sections, no longer
attached to large unions, will try to regain economies of scale in operations
by merging with each other or national unions. International unionism will
continue its decline. And large unions with unlimited jurisdictions, such
as the CEP and CAW, will become centers of merger activity and will
come to rely on absorptions for continued growth.

CHAPTER 4

Great Britain:
The Merger Tradition Continues

In late 1978 and early 1979, British unions were strong enough to launch a series of crippling strikes in the public and private sectors, the so-called winter of discontent, which helped bring to power the Conservative government of Margaret Thatcher. The unions' membership was at its highest level and negotiations with employers were usually contentious. Editorialists wrote of the power of union bosses and the clash between collective bargaining and the public welfare. But through the 1980s, the Conservatives were able to curb the unions, and shrinking employment in core British industries led to severe membership losses.

Declining membership, financial hardship, bargaining setbacks and political impotency forced the unions to explore new ways to recruit and represent workers. Not surprisingly, mergers were a top option. More so than in any other country, unions in Britain have a tradition of turning to mergers to resolve their problems. Mergers are commonly seen as inevitable in the evolution of the labor movement, a natural way to build large unions and to end small ones. This tradition of mergers and a merger-friendly legal framework led in the 1980s and 1990s to an important series of mergers that challenged the federation, reduced union fragmentation, and formed the first modern super-union.

The Context

ECONOMIC DECLINE

The 1980s began with a recession, with unemployment, at 7.0 percent in 1980, rising to 10.5 percent the next year and remaining in double digits until 1988. It then fell for three years, only to rise again in the next recession, reaching 10.0 percent in 1992 and 10.4 percent in 1993. Throughout the decade, productivity growth lagged behind wage growth, causing Britain's competitive position in world markets to deteriorate (Brown and Walsh 1991).

From the mid- to the late-1980s, the decline in manufacturing was largely offset by growth in services. Real personal earnings rose because of tax cuts and low inflation. But inflation was up sharply in 1990, interest rates remained high, and consumers cut spending to repay debts and mortgages. A deep recession followed, with a moderate recovery in 1993 brought on by increased exports (Upham 1993).

Although Britain historically enjoyed trade surpluses in manufactured goods, this ended in the early 1980s because of the strong pound and import penetration in British markets. During the decade, imports grew at twice the rate of exports. In 1983, for the first time since the Industrial Revolution, more manufactured goods were imported than exported. The industries feeling the brunt of foreign competition were electrical components, textiles, clothing, leather, motor vehicles, and chemicals. Manufacturing's share of employment fell from 30 percent in 1980 to 23 percent in 1990 (Edwards et al. 1992). By the end of the 1980s, two million jobs had been lost in manufacturing, about one-quarter of that sector's jobs at the start of the decade (Evans, Ewing, and Nolan 1992). The public sector also contracted. Since 1979, public employment has dropped by 22 percent (down 1.6 million workers); more than half of the loss was in nationalized industries and public corporations (Bailey 1994).

Critics have accused the government of lacking a coherent, comprehensive industrial policy and allowing core industries (e.g., foundries, automobiles, and textiles) to decline. They argue that Britain now competes as a low wage, low labor cost economy, and that this is causing a widening productivity gap between Britain and other major industrial countries (Brown and Walsh 1991; Trades Union Congress 1992). Evans, Ewing, and Nolan (1992), for example, contend that Britain has become "a center for cheap, disposable labour" and, in terms of European wage scales, ranks with Spain and Portugal, rather than France, Germany, or Italy.

Nolan (1989, 84) detects a self-reinforcing relationship between low wages and productivity: "The more employers and successive governments, whether Conservative or Labour, have seen pay restraints as the chief solution to the problems of British industry, the weaker has been the incentive for firms to innovate or modernize, to reduce costs by implementing more efficient technologies."

A recent review shows the British economy recovering from the last recession with growth in the gross domestic product, gains in manufacturing output to meet export demand, competitive exchange rates, only small increases in unit labor costs, low inflation, and rising company profitability (Morris 1995). Britain has attracted more direct foreign investment in new factories and other business operations than any other country in Europe, largely because of its lower labor costs and fewer workplace regulations (Stevenson 1995). But the toll on the union movement has been severe. Whether by policy or lack of policy, the shrinking manufacturing base and reduced public employment have created tremendous membership losses for the unions.

Table 8, based on membership figures submitted by unions to the government's certification officer, shows union membership rising through the 1950s, 1960s, and 1970s, with density gradually increasing. In 1980, union membership was at nearly 13 million and density was 53 percent. Since then, unions lost 3.9 million members, about 30 percent of the total,

Table 8. Union membership and density in the United Kingdom, 1950–1993

Year	Union members (thousands)	Union density[a]
1950	9,289	44%
1955	9,741	45
1960	9,835	44
1965	10,325	44
1970	11,187	49
1975	12,026	51
1980	12,947	53
1985	10,821	43
1990	9,947	33
1992	9,048	32

Sources: 1950–1975: Visser 1989; 1980–1992: Bird and Corcoran 1994.
Note: Includes Great Britain and Northern Ireland. Membership figures for 1950–1992 are unavailable for Great Britain alone. Data are from the surveys conducted by the certification office.
[a]Union membership as a percentage of the labor force.

and density dropped 21 percentage points.[1] In 1992 alone, unions lost more than a half-million members. Data collected as part of the Labour Force Survey show unions losing 1.4 million members from 1989 to 1994 (Corcoran 1995).[2] Union membership, now at its lowest level since the end of World War II, is predicted to fall further, by about 2.4 million members before the end of the century. The result would be a union movement with about half of the 1980 membership ("Think Tank Forecasts" 1993).

Reasons for membership losses include: employment shifts from the more heavily unionized manufacturing sectors to the lesser unionized service sector; new entrants in the labor force who are less likely to favor union representation or share the ideology of unionism (e.g., part-time, temporary and white-collar workers); declining employment in the larger workplaces that are more often unionized than smaller ones; the employers' reluctance to recognize unions at new workplaces; and the contraction of heavily unionized government services.[3]

Some might argue that the severity of the decline in union membership and density is exaggerated in the sense that both were at such high levels initially. The British union movement has certainly not suffered a free-fall in membership similar to that of American unions described in Chapter 2. Union density remains higher in Britain today than in Italy, Germany, Japan, Spain, the United States, or France (Turner 1991; "TUC Membership Figures" 1992). While this is true, we should also keep in mind that the recent declines are without precedent among the British unions, and that sudden, sharp membership losses must be destabilizing for many of Britain's largest unions. For example, from 1980 to 1992, aggregate union membership declined by 30 percent, but was down by 50 percent (about 1 million members) in the Transport and General Workers, 41 percent (626,000 members) in the Amalgamated Engineers, 55 percent (192,000 members) in the United Construction, Allied Trades and Technicians, and 75 percent (278,000 members) in the National Union of Mineworkers (Certification Office for Trade Unions and Employers Associations 1981, 1994).

Most officers of British unions and the Trades Union Congress (TUC), the labor federation, call for a higher priority on membership recruiting and the greater allocation of financial and staff resources for this purpose. In 1987, the TUC created a special committee to lead the effort to revamp organizing techniques, coordinate organizing campaigns, and devise appeals to such lesser unionized groups as part-time and service workers

(Trades Union Congress 1989). From 1985 to 1990, nearly 80 percent of British unions had organizing campaigns, compared to 40 percent between 1980 and 1984 (Mason and Bain 1991).

Organizing in Britain, however, can be extremely difficult because employers are not legally compelled to recognize (or continue to recognize) unions despite the workers' interest (Beaumont and Harris 1995). Under this voluntary system, unions must pressure employers, or appeal to them, to grant recognition. Recent evidence shows that "union recognition became significantly harder to achieve in new establishments in the 1980–1990 time period than it was in earlier years, particularly in the private sector and it was this change . . . that drove the downturn in unionisation" (Disney, Gosling, and Machin 1995, 417). Much of the decline is attributed to management's unfavorable attitude toward unionism in private sector manufacturing. Recognition is also proving more difficult in small firms and the new facilities of multiplant companies (Geroski, Gregg, and Desjonqueres 1995).

In unionized firms, unions often function "as mediating organizations between employers who see some benefit either in the granting of recognition or its maintenance, fearing to deal with an unorganised workforce, and employees who seek various forms of insurance and representation" (Willman 1989, 263). During the 1980s, most unions were able to induce employers to continue recognition by promising orderly industrial relations and flexible work rules; in effect, unions improved their image and showed that employers would benefit in recognizing them.

Employers saw little to gain by withdrawing recognition at one or a few plants, or not extending it to new ones. When employers did withdraw recognition, usually in their attempts to have greater control over pay and productivity, there was little the unions could do. Despite their vulnerability, however, most unions were not concerned about derecognition, which has been confined mostly to smaller and more weakly organized firms. Moreover, derecognition was seldom complete but usually involved one of several unions at a single worksite. Derecognized unions often retained some degree of representation, if only in helping to draft operating procedures.[4]

Fortunately for the British unions, most employers do not try to escape bargaining, apparently out of concern about arousing union opposition or worker discontent in the absence of unions. Many believe that unions play an important role by recognizing management prerogatives at the workplace and channeling conflict (Storey and Sisson 1993). "The overt anti-unionism of some American employers . . . was not replicated in Britain. Where employers recognized unions in 1979 they tended to do so during the 1980s'' (Waddington and Whitston 1994, 198).

But unfortunately for British unions, recognition at new facilities was infrequent and membership gains insufficient to offset the union jobs lost through employment contraction (Millard 1994). For instance, from 1988 to 1992, five union members were lost for every three union members gained through new recognitions (Bassett 1993b). The General, Municipal, Boilermakers (GMB), Britain's fourth-largest union, recently reported a membership turnover of 15 to 20 percent per year and the need to recruit nearly 150,000 new members just to offset annual attrition (General, Municipal, Boilermakers 1993). In the three years since its creation in 1989, the GMB had a net loss of 78,000 members (Certification Office for Trade Unions and Employers' Associations 1990, 1994).

Most British unions are poorly prepared for the task of recruiting members on a large scale and devising appeals for employee support and employer recognition. Mason and Bain (1991, 44) observed: ''The vast majority of trade unions, while attitudinally committed to recruitment campaigning, have not put in place measures which would allow them to methodically organize, finance, and monitor specific campaigns.'' Unions frequently focus organizing campaigns on traditional sources of members, rather than extending recruitment to lesser unionized industries or occupations. This strategy leads to competition between unions and low membership gains rather than expanding the frontiers of unionism (Mason and Bain 1991).

Few unions have organized extensively and most nonunion companies are never approached by union organizers (Kelly 1990). The combination of inexperience, inadequate resources, and reliance on employer recognition has produced only minor gains—105 new recognition agreements covering about 24,000 workers since 1988 (Gall and McKay 1994).

The Transformation of Collective Bargaining

In Britain, collective bargaining agreements are not legally binding documents and their ''negotiation has meant not an occasional and formal agreement but a continuous process of finding compromises'' (Edwards 1995, 48). While this remains so, since 1980 there have been fundamental changes in British collective bargaining. Perhaps most important was decentralization, the shift from multiplant to single-plant bargaining, or from multi-employer and national to single-employer bargaining (Storey and Sisson 1993; Katz 1993). From 1984 to 1990, the proportion of establishments with multi-employer negotiations fell from 20 percent to 11 percent for manual workers, and from 11 percent to 5 percent for nonmanual workers ("Irreversible Decline" 1992).

Decentralization was caused primarily by employers' seeking to weather intense foreign competition by taking greater control over labor costs. In their pursuit of greater flexibility in setting pay and work rules, employers broke from industrywide agreements and negotiated on the company basis, often at the local level. During the later 1980s, national bargaining structures were disbanded in buses, banking, cotton textiles, food retailing, cement, and newspapers (Brown and Walsh 1991). Decentralization also occurred in the public sector; in 1994, more than half of Britain's civil servants were covered by new pay- and job-grading arrangements that were negotiated outside of the national agreements (Baily 1994; "New Moves" 1994).[5]

Though not as pervasive a strategy as decentralization, employers, unions, and the government have sought to simplify bargaining structures and create single-union or single-table negotiations (the latter consists of coordinated bargaining among several unions). Multi-unionism, the presence of several unions representing workers at a single facility, has long been a concern of British employers and union officers. As unions negotiate for neighboring groups of workers, there has been rival, nearly continuous and highly conflictive bargaining (Chaison 1986). In 1990, there was an average of 2.5 bargaining agents at unionized workplaces ("Irreversible Decline" 1992).

Employers initiate a "single-union deal," or negotiations with a single union per workplace, when they grant recognition to only one union, usually as a representative of both manual and nonmanual workers. Along with such status, the employer usually introduces committees for employee participation in decision-making. Unions frequently agree to relax work rules and sign a no-strike clause under which bargaining impasses are resolved by arbitration ("Single-Union Deals in Perspective" 1992).

Unions agreed to single-union deals in the late 1980s to gain a competitive advantage during rival organizing campaigns at new plants and at nonunion companies. Many were signed prior to the opening of new facilities, sometimes after so-called "beauty contests" in which employers chose among the competing unions' proposals. Under such circumstances, unions wooed employers rather than workers (Willman 1989; Swabe 1990; Hunter 1991; "Single-Union Deals in Perspective" 1992).

Although they have received a great deal of publicity, single-union deals are rare, found in only about two percent of workplaces, and their rate of negotiation has dropped sharply since the late 1980s (Gall 1993). This decline occurred because fewer new plants are being opened, particularly by Japanese companies that promoted these arrangements, and because many unions have been discouraged by low membership at plants where they signed single-union deals, the likely result of appealing for recognition to employers rather than workers. As one union officer described it, "In most cases employees do not want to join. And why should they? The union is the employers' choice, not theirs" ("GMB to Avoid 'Beauty Contests.' " 1992, 13). Finally, single-union deals at unionized facilities are widely believed by union officers to be harmful to the growth and solidarity of the British labor movement. In essence, one union gains recognition by displacing others. This violates the Trades Union Congress's policy restricting interunion competition and, as we will see in the case of the electricians' union, it can lead to intense rival organizing and expulsion from the federation.

As an alternative to single-union deals, some unions negotiate jointly in single-table bargaining. Under these arrangements, unions of manual and nonmanual workers coordinate negotiations, agreeing to common pay, job classification systems, similar hours of work, and holidays and pensions. Management promotes single-table bargaining to avoid the conflict and competition of multi-union representation. Smaller unions usually benefit from such negotiations because they can take advantage of the skills, experience, and bargaining power of the large unions sharing the bargaining table. Moreover, single-table bargaining may sometimes be the only effective way for unions and employers to deal with issues such as training and work hours, which extend beyond narrow groups of workers (Marginson and Sisson 1990).

Although employers in Britain have pressed for simplified bargaining arrangements and greater flexibility to control labor costs and increase productivity, they have not retreated from collective bargaining to the extent that employers have in the United States. Swabe (1990, 7) has observed: "Despite all the tales we hear about [British] trade unions and their future, the majority of the structures of collective bargaining remain intact. Employers may have gained ground lost in earlier years, but they have done so mainly through bargaining and by changes in reward systems, not by an onslaught on the institutions and processes of collective bargaining.'' During the 1980s, there were stories in the popular press about the spread of "macho management," but the extreme exploitation of bargaining advantage and union displacement has been rare (Hunter 1991). When they did occur, they were usually in nationalized companies or during industrial restructuring forced by market changes, not because of a transformation of management values (Hyman 1994).

THE CONSERVATIVES' CAMPAIGN TO MARGINALIZE THE UNION MOVEMENT

Since the early 1980s, the British government has tried to marginalize the unions by excluding them from the corridors of power and reducing their size and influence (Marsh 1992). The campaign to diminish the unions' stature began during the government of Margaret Thatcher (1979–1990), but has continued through John Major's administration. It is rooted in the Conservatives' belief in the unrestrained operation of free markets and the need for greater flexibility in production and employment. According to this view, industrial efficiency is generated through competition—only the fittest companies and industries should survive this competition. Union representation is an impediment to competition and economic development. National, multi-employer collective agreements are unresponsive to firm-specific conditions and detract from job creation (Soskice 1984; Nolan 1989; Brown and Wadhwani 1990; Smith and Morton 1993; 1994).

Past British governments attempted to build constructive relations with labor unions. "Through the 1960's and 1970's unions were at the center of the British political stage. Prime ministers at Downing Street warmly and regularly received the leaders of the trade union movement for union militancy could bring down governments, both Conservative and Labour" (Lohr 1988, 7).

The Thatcher administration initially followed a monetarist, free-market approach, and continued the abstentionist tradition by eschewing government intervention in labor relations and not taking sides in labor disputes. Policymakers began to argue, however, that the unions were powerful labor-market monopolies and that collective bargaining contributed to inflationary pressures, inefficiency, and poor economic performance (Soskice 1984; Evans, Ewing, and Nolan 1992). By the mid-1980s, the trade unions and their leaders were being denounced for blocking the free operation of the labor markets and for stifling the individualism of workers.

Thatcher believed "the unions had priced many of their members out of jobs by demanding excessive wages for insufficient output, so British goods became uncompetitive" (Thatcher 1993, 272).

The *Economist* succinctly described Thatcher's fight with the unions: "The trade unions embodied the Britain that Mrs. Thatcher was out to abolish. They existed to protect collective rights and defy the free play of market forces. They were against change because change always threatened some of their members. They were a gift to her: they provided her with an unpopular enemy, a grand fight and a dramatic victory" ("The Thatcher Record" 1992, 18).

Her administration rejected abstentionism and sought instead to intervene in labor disputes and internal governance with aim of dismantling the foundations of union power. Reforms were justified in the name of ending the left's destructive domination of the labor movement, redressing the overbearing power of the unions, and permitting management once more to manage (Thatcher 1993). Tripartitism—structures and policies for the mutual accommodation of the government, labor unions, and employers—no longer seemed desirable. Consensus and compromise became "unacceptable constraints on the determination of the government to pursue a clear political and economic strategy" (Hunter 1991, 135).

The Conservatives carried out their assault against the unions not only through their national economic policy, but also through a stream of legislation—the Employment Acts in 1980, 1982, 1988, and 1990, the 1984 Trade Union Act, and the 1993 Trade Union Reform and Employment Rights Act.[6] These "shatter[ed] the post-war consensus about the values of collective bargaining and the role of trade unions in British society" (Miller and Steele 1993, 224).

Statutory procedures for union recognition by employers were abolished. Wage councils that once imposed minimum pay rates were dismantled. The scope of lawful picketing was limited. Secret ballots for strikes were mandated. Balloting procedures for the election of union officers, the creation of political funds, and compulsory union membership were imposed for the first time. Unions were given a legal personality, enabling them to be sued for a wide variety of activities, including prohibited strikes. Government grants for union balloting and labor-education programs were phased out. The check-off, the employers' deductions of union members' dues, was restricted. Closed shops, arrangements calling for union membership as a condition of employment, were greatly weakened when dismissal for nonmembership became unlawful.[7]

The government also led by example. It became a role model for confrontational employers in bargaining and during strikes. It downsized the unionized public workforce and held public employees to new standards of productivity. In 1984, it banned labor unions at the Government Communications Headquarters, part of NATO's surveillance spy-satellite network, claiming they were incompatible with the national interest, and replaced them with an internal staff association. Legal action by the displaced unions proved ineffective (Pannick 1994). In 1984 the government broke with tradition by directly supporting a public employer, the National Coal Board, in a long and bitter strike. In 1987, it imposed a pay settlement on teachers and suspended their bargaining rights (Towers 1989). A ceiling of 1.5 percent on public-sector wage settlements was announced in 1992, and the federal government proclaimed that raises would have to be self-financing; "Any increases in pay will have to be funded not by increased resources but by better efficiency" ("Public Sector Pay Bargaining" 1994, 12). Finally, large numbers of workers were excluded from the coverage of collective agreements by the withdrawal of bargaining rights or the reclassification of their jobs.

The Conservative Party's 1979 election manifesto proclaimed that the continued nationalization of industries "would further impoverish us and further undermine our freedom" (Fraser and Wilson 1988, 8). It pledged to sell some recently nationalized industries (shipbuilding and aerospace firms) back to private ownership and see to it that others were run efficiently. Immediately after its election victory, the government began a radical program of deregulation and privatization of industry and services. Over the next decade, about 40 percent of the state-owned industrial sector, accounting for 11 percent of gross domestic product and employing 650,000 workers in 1979, was transferred to the private sector (Fraser and Wilson 1988). Also, governments on both national and regional levels promoted privatization and deregulation, introduced compulsory private tendering for government services, pressured unions into pay cuts, and decreased the number of unionized jobs by hiring part-time and temporary workers. Denationalization, the sale of government assets, was actively pursued; among the most prominent targets were British Gas, British Airways, and British Telecom. Companies bought earlier by the government, such as Jaguar and Rolls Royce, were also sold (Kelly 1990; "The Thatcher Record" 1992; Upham 1993; Baily 1994; "Public Sector Pay"

1994). Jobs were slashed in newly privatized industries and in local utilities. For instance, employment fell by over 70,000 workers in British Telecom from 1990 to 1993, and by 26,000 workers in the electrical industry from 1990 to 1994 ("Pay in the Privatized Utilities" 1994).

The government was also a major force behind the decentralization of collective bargaining. It promoted decentralized negotiations and encouraged both private and public employers to pay greater attention to local labor-market conditions in wage negotiations and to resist union claims of comparability on a wider basis (Evans, Ewing, and Nolan 1992). Industrywide agreements were criticized, and the councils that administered them were blamed for rigid national wage rates, and for blocking downward wage flexibility and job creation (Brown and Walsh 1991). Local discretion in wage setting was introduced in education, health services, and local government. Managers were permitted to vary rates of pay in accordance with local labor-market conditions and to introduce appraisal techniques to measure individual performance (Upham 1993). In the water industry, for example, national agreements for manual, staff, and craft groups were replaced by local agreements that were often drafted in single-table negotiations.

Is the British labor movement in a crisis? There is a general consensus that membership losses have been severe and probably irreversible in the short run, that bargaining power has been greatly reduced, and that both of these trends result from economic restructuring, particularly the decline in manufacturing, and laws and actions of hostile Conservative governments. Furthermore, "unions were unable to stem a flood of closures and redundancies, they failed to prevent real wages falling in the depths of recession, they could not prevent changes in working practices and they suffered a number of spectacular strike defeats" (Kelly 1990, 42).

But unions are not in a crisis in either an historical or comparative sense. As one prominent labor leader concluded, contrary to the view of the Conservatives, unions have not become "part of the archaeology of industrial relations . . . doomed to wither and die" (Monks 1994, 42). Overall, the unions were in a stronger position at the start of the 1990s than they were after their last period of significant membership loss in the 1920s. Union membership among manual workers declined at a slower rate than did employment. Union derecognition was not widespread and the majority of large employers still deal with unions. Revenues from dues have been maintained, and though few unions are prospering, most are financially viable. While unions declined nationally, they often maintained a presence at the company and plant levels.

New forms of industrial relations did not supplant collective bargaining. Structures for greater worker participation in decision-making usually complemented union representation rather than replace it. Finally, "macho" anti-union management has not been widespread; few employers became Thatcherite and used the laws to break the unions' power (Kelly 1990; Turner 1991; Martin 1992; "Irreversible Decline" 1992; Marsh 1992: "A Decade of Radical Change" 1993; Hancke 1993; Spencer 1993; Gall and McKay 1994; Monks 1994; Morris 1995).

Although British unions are not in a crisis, the limits to their growth and bargaining power are clear enough for them to consider mergers. Merger-friendly legislation and the longstanding tradition of merging in hard times have been sufficient to overcome merger barriers and create a number of historically important mergers.

The Merger Record

Since 1980, there have been 163 union mergers in Britain—144 absorptions (called "transfers of engagements"), and 19 amalgamations. Merger frequency was erratic, ranging from 4 in 1981 and in 1992, to 32 in 1986 (table 9). Compared to the figures in some earlier periods, particularly 1911 to 1925 and the 1960s and 1970s, recent merger activity is unexceptional (table 10). Excluding the large number of mergers in 1986, the annual rates are lower than those for the 1960s and 1970s. The flurry of mergers in 1986 will not be repeated; these were primarily the absorptions of local government associations into the Federation of Managerial and Professional Officers Unions (19 mergers) and regional textile unions into the General, Municipal, Boilermakers Union (GMB) (10 mergers).

British unions merge for the same reasons as do unions in the United States and Canada, that is, to resolve the problems of financial difficulty and declining membership, and to grow quickly and inexpensively while diversifying jurisdictions (see, e.g., "Union Mergers" 1983; Aston 1987; Merrick 1995; Waddington 1995). For instance, the Association of Professional, Executive, Clerical and Computer Staffs (APEX) was down to about half of its 1979 membership when it amalgamated with the GMB in 1989. With members in airline, insurance, and engineering offices, APEX lacked the size and diversity of membership to counter the effects of unemploy-

Table 9. Union mergers in Great Britain, 1980–1993

Year	Transfers of Engagements[a]	Amalgamations	Total
1980	12	1	13
1981	4	0	4
1982	9	3	12
1983	8	1	9
1984	16	2	18
1985	10	1	11
1986	32	0	32
1987	4	1	5
1988	9	2	11
1989	9	1	10
1990	13	3	16
1991	6	2	8
1992	3	1	4
1993	9	1	10
Total	144	19	163

Source: Certification Office for Trade Unions and Employers' Associations various years.
[a]Includes absorptions and affiliation mergers.

ment and rising employer opposition (Druker 1988). The Amalgamated Textile Workers Union (ATWU) was confined to a declining industry and lost two-thirds of its members in the twelve years prior to its absorption by the GMB (Amalgamated Textile Workers Union 1985).

Many of Britain's largest unions merged to diversify their membership, believing that this would enhance their growth potential by locating them in expanding areas while also reducing the hazards of having members concentrated in declining sectors (Waddington 1992). For example, the GMB absorbed the Greater London Staff Association to expand its base among white-collar local government workers (Waddington 1992). The Electrical, Electronic, Telecommunication and Plumbing Union (EETPU) often merged to strengthen its representation among management and professional staff, thus reducing the impact of the declining membership employment on the union's finances and operations. From 1989 to 1990, the EETPU sought to become a general union and absorbed 12 unions, including those of foremen, powerloom overlookers, prison workers, journalists and film production workers (Waddington 1992). From 1981 to 1985 the Technical, Administrative and Supervisory Section (TASS) of the Engineering Workers, an organization of mostly white-collar workers, extended its membership base to skilled manual workers by absorbing unions of gold and silver workers, sheet-metal workers, patternmakers, and tobacco

Table 10. Union merger activity in Great Britain, 1911–1993[a]

Period	Number of mergers	Average number of mergers per year
1911–1913	52	17.3
1914–1916	63	21.0
1917–1919	128	42.7
1920–1922	137	45.7
1923–1925	35	11.7
1926–1928	27	9.0
1929–1931	35	11.7
1932–1934	29	9.7
1935–1937	29	9.7
1938–1940	17	5.7
1941–1943	21	7.0
1944–1946	38	12.7
1947–1950	37	9.3
1951–1953	9	3.0
1954–1956	16	5.3
1957–1959	6	2.0
1960–1962	17	5.7
1963–1965	32	10.7
1966–1968	33	11.0
1969–1971	54	18.0
1972–1974	54	18.0
1975–1977	41	13.7
1978–1980	35	12.7
1981–1983	25	8.3
1984–1986	59	19.7
1987–1989	25	8.3
1990–1992	28	9.3
1993	10	10.0
Total	1092	13.2

Sources: Buchanan 1974; 1981; Certification Office for Trade Unions and Employers' Association various years.
[a]Includes amalgamations and transfers of engagements (absorptions and affiliation mergers).

workers from 1981 to 1985 (Waddington and Whitston 1994). For all of these merging unions, an important advantage of having diversified membership was that they could offer collective agreements to employers at greenfield sites that covered white-collar, blue-collar, and craft workers (Druker 1988).

Underlying the mergers listed in the tables and appendix to this chapter are some trends that are not readily discernable but that suggest the prominent role of union mergers in British labor relations: labor laws and a merger tradition make merging easier, mergers were often the last step in the evolution of many small, specialized unions, and a merger created a new "super-union."

The Underlying Trends

The Legal Framework

British laws regulate union mergers by establishing procedures for notifying union members of merger terms and determining whether members accept or reject them. This legislation reduces merger barriers by resolving objections quickly, inexpensively, and to finality.

A government agency, the Office of the Certification Officer, scrutinizes transfers of engagements (absorptions and affiliations) and amalgamations.[8]

> The effect of a *transfer of engagement* is to transfer members (and usually the property, funds, etc.) of the transferor union into the transferee union on the terms set out in the instrument of transfer [the merger agreement]. When a transfer takes effect the transferor union ceases to exist. . . . The transferee union, however, continues in being with its legal identity unchanged. The effect of an *amalgamation* is that the two or more amalgamating trade unions are merged, on the terms set out in the instrument of amalgamation, to form a new union with new rules. Upon the amalgamation taking effect, all the amalgamating unions cease to exist. (Certification Office for Trade Unions and Employers' Associations 1994b, 5)

The certification officer ensures that members are fully informed of the merger terms and can approve or reject them without interference or coercion. The officer or his representatives examines the merger documents, the notification of merger terms and the ballots that will be sent to members. He also hears union members' complaints about procedural violations.

When unions transfer engagements, the instrument of transfer must be approved by a simple majority of the voting members of the transferor organization, that is, the union that ceases to exist after the merger. Members of the transferee union, the union that continues after the merger, are not legally required to vote on the merger because their union's identity is not significantly altered. On the other hand, amalgamations must be approved by the members of each amalgamating union because they cease to exist after the merger.[9]

After negotiating a merger, union officers must send a copy of the instrument of transfer (the merger agreement) to the certification officer along with the notice of the merger that they plan to distribute. Revisions may be required if, for example, the instrument of transfer does not adequately describe the merger's impact on the status of the unions and their members, or does not mention changes in dues and benefits. An instrument of amalgamation must include the name and principal purposes of the amalgamated union and its governing structures, the method for selecting officers, the schedule of dues, and the distribution of the properties and assets of the amalgamating unions.

The merging unions must either attach the merger instrument to the notice or summarize its main effects. Under a recent amendment to the legislation, the notice may not contain officers' statements expressing their opinions about the merger or recommendations for its approval, but these may be mailed separately.

Union members must be given an opportunity to cast their ballots without interference or constraint.[10] Once a merger is approved, union officers apply for the registration of the merger instruments. For the next six weeks, members may file complaints about the merger documents or the conduct of the balloting. Complaints must be resolved by the certification office before the merger instruments are registered and the merger becomes final.

When a merger is officially registered, the names of the amalgamating unions or the transferor union (but not the transferee union) are stricken from the lists of federally registered unions. The union created by amalgamation may then apply for registration. Although registration is voluntary, it is an essential preliminary step in a union's application for a certificate of independence. This certificate enables the union to receive tax relief for the cost of members' benefits and provides access to government procedures for recognition as a bargaining agent.

The certification officer does not distribute model documents for mergers, nor does it directly assist unions drafting them. The officer does interpret merger requirements and revise documents, however, and may provide financial assistance for postal ballots. Mergers take at least fifteen weeks to complete—nine weeks to hold an election after submitting a merger proposal and six weeks for the filing of objections before the registration of merger documents.

The British legal framework has affected merger form and frequency by changing the stringency of merger approval.[11] The first merger law, the 1876 Trade Union (Amendment) Act, required that merger proposals be approved by at least two-thirds of each participating union's members, not merely those voting. Few mergers occurred under the 1876 act. In 1917, the Trade Union (Amalgamation) Act sought to reduce jurisdictional overlapping and interunion disputes by encouraging mergers. It called for approval by 50 percent of each union's members, but the votes in favor of merger had to exceed those against by at least 20 percent. Although this formula was open to conflicting interpretations, it sufficiently relaxed the voting requirements to start a merger wave that lasted for five years and averaged over 40 mergers per year (see table 10).

In 1940, section 6 of the Societies (Miscellaneous Provisions) Act amended the 1917 act by creating separate procedures for transfers of engagements. Two-thirds of the members of the transferor union had to consent. Balloting among the members of the transferee (absorbing) union was not required. Merger activity, however, was low. Under pressure from the Trades Union Congress, Parliament passed legislation in 1964 to encourage union mergers; majority approval was needed from the *voting* members of each amalgamating union or from the *voting* members of *only* the transferor union in a transfer of engagements. "Apathy can no longer be a bar to a successful merger" (Elias 1973, 129). The result was a merger wave that continued through the mid-1970s.

Although the certification officer and his staff believe mergers to be generally beneficial, their role is protecting union members' rights rather than promoting mergers, a neutral role not likely to change in the near future because amendment of merger legislation is not a high priority for the current or foreseeable administrations. Conservatives would find it difficult to fault the present procedures after arguing for so many years for a more efficient union movement and for the protection of union members' voice in union governance. Labour does not see changes in merger procedures as an important issue. Rather, once elected, a Labour government would try to reverse the legislation of the past fifteen years (e.g., by restricting the employers' ability to discharge strikers) and would introduce procedures for designating unions as representatives.

The effectiveness and broad acceptance of the British legislation lies in its standardization of the merger approval process and its channeling of members' and officers' opposition through prescribed procedures.[12] Unions must still offer satisfactory terms if merger negotiations are to succeed, but once merger committees reach a settlement, the remaining process is straightforward, quick, and inexpensive relative to the alternative—court actions or internal political contests. Recall the long, bitter merger campaigns of the Typographical Union and the Health Care Employees in the United States and the challenge to the merger of the fishermen's local in Canada where merger approval does not follow a uniform, externally administered process.

THE BRITISH TRADITION OF UNION MERGERS

British unions have a long tradition of forming, dissolving, and expanding into new organizing territories through mergers. Since 1911, there have been nearly 1,100 union mergers (see table 10).

Most large unions evolved through mergers. For example, Unison, the largest union in 1994, was formed by a three-union amalgamation in 1993. The Transport and General Workers Union, Britain's second-largest union, was created by an amalgamation of 18 unions in 1922 and it absorbed 60 unions during its first half-century. The Amalgamated Engineering and Electrical Union, the third-largest union, was formed by the 1992 merger of the Amalgamated Engineering Union and the Electrical, Electronic, Telecommunications and Plumbing Union. The former had been through 101 mergers since the early nineteenth century, while the latter had absorbed 17 unions since 1980. The General, Municipal, Boilermakers (GMB), the fourth-largest union, was created by an amalgamation in 1989 and has since absorbed 4 unions. Indeed, the Royal College of Nursing is the only one of Britain's 10 largest unions that was not involved in a merger over the prior 5 years (Bird and Corcoran 1994).

Because of the frequency and historical importance of mergers, union officers and members do not see them as extraordinary events or radical solutions to union problems. Mergers appear as steps in the natural evolution of the union movement, the inevitable streamlining of fragmented union structures. As a result, union officers can often initiate merger discussions without authorization from the membership. Officers and staff tend to be experienced in merger negotiations and members are not predisposed to reject mergers. At any time in Britain, merger contacts are being made, officers are weighing merger terms, and merger negotiations are being started or recessed (Chaison 1986).

Mergers figure prominently in prescriptions for revitalizing the labor movement, making unions more effective and curbing interunion conflict. For example, a royal commission examining the state of industrial relations in the late 1960s, the Donovan Commission, expressed concerns about the number of unions operating in Britain and suggested that "a very real contribution could be made to the problem of multi-unionism if some of the more important and wide ranging organizations [unions] could be induced to combine with each other" (Royal Commission on Trade Union and Employers Associations 1969, 181). It added: "We consider that there is scope for many more mergers between unions. . . . It seems to us that it would be practicable as well as useful to work towards the goal of one or at most two craft unions for the great bulk of craftsmen in [the engineering and construction industry]" (Royal Commission on Trade Unions and Employers Associations 1969, 182). The commission affirmed that decisions to merge rest with individual unions, but it suggested that the Trades Union Congress take the lead in promoting mergers.

In brief, the British merger tradition is derived from and perpetuates a large and continuing stream of union mergers. Unions have been inclined to turn to mergers in hard times, to use mergers as a first rather than last option for structural reform. Merging seems logical in a general sense, and the historical record suggests that British union officers and members are less concerned with whether merging is right in principle than with whether the right merger terms are being offered.

MERGERS AND THE SMALL UNION

The British union movement is highly fragmented. In 1992, 91 percent of the unions had fewer than 50,000 members and 74 percent had fewer than 5,000 members (Certification Officer for Trade Unions and Employers Associations 1994a). Although small size is commonly considered a handicap, there is no consensus about the minimum size necessary for representational effectiveness and financial viability. Sherman (1986), for instance, has argued that British unions with fewer than 70,000 members were not likely to remain viable. Willman (1989) saw economies of scale in unions with over 200,000 members. Undy et al. (1981) reported that officers' believed unions should have between 300,000 and 350,000 members to be influential. John Edmunds, general-secretary of the GMB and a major proponent of union mergers, has claimed that unions should have at least 600,000 members if they intended to service a national membership (Tiemann 1993a).

Snape and Bamber (1989, 102) have described the problems of small managerial and professional unions, but they appear relevant to others in Britain: "Most small unions have limited finance and expertise, and may be unable to provide a wide range of services to members, and they cannot benefit from economies of scale. Such problems can threaten the union's viability." In many instances, small unions "had their members scattered between various employers, making it difficult and expensive for them to recruit, service and retain members" (104). Finally, "the employer knows that a small closed organization [a union with a narrow jurisdiction] is less able to finance prolonged industrial action, given its limited resources" (105).

Officers of small British unions respond to critics by arguing that their organizations are quite capable of representing members' interests when they concentrate on specialized occupations and limit themselves to regions or local communities. They also claim that smaller unions have greater membership participation and attendance at their meetings, and provide for closer contact between members and officers than do large unions (Tiemann 1993a). Small unions may also join together and receive the benefits of greater size. The General Federation of Trade Unions, an association with 30 small affiliates, provides research, educational, legal, and other specialized services which most small unions could not afford individually ("Small Unions" 1992).

Although small size does have its advantages, small unions are nonetheless threatened by forces over which they have little control. First, financial stability is uncertain. The 1993 Trade Union Reform and Employment Rights Act requires that dues check-offs be periodically approved by union members. Although it is too early to determine the law's full impact, the new requirements could result in a substantial decline in dues income. About 80 percent of union members in Britain pay dues through the check-off and in mid-1994 it was reported that 10 to 20 percent of them had not signed up to continue dues payments despite the passing of the deadline to reconfirm ("Check-off Renewals" 1994; Morris 1995). Small unions may feel the brunt of this financial loss because they commonly operate under tight budgets and cannot readily adjust by combining departments and reducing staff.

Moreover, as they intensify organizing efforts, large general unions such as the Transport and General Workers and the GMB will challenge smaller unions for representation rights. In contests for workers' support, larger unions will offer a broad array of membership services as well as industry divisions and regional structures which allow bargaining and administrative autonomy on local levels. They will argue that the benefits of small size can be found in a large union, but that the benefits of a large one cannot be found in a small one (Chaison 1995).

Like their compatriots elsewhere, officers of small British unions reject proposals that end their jobs, submerge their members' interests in large unions, end cherished union traditions, force local branches to merge, or reduce local autonomy in bargaining. They are receptive to proposals that create regional or industrial sections for their unions and that assure the continued employment of their union's officers and staff. Some larger unions have structures that facilitate these arrangements. For example, the GMB has 8 semi-autonomous industrial sectors, each with its own full-time officers, periodicals and conferences (Willman, Morris, and Aston, 1993). In its merger proposal to the Furniture, Timber and Allied Trades Union (FTAT), the GMB offered to create a new section with 67,000 members built around the FTAT's members and officers. This would "enable FTAT activists at all levels and FTAT officers to have a crucial role in forming the shape, methods and functions of the new Section" (General, Municipal, Boilermakers 1992, 4). The new section would hold conferences and be governed by its own national committee, and all FTAT officers and staff were guaranteed continuity of employment at GMB at terms no less favorable than they enjoyed at FTAT.

As large, absorbing unions offer attractive arrangements through their industry structures, it will be increasingly difficult for officers of smaller unions to resist merger proposals. The most important remaining barriers will form around the officers' and members' concerns about ending close attachments to local communities and diluting traditions which often date back to their unions' creation in the last century as benevolent and protective associations. But such concerns can be assuaged by guarantees of autonomy as locals or sections within larger unions.[13] These arrangements may be far more preferable than going head to head with large, general unions in organizing campaigns or seeing the quality of services deteriorate as membership declines. In short, many of those unions preferring to retain the benefits of small size may have to find ways to do so within large unions.[14] Large unions, attracted to the fast growth possible through mergers, should prove accommodative.

MERGERS AND THE TRADES UNION CONGRESS

Despite the broad acceptance of mergers among British unions, the Trades Union Congress (TUC) must refrain from direct involvement in mergers. Similar to the American AFL-CIO and the Canadian CLC, the TUC cannot intrude in affiliates' internal affairs by arranging or negotiating mergers. Anything beyond the most general suggestions about the need to simplify union structure and reduce jurisdictional overlap by creating fewer but larger unions would be interpreted as a challenge to affiliates' autonomy.

The TUC's general council comments periodically on the need for greater coordination among the numerous British unions, suggesting that the most effective way to achieve this is through mergers (Donoughue, Oakley, and Alker 1963). But the TUC has been involved in union mergers only tangentially. First, it helped accelerate the merger pace by successfully lobbying for the amendment of the 1964 Trade Union (Amalgamation) Act. This legislation relaxed the voting requirements for transfers of engagements, causing the number of mergers to double during the 1960s (Buchanan 1981).

Second, the federation tried to reduce the number of unions operating in the same industries by convening sectoral meetings and chartering industrial committees in the hope of building sufficient interest and trust among officers to start merger discussions. The federation proposed 15 industrial groupings and recommended that 50 unions be merged into them (Lover 1980). "The TUC made a major effort to exhort unions in the same sector to amalgamate; a few did [for example, in printing], but most did not" (Trades Union Congress 1988, 13).

The TUC has not been able to promote specific mergers because the final choice of merger partner and terms remains with union officers and members. For instance, it proposed the creation of a giant metal-trades union through mergers by the Sheet Metal Workers; the Heating and Domestic Engineers; the Plumbers; the Boilermakers; and the Construction Engineers. But unity could not be imposed; the first two unions merged, but the Construction Engineers joined with the Amalgamated Union of Engineering Workers and the Plumbers merged with an electricians' union (Lover 1980).

Finally, the TUC's officers and staff mediate at stalled merger negotiations and provide advice on drafting merger documents. This assistance is always at the request of the negotiating parties. The neutrality of the TUC is evident in the cautious wording of its merger policy—Principle 1(d) of the *Disputes Principles and Procedures*:

> Mergers between affiliated unions in frequent contact with one another are in general a desirable means of strengthening trade union organisation and the TUC General Council will therefore be glad to provide advice and assistance to unions considering mergers.
>
> Affiliated unions should consult other affiliates with an interest when they are considering a merger with a non-affiliated organization. In the event of disagreement it is open to any affiliated union involved to refer the matter to the TUC for advice and conciliation but not adjudication by a Disputes Committee unless by agreement between all the affiliated unions concerned.
>
> Affiliated unions will of course appreciate that it is a matter of good trade union practice not to intervene in any way in a ballot being conducted by other unions about a merger. (Trades Union Congress 1993, 11–12)

Maintaining neutrality can be difficult when affiliated unions object to each others' mergers. This was evident in the dispute over the 1992 amalgamation of the Amalgamated Engineering Union (AEU) and the Electrical, Electronic, Telecommunications and Plumbing Union (EETPU).

The AEU had felt the full impact of declining employment in the manufacturing sector, its core jurisdiction. Membership dropped by about two-thirds, from 1,510,000 in 1980 to 541,000 in 1992, despite its absorption of 7 unions during those years. In 1985, its Technical, Administrative and Supervisory Section seceded, taking with it over 200,000 members. The EETPU was also active in mergers, absorbing 18 unions ranging from powerloom operators to probation officers. Nonetheless, heavy job losses caused its membership to fall from 444,000 to 343,000 (Certification Office for Trade Unions and Employers' Associations 1981; Amalgamated Engineering and Electrical Union 1994).

The roots of the AEU–EETPU amalgamation movement can be traced to 1986 when the two joined with other TUC affiliates, the Union of Construction, Allied Trades and Technicians (UCATT) and the Institute of Professional Civil Servants (IPCS), to form an organization of right-of-center affiliates called "Project 2000." The proposed affiliation was intended to curb the rising power of left-of-center unions in the TUC. When UCATT and IPCS dropped out, the AEU and EETPU continued their alliance and started merger discussions. In 1989, the AEU's national committee rejected a merger proposal because it was concerned about differences in the selection of officers, the powers of the regional bodies, and the possibility that merger with EETPU, by then expelled from the TUC, would jeopardize the AEU's affiliation in the TUC ("United Kingdom: Union Mergers" 1992).

Through the 1980s, the EETPU had recruited aggressively with apparently little concern for other unions' jurisdictions. It occasionally sought a competitive advantage by offering single-union deals to employers at unionized and nonunion plants, trading the right to strike for the arbitration of unresolved bargaining issues ("Single-Union Deals Examined" 1993). The EETPU's relationship with the TUC deteriorated because of disagreement over its single-union deals at newspaper plants. The EETPU also supported the use of publicly available funds for union-officer ballots despite federation policy again this practice (Hall 1988).

At a plant of Orion Electric, the EETPU sought and gained employer recognition after the Transport and General Workers Union (TGWU) had already begun an organizing campaign. At two transport depots of the firm of Christian Salvesen, the EETPU recruited members even though three TUC affiliates represented workers at the company's other depots. Complaints were filed with the TUC disputes committee, which decided that in both instances the EETPU had failed to consult with other unions. The EETPU was instructed to cancel its recognition agreements and abide by the federations' Bridlington Principles restricting rival organizing. When the EETPU failed to do so, it was expelled at the 1988 meeting of the TUC. At that time, the EETPU had 336,000 members, or 3.6 percent of the TUC's total membership (Kelly and Richardson 1989).

In its appeal of the suspension, the EETPU was unable to gain the support of affiliates aside from the AEU. Seeing little chance of a change in federation policy and the possibility of intensive organizing rivalry, the EETPU turned to the merger with the AEU, a large TUC affiliate, for protection and as a way to reenter to the federation (Willman, Morris, and Aston 1993).

Negotiations with the AEU proceeded quickly because the most contentious issues were left for resolution after merger (e.g., dues schedules, financial practices, officer compensation and duties). On March 4, 1992, the members of the AEU and the EETPU approved a merger agreement by 87 percent and 85 percent, respectively, and formed the Amalgamated Engineering and Electrical Union (AEEU). The agreement called for lesser integration than customarily found in amalgamations; the two unions formed separate and largely autonomous sections with their own budgets, assets, and conferences. The AEU section continued its practice of electing officers, while most in the EETPU remained appointed. The executive committees of the two unions would meet jointly as the new union's governing body. It was agreed that within four years of the merger, a new constitution would be presented to the membership for their approval ("Electricians and AEU" 1992; Wheal 1992).

The merger seemed like a natural combination. Both unions had suffered severe membership losses and were major proponents of using single-union deals to gain employer recognition. New technologies and changes in work rules had blurred the boundaries between the two unions' jurisdictions. Both were advocates of the "new realism," the philosophy of right-of-center unions that emphasized greater job-related workplace representation and less political involvement ("United Kingdom: Union Mergers" 1992; Tieman 1991, 1993a). But the EETPU's pariah status as an expelled union provoked affiliates' opposition to the merger. Since its expulsion, the EETPU had been sharply criticized by affiliates for recruiting their members ("poaching"); these unions were now concerned that the merger would lead to reaffiliation without withdrawal from the contested bargaining units.

In principle, federations object to the return of an expelled union through the back door by merging with an affiliate and without resolving the issues that caused the expulsion (Chaison 1986). (This was evident in the AFL-CIO's strenuous opposition to a merger between the affiliated ITU and the expelled Teamsters, described in chapter 2.) As a practical matter, however, the TUC was hesitant to turn away the AEEU's request for affiliation.[15] The federation was in financial trouble because its affiliates' declining membership led to lower per capita dues payments. In 1993, the TUC officers were considering laying off a fifth of its staff. The AEEU would bring in more than £1.2 million and return the TUC's second-largest affiliate (Tieman 1993b). The TUC also feared that rejection of the AEEU would lead it to form a rival federation of right-of-center unions. Moreover, if the EETPU sections of the AEEU remained outside the federation, they could continue to use single-union deals to gain a competitive advantage over TUC affiliates, which might derail the federation's campaign to promote single-table bargaining (Hall 1988).

TUC affiliates insisted that the AEEU relinquish the members that the EETPU had recruited in rival contests. Officers of eleven unions wrote to

John Monks, the federation's general secretary, objecting to the proposed merger, and later met with him to express their concerns. Other affiliates submitted their concerns in writing (Trades Union Congress 1993c).

At the TUC's 125th congress in September 1993, Monks successfully averted a walk-out of affiliates by proposing a plan for the readmission of the AEEU. The AEEU agreed to abide by the rules and constitution of the TUC, its engineering section would affiliate, and it would consult other unions before recruiting in their jurisdictions. The EETPU Section promised to act in an "honorable fashion" (Trades Union Congress 1993c, 517). The TUC approved the merged union's affiliation by a vote of 4,303,000 to 2,837,000. Some dissenting unions considered the terms too lenient and, believing that rival organizing would only continue, threatened to revive the issue at future congresses ("125th TUC Congress" 1993).

The AEEU–EETPU merger shows the difficult position of the TUC in maintaining its neutrality in affiliates' mergers. The relevant sections of the Bridlington Principles cited earlier prohibit the unilateral resolution of contested mergers by adjudication through the TUC's disputes committee. Moreover, the TUC cannot command an affiliate to abandon a merger or select another merger partner. It can only suggest the costs of a disapproved merger in terms of sanctions (the federation's refusal to continue affiliation or to reaffiliate the new union) and then propose a compromise. This worked in the case of the AEEU because the AEU, EETPU and their combined union saw that they gained more in the federation than outside it. The federation was flexible in its terms of re-entry because it could ill-afford to lose the dues income of a large union or to face a rival organization centered around an expelled union. If more demanding conditions for re-entry had been proposed and if leaders had been intransigent, the merger could easily have created a schism within the TUC.

UNISON, THE NEW SUPER-UNION

Over the past decade, there have been numerous references in the popular press and the academic literature to the coming age of the super-unions. A super-union is commonly described as a union formed by amalgamation, using absorptions as its primary growth strategy, and so large that it can shift the balance of power in the labor movement.[16] It has been predicted that by the end of this century there will be a "super-bloc" of 4 or 5 super-unions, each with 1 to 2 million members, surrounded by a few small, highly specialized unions. Although this is pure speculation, a recent merger did create Unison (or the Public Service Union)—the first, modern British super-union.

Britain has had many huge unions. The AEU counted one-and-half million members in 1980 and the TGWU once had more than two million members (Certification Officer for Trade Unions and Employers' Associations 1981). But Unison is important as a new super-union not only because of its size—with 1.4 million members, the largest union—but because of its formation through a three-union amalgamation. The creation of Unison shows the kind of structural and political compromises that will be needed to build future super-unions.

Unison was formed in July 1993 from the merger of the National and Local Government Officers Association (NALGO), the National Union of Public Employees (NUPE), and the Confederation of Health Service Employees (COHSE). NUPE and COHSE had tried to merge in the early 1960s, but negotiations were unsuccessful. NUPE and NALGO started merger discussions in 1988, and COHSE joined in when a settlement seemed likely in 1989.

The Unison merger was primarily a reaction to the changes in public employment reviewed earlier. In particular, the three unions' officers were concerned about denationalization of government-owned companies, the spread of privatization at the federal level, and the new requirement for compulsory competitive tendering (government councils' solicitation of private tenders for the continuation of services). Bargaining was also decentralizing and becoming more contentious and complex, which strained the unions' staff and resources at branch levels. With government employment contracting, growth was highly unlikely for public-employee unions. Recruiting outside of the public sector proved difficult; for instance, NALGO tried to recruit private-sector members in the 1980's, but was met by stiff employer resistance and opposition from private-sector white-collar unions ("Union Mergers" 1992). Merger proponents argued that a combined public-sector union would be financially stable, more effective in negotiations, capable of representing all employees in a broad unit in single-union deals, and would have a substantial competitive advantage over the small professional unions to which many public workers belonged (Bailey 1994).

The three unions were not perfectly matched. At the time of the merger, there were 744,000 members in NALGO, 579,000 members in NUPE, and only 203,000 members in COHSE. NUPE and COHSE had been losing members while NALGO was fairly stable. NALGO had more than twice the financial assets of NUPE and COHSE combined (Donaldson 1992). NUPE and COHSE were affiliated with the Labour Party, while NALGO was politically unaffiliated and determined to remain so. When combined, the three unions had an exceptionally diverse membership—part-time workers earning £3,000 per year and chief executives earning £70,000, workers who deliver school meals as well as hospital administrators. Seventy-nine percent of COHSE's members were women compared to 74 percent for NUPE and 53 percent for NALGO. NALGO was primarily a white collar union, while NUPE was blue collar. ("Toward a Public Service Super-Union" 1991; Donaldson 1992).

The officers negotiating amalgamation had to create structures that furthered the interests of a diverse membership, preserved the members' identities in a huge union, and resolved differences in political affiliation. The merger committee decided to create a completely new union, rather than merely joining the three unions' structures (COHSE-NALGO-NUPE 1991). At the same time, however, the committee realized that "it would be unlikely that a new union could be brought into being by a 'big bang' approach" (COHSE-NALGO-NUPE 1992, 5), so it adopted a transitional governing structure. The three executive committees formed the Unison executive for the first two years. Their officers served in their positions, with NALGO's top officer taking the lead (Unison 1993). This compromise resulted in a 127-member executive committee. Occupational interests were furthered in service groups for electricity, health care, higher education, local government, public transport, and water (Cohen 1994). These groups were designed to negotiate agreements and carry out policies promoting the professional or occupational concerns for members. Members elect officials and send delegates to each service group's governing conferences (COHSE-NALGO-NUPE 1991, 1992).[17]

A merger proposal was circulated to the COHSE, NALGO, and NUPE membership, then debated and approved at their national conferences. A rule book (constitution) was then proposed, rewritten after debate, and circulated along with the instrument of merger and the ballot paper (NUPE 1993). The merger agreement was approved by 94 percent of the NUPE and COHSE members casting ballots, with 74 percent in favor from NALGO. The latter had the strongest reservations regarding protections for the members' occupational interests and the continuation of political affiliation (Milne 1992).

The status of political funds collected by the three unions was probably the most difficult issue in merger negotiations. NALGO's fund was independent of a political party, but those of NUPE and COHSE were affiliated with the Labour Party. It was agreed that there would be two separate political funds during an interim postmerger period—the former NALGO Political Fund and the combined COHSE/NUPE Political Fund. Former NALGO members, or those who joined branches that once were part of NALGO, would contribute to the NALGO fund. Past or new members of COHSE and NUPE branches would pay into the new, combined fund. Members of newly formed or amalgamated branches could elect to contribute to either fund. When an interim period ended on January 1, 1996, two new funds would be created from the earlier ones—a General Political Fund and an Affiliated Political Fund that was linked to the Labour Party. Unison members would be able to contribute to either or both funds, regardless of their prior affiliation (COHSE-NALGO-NUPE 1992; Unison 1993).

When the amalgamation was approved, the new union was registered with the certification office and its predecessors were deregistered. Unison is massive—Western Europe's third-largest union and Britain's largest, exceeding the nearest in size, the Transport and General Workers Union by a half-million members. It accounts for 1 of every 6 union members in Britain, has over 70,000 stewards and local officials, and has annual expenditures of £100 million, or about one quarter of the funds spent by all TUC affiliates (COHSE-NALGO-NUPE 1991; Trades Union Congress 1993a; Certification Office for Trade Unions and Employers Associations 1994a).

The formation of Unison left observers asking whether such super-unions might eventually displace the TUC. Some, for instance John Edmonds, the GMB's leader, believe that super-unions will remain TUC affiliates, but they will represent their own interests to employer groups and legislators. The federation will be left to deal with international labor relationships, and provide specialized services (education and training, health and safety) for smaller affiliates (Milne 1990). Moreover, it has been argued that when a few unions have a large share of the TUC's members, they might dominate the federation to the detriment of smaller unions and prompt the latter to leave or form an opposition coalition. The TUC might also be paralyzed in disputes between powerful left-of-center and right-of-center super-unions (McIlroy 1992; Bassett 1993a).

But it is more probable that the impact of super-unions has been exaggerated. Super-unions are not true alternatives to the TUC because they cannot represent the labor movement, nationally and internationally, to governments and other institutions, as the federation does. Furthermore, a crucial function of the TUC has been its service as a neutral umpire regulating and coordinating interunion relations. (Recall the TUC's handling of the AEEU affiliation discussed earlier.) This is something that super-unions are too partisan to do effectively. Finally, super-unions may shift the balance of power within the federation, moving it, for instance, toward the left or the right or toward the public- or private-sector unions. But these super-union biases could actually increase the TUC's power by allowing it to assume the role of a neutral mediator between union factions and serve as the unified voice of labor in negotiations with the government (Turner 1964).

When we speculate about possible new British super-unions, we should also keep in mind that these are not easily built and that seemingly logical mergers are not always proposed or agreed to. For example, plans for joining eight unions in telecommunications, postal, print, broadcasting, and rail and sea transport have been mentioned over the years but no new super-union has emerged. Plans were apparently diverted by officers who felt that the various unions did not have common interests ("Union Merger Moves" 1989; "More Union Mergers" 1991; "Where are the Super-Unions?" 1992). A merger between the GMB and TGWU, the two largest unions with unlimited jurisdictions, would have created a super-union with over 2 million members. Merger negotiations ended in 1994, primarily because of GMB officers' concerns over the governance of regional bodies and the power of TGWU officers and committees. Reports have also circulated about a proposed merger of the TGWU and the Manufacturing, Science and Finance Union, which have a combined membership of 1.5 million. This merger is no closer to fruition than when first proposed more than five years ago ("Union Merger Moves" 1989; Wheal 1992).

Although the creation of the next super-union is difficult to predict, its key characteristics are apparent now. Following the example of Unison (and such large general unions as TGWU and GMB), the super-unions will have semi-autonomous industry or craft sections to preserve the interests of its diverse membership. Formed by amalgamation, their decentralized structure will attract the numerous smaller, specialized unions by allowing for bargaining autonomy and self-governance and for the continued employment of their officers and staff. The initial amalgamation will probably join unions in similar jurisdictions but subsequent absorptions and affiliations will be without regard to industry or occupation.

Despite recent descriptions of ''merger mania'' and ''rush to merger,'' there has not been an accelerated merger pace in Britain since 1980.[18] The recent merger trend has been erratic, not comparable to the upswing in the 1960s and 1970s. But, in a qualitative sense, the recent mergers are extremely important. Mergers have been major industrial relations events in Britain, nearly tearing apart the TUC, ending small, highly specialized unions, increasing the size and diversity of the largest unions, and creating the first new super-union.

A century of union fragmentation and a decade and a half of hostile administrations and laws aimed at reducing union power have formed the preconditions for merger. The organizing task and the decentralization of bargaining placed new burdens on union staff and finances. A tradition of mergers and a merger-friendly legal framework shortened and smoothed the route to merger and reduced the impact of opposition to mergers. British union officers continue to explore merger possibilities because mergers, the traditional wisdom tells them, are the natural, expedient way to grow and survive in hard times.

CHAPTER 5

Australia: Rationalization
through Amalgamation

In Australia, labor laws and the labor federation actively promoted union mergers to rationalize and simplify union structure and to prepare the unions for a new industrial relations system. Mergers were seen as crucial to the structural reform of the unions and followed from a broad consensus that such reforms were needed if the unions were to remain effective, relevant worker representatives. The government and federation strongly encouraged mergers in more than a general sense, however; they also showed an unambiguous preference for those mergers reducing the number of small unions and the presence of several unions at individual workplaces. "The Australian experience has been characterized by a centrally imposed and very clear conception of what constitutes an optimum union structure in the 1990s and a very deliberate and coercive use of collective bargaining law to achieve that structure" (Bennett 1994, 209).

The merger campaign was hugely successful. Since 1983, the number of unions registered with the federal government was reduced by two-thirds, largely as the result of quick and complex sequences of mergers (Kerslake 1995).

The Context

TOWARD A MORE PRODUCTIVE AND COMPETITIVE ECONOMY

In the years between the severe recessions of the early 1980s and the early 1990s, there was a growing concern in Australia about the weaknesses of the economy and the nation's ability to compete in world markets while maintaining a high standard of living. Nearly all signs pointed to hard times ahead. The economy had become dependent on export income generated primarily through the sale of commodities whose prices fluctuated according to international markets (Kyloh 1989). A continuing balance of payments deficit had increased foreign debt and constrained the domestic economy (Hancock and Rawson 1993). The government's trade liberalization policies correctly recognized that protectionism was the cause rather than the solution of economic problems, but their implementation unleashed "competitive forces on a scale never before seen in Australia" (Castle and Haworth 1993, 24).

Labor-market conditions deteriorated; there was double-digit unemployment during the recessions of the early 1980s and 1990s, with heavy job losses in manufacturing as well as among white-collar workers. Emigration was high among skilled workers. Labor productivity was sluggish through the decade (Niland and Spooner 1992; Sloan 1992; Bureau of International Labor Affairs 1994). The general consensus was that nothing less than the future of the industrial economy was in jeopardy. There had to be greater productivity to survive the new, intense international competition. But improving productivity depended on the reform of the industrial relations system. "Australia's productivity achievements are mediocre and the industrial relations system has been 'lead in the saddle bags' which has retarded them" (Hancock and Rawson 1993, 505).

There were numerous restrictive work rules, rigid demarcations between jobs, poor negotiating skills on the part of both union and employer representatives, inadequate on-the-job training, and no clear paths for career progression. A series of commission reports and policy papers proclaimed the obvious need for internationally competitive enterprises with high productivity growth. To create these enterprises, the reports called for increased labor flexibility and skill formation alongside controlled layoffs and unemployment (Frenkel 1993; Hancock and Rawson 1993). But the structures and process that had come to be known as the Australian model of industrial relations were well-entrenched; reforms would have to occur within the context of a long established, pervasive system of national wage adjustments and through close ties between the government and the unions as represented by the powerful federation, the Australian Council of Trade Unions (ACTU).

Under the centralized system of wage determination, the dominant feature of the Australian model, employers and unions had become dependent on third-party decision-making and were often unable to resolve their differences through direct negotiations. Tribunals set wages and working conditions with little assistance or encouragement to the parties. "Custom and practice" were often protected through their legal standing, thus shielding unproductive work rules from change (Niland and Spooner 1992). Policymakers seeking reforms concluded that they would have to dismantle a tribunal system dating back to the start of the century. As the future of this system was debated, its highly fragmented union movement came under close scrutiny.

UNION MEMBERSHIP AND FRAGMENTATION

Through the 1980s, the membership of the Australian unions was nearly unchanged (a net gain of 2,000 members), but in the 1990s membership fell sharply. Unions lost 151,000 members from 1990 to 1992, and 226,000 members from 1992 to 1994 (see table 11). Since 1990, union membership has declined by 14 percent. Between 1980 and 1995, the labor force expanded. Consequently, union density as a proportion of employment has fallen steadily, from 50 percent in 1982 to 41 percent in 1990 and 35 percent in 1994. Membership losses have been attributed to employment shifts from more heavily unionized sectors to lesser unionized ones (e.g., from manufacturing to services). In manufacturing, unions lost more than 200,000 members from 1982 to 1993 and density fell from 54 to 43 percent (Australian Council of Trade Unions 1995). Losses due to employment shifts have been compounded by increased employer opposition to unions, the difficulty of retaining union members under new legislation and the rising number of small enterprises and part-time workers—sectors where unions are less experienced in recruiting and rep-

Table 11. Union membership and density in Australia, 1982–1994

Year	Membership (thousands)	Density[a]
1982	2,658	50%
1986	2,594	46
1988	2,536	42
1990	2,660	41
1992	2,509	40
1994	2,283	35

Source: Australian Council of Trade Unions 1995.
[a]Density is union membership as percentage of employed wage and salary workers.

resenting workers. Since the early 1980s, Australian unions have recruited only 7 of every 100 new workers added to the labor force (Frenkel 1993; Bureau of International Labor Affairs 1994).[1] Cooper and Walton (1996, 3) observed that "the depression of the 1930s was the only period this century where membership loss was as fast and as extensive as that in recent years."

Union fragmentation and multi-unionism were common characteristics of the Australian labor movement. In 1980 there were 316 unions; 96 percent had fewer than 50,000 members and 80 percent had fewer than 10,000 members (Cameron 1980). Most unions were craft-based, composed of employees doing similar work though in different industries. In 1981, for example, there were 26 unions representing workers in manufacturing and 55 unions in transportation (Plowman 1981). Several unions customarily represented workers at individual workplaces. A 1989 survey found a single representative at only about 20 percent of unionized plants; in about one-third there were more than 6 unions (Kollmorgen and Naughton 1991).

Union fragmentation and multi-unionism resulted from the state and federal system of industrial relations tribunals. Rather than having to overcome employer campaigns, union organizers had only to convince tribunals that their union is the best one to represent a particular category of workers. Once recognized, the union enjoyed protection from displacement by other unions and could represent members at tribunal hearings (Deery 1983).

Over the years, there were numerous proposals to reform union structure, primarily by reducing the number of unions through mergers into industrywide unions (Gill and Griffin 1981). But it was not until the recent reappraisals of the entire system of worker representation that reforms seemed possible. In the 1980s, the largely academic debates over the effectiveness of different union sizes and types were replaced by debates in the legislature and the federation congresses over what the new union movement should look like.

THE TRANSFORMATION OF WORKER REPRESENTATION

Frenkel (1993, 249) has observed that "the Australian union movement is in the early stages of a transformation as significant as that experienced in the first decade of the century" when its system of awards (arbitration decisions) was introduced. Niland and Spooner (1992, 230) see "industrial relations in Australia . . . in a major transformation phase, the likes of which has not been seen for many generations.'' Tremendous change has occurred on two levels—through the system of national consensus agreements between labor and the government (the Accords) and through the tribunals which determined wages and working conditions.

A detailed description of the Australian approach to labor–management relations is beyond the scope of this chapter. It is important, however, to review its fundamental premises and structures because their recent evolution provides the context for the wave of union mergers.

Legislation establishes independent tribunals that set wages and conditions of employment through awards and orders. The federal tribunal, the Australian Industrial Relations Commission and its predecessors (collectively called the ''commission'' in this chapter) have until recently implemented the government's wage policy (albeit with some modifications) though not legally required to do so (Niland and Spooner 1992). A basic principle of the awards was that ''workers doing the same job, regardless of the situation of different employers, deserve 'comparative wage justice', i.e., equal pay for equal work'' (Bureau of International Labor Affairs 1994, 4). Awards to one group of workers usually quickly spread to others doing the same work in the economy and then, through a complex system of historical precedents, wages of workers in other occupations were then adjusted accordingly.

This highly centralized system was repeatedly criticized as a source of inefficiency and labor-market inflexibility. Awards created large numbers of narrowly defined job classifications and inhibited productivity and flexibility (Kyloh 1989). They usually covered occupational groups in specific industries, thus entrenching highly specialized, occupationally based unions. A typical manufacturing plant might deal with five to ten unions, each with its own representational rights. Work was organized according to the union and award coverage and the result was a proliferation of restrictive work practices and demarcations between jobs (Niland and Spooner 1992).

Critics argued that weakening the awards system was a crucial precondition for greater industrial productivity and flexibility because only then could unions and employers deal directly with one another. But it was also understood that some elements of the system would continue to underpin negotiated settlements. Tribunals should co-exist with union–management negotiations.

When it was introduced in the Conciliation and Arbitration Act of 1904, arbitration was meant to supplement rather than substitute for collective bargaining. Negotiations before awards were encouraged. Labor–management agreements could be certified and have the legal status of awards. Awards imposed by tribunals commonly contained clauses already agreed to by unions and employers. Employers also frequently agreed to "over-award" payments and working conditions that were better than those described in awards, usually in response to unions' demands and strike threats, or the need to attract workers in difficult labor markets, reduce turnover, and reward seniority (Deery 1989; Parliamentary Research Service 1993; Hancock and Rawson 1993).

Speaking at an international labor relations conference, in 1992, Prime Minister Paul Keating proclaimed that the system of arbitration and conciliation had "served quite well . . . but the news I have to deliver today to those who still think Australian industrial relations is run this way, is that it is finished. Not only is the old system finished, but we are rapidly phasing out its replacement, and have now begun to do things in a new way" (Keating 1992:1). The awards system would have to give way to a movement for flexibility and decentralization in worker representation.

In the later 1970s and the early 1980s, the government of Malcolm Fraser sought to "fight inflation first"; this often meant reversing the "wage overshoot" in awards. The government intervened in national wage cases to persuade the commission that it should award increases at less than full indexation, that is, less than the rate of inflation. But as real wages subsequently fell, unions resorted to strikes to gain increases beyond the award rates (Hagan 1989). Wage inflation broke out in 1981 and 1982, that, combined with a downturn in aggregate demand, resulted in high unemployment. Kenyon and Lewis have observed that "[t]he experience of the . . . early 1980s [was] that any rapid wage gains were eroded by inflation, that unemployment resulted and that it persisted. The persistence of unemployment was leading to increased duration of unemployment and creating the beginnings of an Australian 'under class' who were excluded from the economic mainstream" (1993, 53). The ACTU and the Labour Party entered into a partnership to maintain standards of living while moderating wage claims and boosting employment. The agreement they reached, known as the Accord, contributed to Labour's election victory in 1983. When it assumed office, the government convened an economic summit conference at which business interests endorsed the Accord (Hagan 1989; Dabscheck 1993; Kenyon and Lewis 1993).[2]

By backing the Accord, the ACTU and the unions had essentially shifted their primary concern from money wages to the "social wage," which took into consideration taxation, government expenditures on social services, and pensions (Hagan 1989). In return for full wage indexation (adjustments to compensate for inflation) and job creation, the unions agreed not to strike if dissatisfied with the commission's awards. (Hagan 1989).

Under the Accord, the government sought to reduce unemployment without inflation and unions promised to exercise moderation. But the ACTU had also now assumed a consulting role in matters broadly affecting unions, their members, and workers in general, including such issues as industrial development, economic planning, and social policies. The Accord was renegotiated several times but reached a turning point in 1987. Under the pressure of deteriorating economic conditions, the unions agreed to an end to indexation. A new two-tiered system was introduced; the first tier provided wage raises for all affected workers; the second tier tied additional wage increases to negotiated improvements in work practices that led to greater productivity and efficiency (Niland and Spooner 1992). In other words, the key characteristics of the Australian model— centralism and uniformity—were continued, but negotiations over productivity at the industry or enterprise level were simultaneously promoted. "The productivity bargaining element represents the first instance, at least since the Great Depression, in which the Commission placed caveats upon national wage increases" (Niland and Spooner 1992, 222).

This new approach produced some gains in productivity (Niland and Spooner 1992, 222–23), but by 1988 there was increased concern among the unions that too much was being traded for second-tier wage increases. Under the next Accord (Mark IV), signed in August 1988, wage increases were tied to the unions' demonstrated commitment to achieving greater efficiency at industry and enterprise levels, and not asking for further wage increases for a year.

Differences in the orientations of the Accords and the commission had to be reconciled. In an award in April 1991, the commission declined to add union–management bargaining at the enterprise level to the enumerated principles for wage determination. The ACTU objected and was joined by the government. The commission had refused to accept an important Accord feature, the decentralization of bargaining to the workplace level, because it believed "unions and the employers are not yet on a mature enough footing to continue towards enterprise bargaining" (Jameson 1992, 167). The government's opposition to and its disassociation from the award meant that "the concept of the Commission as an umpire had been dealt a heavy blow'' (Ludeke 1993, 317). But in another wage case, presented in October 1991, the principle of enterprise bargaining was introduced and integrated with existing criteria for wage determination. There was no repeated criticism of the commission.

A tension was developing between the commission's awards of allowable wage increases, and the Accord partners' desire to fashion their own wage policy (Hancock and Rawson 1993). In February 1993, the government announced Accord Mark VII, titled *Putting Jobs First,* it was to last for three years. Its objective was to increase employment, maintain low levels of inflation, encourage bargaining at industry and workplace levels, and provide a safety net of minimum-award wages and conditions. The Accord linked greater international competitiveness, economic recovery, and employment growth to the increased flexibility in setting wages and working conditions that was forthcoming from workplace bargaining. Unions and employers were urged to negotiate linkages between wage increases and productivity improvements from work reorganization and redesign. If the parties were unable to reach such an agreement, they could apply for the intervention of the commission, which might require further negotiations and then entertain applications for conciliation and, if necessary, arbitration. It was understood that the awards system would underpin rather than substitute for workplace bargaining (Ludeke 1993).

Accord Mark VII radically transformed the Australian industrial relations system:

> Under the agreement with the ACTU, the federal government has accepted assurances that the current low inflation rate will be maintained. The government also accepts that the union movement has the ability to control the timing and extent of claims. The point of these assurances is that wage demands will not exceed economic capacity; in other words, the ACTU will carry the major public interest responsibility formerly held by the commission. . . . [T]he Australian Industrial Relations Commission has been displaced from its historic role and responsibilities and the centerpiece of the new system will be the trade union movement. (Ludeke 1993, 327)

The second step in the transformation of the Australian system is the Industrial Relations Reform Act of 1993, which effectively moved ''the wage setting process away from the old national wage cases and toward workplace agreements'' (Brereton 1993, 53). The act distinguishes between a bargaining stream and an arbitrated award safety net. Its intent is to provide "employers with the flexibility they need to improve productivity and compete internationally, while recognizing that employee protection is crucial to the success of enterprise bargaining" (Minister for Industrial Relations 1993, 1).

Briefly, the act allows the commission to establish minimum entitlements but they are meant to be national safety-net provisions. Guaranteed minimum entitlements are extended to all workers in the form of minimum wages, equal pay for work of equal value by men and women, rights to layoff pay, protection against unfair dismissal, and up to twelve months parental leave. The commission maintains and updates the award safety net, implements minimum-entitlements legislation, makes pay-rate awards when appropriate, and assists negotiations at the enterprise level through conciliation. The commission approves agreements that reduce entitlements and employee protection when it believes these are not contrary to the public interest.

In a particularly controversial section detailing the bargaining stream, the act distinguishes between certified agreements and enterprise-flexibility agreements. Certified agreements are negotiated between unions and employers and are approved by the commission. Enterprise-flexibility agreements may be negotiated between employers and employees; if unions are present at the workplace, they may participate in negotiations and present their case before the commission prior to the agreements' approval (Minister for Industrial Relations 1993; G. Smith 1994). Flexibility agreements are intended to change the general conditions of awards to suit the particular needs of individual enterprises or workplaces.[3]

The Act continues the decentralizing trend of the Accords, and most likely makes it irreversible. Its objective is to have 80 percent of employees covered by federal legislation involved in direct collective bargaining before the end of 1996 (G. Smith 1994). G. R. Smith, a member of the commission, stated in 1994 that "the clear direction and commitment of the government is to ensure that the primary industrial relations instruments will be agreements at the enterprise level" (G. Smith 1994, 15). While some sections of the act may have to be modified because of legal challenges from employer organizations and state governments, the overall trend is clear: "the significance of the changes ensures that there will be no return to the basic model of conciliation and arbitration. . . . The changes are profound, and the debate will be vigorous in the years ahead" (G. Smith 1994, 17). By August 1994, 2,460 agreements had been signed, covering 1.3 million workers or about 55 percent of workers covered by federal awards (Griffin 1994).

A substantial burden was placed on unions because of the break with the centralized awards system and the swift move to enterprise bargaining. At the many workplaces where several unions share bargaining rights, some will now have to take the lead in negotiations while others follow (Bureau of International Labor Affairs 1994). Union officers will have to learn how to approach the commission and argue against the approval of nonunion flexibility agreements.[4] If they cannot, their unions' role may be usurped. Union officers also have little experience in problem-solving and increasing productivity at the enterprise level—key activities under enterprise negotiations (Green 1993).

The unions were once secure in the all-embracing legal framework of the tribunal system and they were able to shape and police awards. But they were usually inactive at workplaces. For example, a 1991 survey showed unions actively representing workers (i.e., establishing union committees, holding regular meetings, and having officers who spent at least an hour per week on union work) at about one-quarter of unionized workplaces. In about a third of workplaces, there was no union activity at all (Davis and Lansbury 1993). An officer of the Metal and Engineering Workers Union commented on the task ahead:

If our members are being faced with enterprise bargaining, we must be in a position to provide them with appropriate advice and to take some leadership on the issue. . . . Organisers must be equipped to deal with issues that they have never dealt with before: that is, understanding the driving factors for improved productivity at the plant level . . . and convincing management that total managerial prerogative is not the recipe for improved productive performance and that they must divest their complete managerial control and use the intellectual capacity of the workforce and empower workers. ("Enterprise Bargaining" 1992, 5)

This new approach to worker representation demands greater expertise and involvement of union staff and an end to multi-unionism. The ACTU and the government saw union mergers as crucial to the development of this approach. The transformation of industrial relations called for nothing less than the transformation of the unions.

The Merger Record

Table 12 shows the number of union mergers per year between 1951 and 1994, and Table 13 indicates the form and frequency of mergers per year between 1980 and 1994. The trend is obvious; a slow merger pace over the first three decades followed by a tremendous increase in the latter years. The average number of mergers per year went from less than one between 1951 and 1980 to two per year between 1981 and 1990, and to

Table 12. Union merger activity in Australia, 1951–1994

Period	Number of union mergers	Average annual number of mergers
1951–1960	2	0.2
1961–1970	9	0.9
1971–1980	9	0.9
1981–1990	20	2.0
1991–1994	66	16.5

Source: 1951–1980: Griffin and Scarcebrook 1989; 1981–1994: Appendix 4.

Table 13. Union mergers in Australia, 1980–1994

Year	Absorptions and affiliations	Amalgamations	Total mergers
1980	0	0	0
1981	0	0	0
1982	1	0	1
1983	0	0	0
1984	1	0	1
1985	1	0	1
1986	2	1	3
1987	0	2	2
1988	2	2	4
1989	1	4	5
1990	1	2	3
1991	20	11	31
1992	10	12	22
1993	4	4	8
1994	2	3	5
Total	45	41	86

Source: Appendix 4.

more than 16 per year between 1991 and 1994. Table 13 shows the merger wave—31 mergers in 1991 and 22 in 1992—subsiding in 1993 and 1994.

Underlying the list of merging unions in appendix 4 is a characteristic unique to Australia—the long, complex sequences of mergers among unions in related jurisdictions. These were generally started by amalgamations, which were then followed by a series of absorptions and affilia-tions, and occasionally additional amalgamations. For instance, the Australian Municipal, Administrative, Clerical and Services Union (ASU) was formed in 1991 by an amalgamation of the Municipal Officers Association, the Australian Transport Officers Federation, and the Technical Service Guild. By the end of 1994, the ASU had absorbed the Australian Social Welfare Union, the Australian Shipping and Travel Officers Association, the Federated Clerks Union, the Federated Municipal and Shire Council Employees Union, and the Totalisator Employees Association of Victoria.

The Public Sector Union (PSU) was created in 1989 through the amalgamation of the Administrative and Clerical Officers Association, the ABC Staff Association, and the Australian Public Service Association. In 1990, taxation department members broke away from the Federal Clerks Union and joined the PSU. The Meat Inspectors also joined the PSU that year.

The Media, Entertainment and Arts Alliance was created by the merger of Actors Equity, the Australian Journalists Association, the Australian Theatrical and Amusement Employees Association, and the Australian Commercial and Industrial Artists Association. Since then, the Alliance has absorbed the Professional Rugby Players Union, the Soccer Players Association, and the Artworkers Union of New South Wales ("Meet Australia's Super Unions" 1993; "A United Voice" 1994; "Union Amalgamations" 1994).

In contrast to the composition of mergers in the United States, Canada, and Great Britain, a large share of recent Australian mergers were amalgamations—30 of the 66 mergers since 1991. These generally combine unions operating in the same jurisdictions and follow the ACTU's plan to rationalize union structure. They usually entail low degrees of integration to allay fears of the submergence of members' interests in the new unions. For example, the five occupational sections of the amalgamated Media, Entertainment and Arts Alliance deal with professional issues, elect their own officers, and send representatives to branch councils in each state and to their union's federal council ("A United Voice" 1994). In the merger forming the Construction, Forestry, Mining and Energy Union, each predecessor union remains an autonomous entity with its own policymaking bodies and leadership ("Rebuilding Australia" 1992, 31).

What caused the 1991–1992 merger wave and the sequential nature of the union mergers in Australia? Prior to the 1980s, there was little incentive for unions to merge. Improved wages or working conditions could be achieved through an awards system which perpetuated narrowly based occupational unions (Frenkel 1993). When mergers did occur they were motivated primarily by a) financial hardships caused by declining membership and employer sanctions during illegal work stoppages, and b) the need for a few small, highly specialized unions to achieve economies of scale in operations (Hocking 1990; Jameson 1992, 1993; Frenkel 1993).

In the late 1980s and early 1990s, union officers were becoming more receptive to merger overtures because they recognized how much enterprise bargaining would strain their unions' staff and financial resources, both at national levels where negotiations had to be coordinated and assisted, and at the branches where negotiations were often carried out for the first time. For instance, an officer of the Australian Journalists Association, which amalgamated with two other unions in 1992, observed that his union "would never have had the resources to deal with enterprise bargaining. For example, instead of negotiating the metropolitan daily newspapers award with one employer group, we now have to negotiate separately with half-a-dozen different employers" ("A United Voice" 1994, 30). More important, however, new legislation and federation policies directly affected the form and frequency of mergers during early 1990s.

The Underlying Trends

THE IMPACT OF LEGISLATION ON MERGER FORM AND FREQUENCY

Put simply, recent Australian public policy aims to reform union structure by assisting, encouraging, and sometimes prodding small unions to combine either with each other or into large unions. The objective is industrywide unions.

In 1985, the influential Hancock Committee, formed to examine the state of union structure and labor relations, recommended that the creation of industry-based unions be encouraged to reduce jurisdictional disputes and enable unions to identify with the interests of their industries. The committee, however, recognized the difficulty of defining industries and compelling unions to merge according to some predetermined pattern: "We must . . . look at the reality of the situation. We must be conscious, in particular, of the bonds of history, customs and practice, the questionable relevance of overseas comparisons and the impracticality of attempts to 'direct', by legislation, a free trade union movement down a path of restructuring that it does not wish to follow" (quoted in Creighton, Ford, and Mitchell 1993, 1100). Nonetheless, the government soon moved down the path of restructuring by threatening the status of small unions and by changing the requirements for merger approval.

The Minimize-Size Threshold. In Australia, registration with the federal government bestows on a union a legal personality, protects its status from opposing employers and unions, and enables it to participate in the labor relations process.

> Registration all but assures a union's continued existence. Once registered, a union has the almost permanent right to represent workers of a particular class . . . to seek exclusive award coverage for its members and to be protected against competition for its membership from rival bodies. Access to the awards system provides a mechanism by which unions can obtain benefits for their members which are legally binding on employers. (Sloan 1992, 75)

Changes in the conditions for registration have been used to compel unions to merge. The Industrial Relations Act 1988 required that unions have at least 1,000 members to register. For the prior 84 years, the minimum size had been 100 (Stewart 1989). Unions that were already registered and that had less than 1,000 members would be reviewed by the commission during a twelve-month period and might lose their registration. In March 1991, the Industrial Relations Legislation Amendment Act 1990 raised the minimum size to 10,000 members; smaller unions would have their registration withdrawn unless their presence was justified by special circumstances. The continued registration of unions with up to 1,000 members would be reviewed from March 1, 1992 to February 28, 1993, and over the next year there would be a review of those with up to 10,000 members.[5]

For the smaller unions confined to narrow jurisdictions and seeing little chance of growth, the new size threshold became the ultimate motivating force for merger. Ninety-two of the 149 federally registered unions fell under the 10,000-member minimum and faced the loss of registration if they were unable quickly to find a merger partner. It was difficult to prove that continued registration was justified by special circumstances, for example, the quality of representation or continuing, fruitful attempts to increase membership ("Changes to the Industrial Relations Act, 1988" 1991; Andrades 1991; Kollmorgen and Naughton 1991).

The Confederation of Australian Industry opposed the new size threshold, protesting that there should not be a public policy of favoring bigger unions solely for their own sake ("Changes to the Industrial Relations Act, 1988" 1991). In November 1990, it filed a complaint with the Committee on Freedom of Association of the International Labour Organization (ILO) and claimed that the new size requirement infringed on the ILO's principles of freedom of association. In 1992, the committee announced that it would request that the ILO's governing body ask the Australian government to rescind the 10,000-member requirement. The government responded by restoring the original size threshold of 100 members. This ended the proceedings before the ILO.

The ILO's Freedom of Association and Protection of the Right to Organize Convention of 1984 states in that "workers and employers . . . shall have the right to establish and, subject only to the rules of the organization concerned, to join organizations of their own choosing without previous authorization" (Creighton, Ford, and Mitchell 1993, 1102). This statement has been interpreted to mean that "trade union pluralism must be at least *possible*, even if it does not exist in practice" (Creighton, Ford, and Mitchell 1993, 1102). The minimum-size threshold in effect denies workers the right to be represented by small unions, which violates the ILO's principle. Thus, the Australian government could not use the minimum-size threshold to compel mergers or dissolve small unions. For the four-year period during which the new size thresholds were in force, however, there was exceptional pressure for mergers; nearly 80 percent of the mergers during that period involved unions with fewer than 10,000 members (Creighton, Ford, and Mitchell 1993).

The Regulation of the Merger Process. Another way the state can alter the pace of mergers is to modify the procedures for merger approval. Prior to 1972, there were no formal merger procedures. The registrar of unions did not have to be informed of mergers (Griffin and Scarcebrook 1989). Absorbing or amalgamating unions merely widened their eligibility for membership rules. Unions that were absorbed or affiliating canceled their registration. Ballots were not required, although the cancellation of the registration did have to be approved by votes of the absorbed or affiliated union's members (Kerslake 1995).

In 1972, the Amalgamated Engineering Union, the Boilermakers' and Blacksmiths Society, and the Sheet Metal Workers, Agricultural Implement and Stovemaking Industrial Union merged to form the Amalgamated Metal Workers' Union. With a membership of over 100,000, this became Australia's largest union. Its history was one of militancy and left-of-center leadership, and this concerned the federal government and the Democratic Labour Party. The party wanted the government to legislate retroactively to invalidate the merger but the government refused to do so; instead it made further mergers of large unions highly unlikely. Under amendments to the legislation, a merger was approved when at least half the members eligible to vote in each union actually did so and majorities were cast in favor of the merger. Moreover, when a large union absorbed a smaller one with total membership exceeding 5 percent of its total membership, the members of both unions had to be balloted. Otherwise, only the small union's members had to vote (Kerslake 1995).

Large unions were frequently unable to achieve a 50 percent turnout for an election. The voter turnouts for the Metal Workers merger, completed prior to the new requirement, had been 9 percent of the Engineering Union, 40 percent for the Boilermakers and 36 percent for the Sheet Metal Workers (Bennett 1994). Under the new requirements, a proposed merger between the Textile Workers Union and the Boot Trade Employees Federation failed because not enough members voted, despite the strong support for merger among those who did (Deery 1983; Griffin 1992). One study showed that the probability of a union with 10,000 members achieving a 50 percent ballot return was about 12 percent. For a union to have a better than even chance of a 50 percent return, it would have to have fewer than 700 members (Deery 1983).

The amended legislation halted the merger process. Between 1972 and 1983, there were only 5 mergers under the federal jurisdiction. In 4 mergers, the larger unions were exempt from merger votes because of the relative size of the smaller ones.

The turnout requirement was amended in 1983 by a government seeking to reduce union fragmentation and overlapping union jurisdictions. Under the new rules, if the commission declared that a proposed merger was in the public interest while also in the best interests of the unions concerned, the minimum voting requirement was reduced to 25 percent. A community of interest between the proposed merger partners could be established by, for example, one union's members being eligible to join the other, employed at the same or related work or by companies in the same industry, or bound by the same awards. The 50 percent turnout requirement remained for unions that could not establish a community of interest. There were 11 mergers in the first 6 years of the new voting requirement, compared to 6 mergers during the 12 years of the earlier procedures (Hocking 1990; Creighton, Ford, and Mitchell 1993; Kerslake 1995).

The government's preference for mergers of similar unions became even more apparent in the Industrial Relations Act 1988. The 25 percent turnout requirement was eliminated. If a community of interest could be demonstrated, the merger need only be approved by a majority of members casting ballots. When a community of interest was not declared, at least 25 percent of the members must cast votes (Hocking 1990; Creighton, Ford, and Mitchell 1993).

The next amendment, the Industrial Relations Legislation Amendment Act 1990, also strongly favored union mergers. Among its objectives were "to encourage and facilitate the amalgamation of organizations, and . . . to encourage and facilitate the development of organizations, particularly by reducing the number of organizations that are in an industry or enterprise" (Andrades 1991, 602) The merger process was expedited; the time between the union resolutions approving merger and the publication of the notice of the merger ballot was condensed from about two years to six months. The definition of a community of interest was relaxed. Requirements to obtain an exemption from a merger ballot were relaxed; a large union may receive an exemption if the membership of a smaller union did not exceed 25 percent of its members (the figure was previously 5 percent) (Andrades 1991).[6] Ross and Johnstone (1991, 184) reported: "A number of organizations are looking at a series of amalgamations [i.e., absorptions or affiliations] with relatively small organizations. If the 5% exception rate had not been lifted they may have forced the prospect of a series of [merger] ballots—this may have had an adverse impact on membership support and would be expensive."

Despite the recent amendments relaxing voting requirements, it is worth noting that the Australian union merger process remains quite complicated; the law "still makes exceedingly elaborate provision for what is, in most other countries, a relatively simple process, the legality and effect of which depends largely upon adherence to the terms of the rules of the organizations concerned" (Creighton, Ford, and Mitchell 1993, 1129). A scheme of amalgamation must be drawn up, an application made to the Industrial Registry for processing, hearings conducted by a designated presidential member of the commission, ballot determinations made by a Returns Officer of the Australian Electoral Commission and, if merger is approved by voters, a date fixed when the merger takes effect. There are additional procedures if the merger entails an extension of the union's eligibility rules (Ross and Johnstone 1991; Kerslake 1995). Despite these steps and requirements, described in 27 pages of the Industrial Relations Legislation Amendment Act of 1990, the process promotes mergers by serving as the exclusive means for handling members' and officers' objections, determining membership support, and assuring the legal status of the postmerger union. In a manner similar to the British procedures discussed in chapter 4, the Australian legislation channels and resolves merger opposition from members and officers, thus reducing the costs, time delays and unpredictability of primary merger barriers. Far more so than in Britain, however, the Australian procedures are shaped by the government's preference—the absence of a voter turnout requirement is meant to encourage mergers in general, the 25-percent ballot exemption promotes mergers of small unions into larger ones, and the community of interest declaration encourages mergers of unions in similar jurisdictions. Within this positive legal framework, the labor federation was able to design and carry out a merger program that reshaped the Australian union movement.

The ACTU's Merger Campaign and Strategic Unionism

The ACTU has always favored union mergers and the resulting rationalization of union structure (i.e., the reduction in union fragmentation, multiunionism, and jurisdictional overlap). At its first congress in 1927, the ACTU called for "the transformation of the trade union movement from the craft to the industrial basis by the establishment of one union in each industry" (Deery 1983, 191). By the late 1980s, it had devised a blueprint for large industry-based unions to be created through series of mergers.

In 1986, representatives of the ACTU and the Australian Trade Development Council went on a fact-finding mission to Sweden, Norway, Austria, West Germany, and the United Kingdom—countries whose economies seemed similar to Australia's. The mission's report, *Australia Reconstructed* (Australian Council of Trade Unions and the Trade Development

Council 1987), called for strategic unionism, a new role for unions that went beyond a narrow focus on wages and working conditions.

Strategic unionism entails the development of broad-based, integrated union strategies for full employment, greater productivity, more favorable trade and industrial policies, participation on tripartite boards, stronger union organization at the workplace level, and a demonstrated commitment to economic growth and wealth creation. In its broadest sense, it is labor's belief that capitalism can be altered through the united labor movement's participation in a social democratic political system (Frenkel 1993). A fundamental premise of strategic unionism is that unions should be "moving from being reactive to events, to becoming proactive, taking initiatives and setting the agenda" (Ogden 1993, 40). And it was in such a proactive mode that the ACTU set out to build larger unions.

The authors of *Australia Reconstructed* have argued that:

> Australia needs to develop a smaller number of larger unions. Through amalgamations, substantially more resources become available to increase the range and quality of services provided to members. Specifically, more research, education and organization resources are freed and duplication is avoided. Union members get more efficient service and more value for their money because amalgamation simplified union structure, allowing greater co-ordination and cohesion between unions at all levels. (Australian Council of Trade Unions and the Trade Development Council 1987, 229)

They proposed that a series of mergers reduce the number of affiliated unions to no more than 20 by 1991. Existing unions should combine, new unions should not be formed and, if necessary, the ACTU should revise union jurisdictions ("ACTU/TDC Mission to Western Europe" 1987). Bill Kelty, the ACTU secretary, would serve as "chief architect and executor" of the merger plan (Martin 1992, 139). At the ACTU's 1987 congress, Kelty warned union officers that without mergers and larger unions with better resources "unionism will decay and decline to the point of irrelevancy" (Davis 1988, 120). This theme was repeated throughout the federation's discussion paper, *Future Strategies For the Trade Union Movement* (Australian Council of Trade Unions 1987).

At the 1989 ACTU congress, federation officers claimed that the narrow union jurisdictions and job classifications specified in awards had limited the unions' ability to respond to workplace changes, protect jobs, and increase flexibility. They argued that unions must merge to expand their coverage and increase their effectiveness. There should be no more than two or three unions for each industry and these should operate as single bargaining agents at plants and companies. Industry-based unions were the surest guarantee of union strength at the workplace. Unions had to break out of a vicious circle of small size, specialized membership, scarce resources, and minimal growth potential. Some congress delegates opposed the proposal, claiming that plans for restructuring should come from membership ballots and not be imposed from above. But a motion to approve a comprehensive plan for restructuring was carried with only a few dissenting votes (Davis 1990).

In its subsequent congresses and policy papers, the ACTU's officers laid out their master plan for restructuring through mergers. "Amalgamations that seek to reduce the number of unions should be supported by the [labor] movement as a whole provided . . . there is a real community of interest between the unions concerned . . . and the amalgamation does not result in an increase in the number of unions covering the same classification of workers in the same industry" (Australian Council of Trade Unions 1992, 125). Moreover, 17 to 20 unions should be created in "clearly defined industry or occupationally representative streams" (Australian Council of Trade Unions 1992, 126). The ACTU would encourage mergers, facilitate merger discussions, assist unions to meet statutory obligations, develop campaign materials to promote mergers, and press for merger legislation (Australian Council of Trade Unions 1992). One observer portrayed the ACTU's plan as "the most far reaching and detailed reorganization programme ever undertaken by an established, autonomous trade union movement of its own volition" (Martin 1992, 140).

Jurisdictional boundaries were redrawn and multi-unionism reduced through the federation's designation of "principal unions," "significant unions," and "other unions." A "principal union" has the capacity to recruit all workers in an industry or occupation, while a "significant union" has substantial membership in the industry or occupation and agrees to be part of a single bargaining unit led by the principal union. An "other union" does not have substantial membership in the industry or occupation. It can continue to represent workers who wish to be represented by it, but it cannot prevent workers from joining the principal union in their industry or occupation, and it must agree to be part of a single bargaining unit. Under this plan, competing bargaining units within enterprises or industries would be consolidated. Unions could not extend their membership beyond the coverage specified in their constitutions other than when assigned principal-union status by the ACTU.

The primacy of the principal unions and the plan for a few large unions formed mostly on the industry basis conflicted with the growing movement toward bargaining at the enterprise level. The ACTU argued against the registration of unions confined to enterprises, claiming that this practice "will reduce the effective representation of workers' interests and runs counter to the policy of promoting fewer, larger and more effective unions" (Australian Council of Trade Unions 1992, 132).

Despite the ACTU's intentions, the designation of principal unions did not automatically simplify union jurisdictions and bargaining arrangements. The new unions formed by mergers had extremely diverse memberships (Ewer and Yates 1995). For example, the Australian Workers Union has principal-union status in 31 industrial sectors, the Federated Miscellaneous Workers is a principal union in 36 sectors and the National Union of Workers is principal union in 28 sectors (Plowman 1992). The designations did, however, raise concerns among union officers about their organizations' future growth and influence in the absence of mergers. "The ACTU held up the carrot of principal union status as an inducement to some unions to merge" (Griffin 1992, 221). Failure to merge could mean not receiving principal-union status, even being relegated to other-union status because other unions have larger shares of the members in an industry or occupation. This "negative" motivation to merge was countered by an inducement; the ACTU negotiated with the federal government to create a fund to help financially support merger campaigns (Ewer and Yates 1995).

In the later 1980s, once again moving proactively as dictated by the principles of strategic unionism, the ACTU began to reveal the details of a sweeping merger plan. Through sequences of mergers, affiliates would merge into eighteen large industrywide, multi-industry or multicraft unions. The jurisdictions of the new unions were administrative services and local government; building, construction, mining and timber industries; communications and electrical; distribution, warehousing, and manufacturing; education; finance; health; hospitality, liquor and miscellaneous workers; manufacturing; maritime and stevedoring; media and entertainment; professional and managerial, public sector; public transport; transport; retail; rural industries, infrastructure, and manufacturing; and emergency services (Australian Council of Trade Unions 1993).[7]

The ACTU had first increased the motivation to merge by arguing persuasively that mergers were central to strategic unionism and the only structural reform that could assure the vitality and relevancy of unions into the next century. Mergers must have seemed inevitable to officers whose unions' representative status was threatened by the devolution of the tribunal's powers, the new minimum size requirements, and the spread of enterprise bargaining. Then the ACTU's creation of principal, significant and other union status increased the motivation to merge even more by raising the possibility that representation would be immediately jeopardized if a merger partner in the same industry or occupation could not be found. The federation's blueprint for mergers (Australian Council of Trade Unions 1993) showed who should merge with whom, and how planned sequences of mergers would lead to a simpler, more rational and assumedly more effective union structure.

In Australia, union mergers have been more important than the United States, Canada, or Britain. The structural reform of the union movement, that is, the reduction of union fragmentation at the national level and multi-unionism at the workplace and enterprise levels, was a well-publicized objective of the government and the federation. First, the changes in the minimum-size threshold were unmistakable signs that the government believed bigger unions were better unions and small unions must grow, merge, or perish. Modifications of the procedures for approving mergers favored combinations of unions with similar jurisdictions and of small unions into much larger ones. Second, the ACTU's policy was unambiguous; with few exceptions, small, highly specialized unions had no future in the new Australian industrial relations system. The designation of union types prodded unions into mergers and the federation' merger blueprint set out the sequences of mergers needed to rationalize union structure.

The 1990s have seen truly momentous changes, but the Australian industrial relations system remains in a state of flux. First, on March 2, 1996, a conservative coalition of the Liberal and National parties defeated the Labour Party in the federal election. The impact of the change in government is presently difficult to determine because the platform of the victorious parties avoided radical changes in economic and social programs, instead emphasizing policies close to those of Labour—that is, the revival the economy and the reduction of unemployment. Furthermore, the coalition was unable to win control of the upper house of Parliament. Government representatives have commented, however, about the need to curb excessive union power, and they might attempt to further decentralize collective bargaining (Colley 1996; Cooper and Walton 1996; "Labor Ousted in Australia" 1996).

Second, enterprise bargaining is not uniformly favored by the unions. One union's report, for example, called enterprise bargaining "the wrong policy at the wrong time" and claimed that "what is being sold to Australian unions is a hybrid system that combines the worst aspects of the American system of localized collective bargaining with the legalism of the Australian system" (O'Reilly 1993, 23). In another union, an officer was concerned that the spread of enterprise bargaining would evolve into a free-for-all between labor and management in a deregulated industrial relations system; but then "enterprise bargaining based on productive performance under a regulated framework . . . which maintains basic wages and conditions, can push the performance of the whole economy ahead" ("Enterprise Bargaining" 1992, 2). A Labour parliamentarian feared that decentralized bargaining could be used to "screw down rates for workers already on low rates, and whose terms and conditions have little to do with Australia's competitiveness" (Rees 1993, 77).

The impact of the ACTU's merger program is questionable. Mergers have been criticized as "misguided and flawed in their outcomes," creating "fiefdoms of power for bureaucrats," and the results of the ACTU's "frenzy of centralisation" (Way 1993, 68). Several mergers occurred between unions with similar political leanings but without regard to the ACTU master plan (Strauss 1993). Some argue that the mergers are creating general or conglomerate unions, that is, multicraft and multi-industry unions, and that these will block future restructuring along single-industry lines, while reducing union solidarity by combining workers with different occupational cultures (Stewart 1989; Ewer and Yates 1995). There are also reports that newly formed unions are in financial difficulty because they had to assume the liabilities of small unions and guarantee continued employment for those unions' officers and staff, or offer expensive inducements for them to retire ("Meet Australia's Super Unions" 1993). Despite their intentions, mergers that carry financial burdens cannot readily increase recruitment or strengthen workplace representation.

Moreover, amalgamations are occurring with low degrees of integration. Critics claim that autonomous divisions increase the chances of factionalism and duplicate union services. An officer of a recently merged union probably expressed the concerns of many others when he asked, "Is it possible for us to develop the appropriate horizontal links across a divisional structure that will enable the union to hang together in a cohesive fashion?'' (''Union Vows to Defend Wages'' 1990, 2). Finally, there is some evidence that the creation of huge new unions through sequences of mergers often did not significantly reduce the number of unions operating at the enterprise level. Mergers often did not join unions that negotiated side by side (Hilmer et al. 1993).

While questions remain about the future directions of the Australian industrial system and the outcomes of recent mergers, there can be little doubt that union structure has been radically altered by a merger wave of tremendous breadth and suddenness. Legislative changes made mergers easier and the minimum-size requirement suddenly increased the motivation to merge, but it was the ACTU's vision of a new unionism that gave form and reason to the merger wave. ACTU policymakers realized that if the unions did not control structural change it could be imposed on them by federal or state governments, perhaps hostile ones, and that change might not necessarily benefit unions and their members (Davis 1992; Bennett 1994). The ACTU promoted mergers ''as a self-structuring mechanism under which unions can be the source rather than the object of structural reform'' (Kollmorgan and Naughton 1991, 387).

The roles of enterprise bargaining and the tribunal system are evolving as the new government, the unions, and employers vie to shape the contours of the new Australian model. What is obvious, however, is that a sweeping and irreversible restructuring of the union movement has occurred through the encouragement, guidance, and pressure of federation and public policy. The connections between union mergers, structural reform, greater productivity, and national competitiveness seemed so strong and so clear that the decision of when and how to merge could not be left entirely to the unions themselves.

CHAPTER 6

New Zealand: In The Aftermath
of the 1,000-Member Rule

Labor laws passed in 1987 and 1991 had a profound effect on union structure and worker representation in New Zealand. The objectives of the two laws were quite different. The Labour Relations Act of 1987 sought to strengthen the unions, to make them "viable" by forcing the smallest unions either to grow, merge or lose bargaining rights. It also continued the system of centralized negotiations and arbitration. Soon after its passage, there was a tremendous merger wave involving small unions.

The Employment Contracts Act of 1991, in contrast, was a radical departure from previous labor policy. Contract negotiations were deregulated and individual representation was promoted as an alternative to collective bargaining. While this threatened the legitimacy and survival of all unions, a second merger wave did not occur, largely because the merger potential had been spent in the preceding four years.

The Context

THE CRISIS IN THE ECONOMY

Beginning in the early 1970s, New Zealand suffered high inflation and economic stagnation. The country's economic problems reached crisis proportions in the 1980s; "productivity growth rate ran 50 percent lower and the inflation rate 50 percent higher than her trading partners" (Plowman and Street 1993, 93). Profits and real wages fell, and public and private debt increased. Unemployment rose from 3.8 percent in 1985 to 9.7 percent in mid-1993 as employment declined while the size of the labor force remained stable. Long-term unemployment quadrupled (Silverstone and Daldy 1993).

New Zealand's stagnant economy can be traced to its dependence on primary agricultural and natural-resource commodities. Internationally, it was able to maintain a competitive position only through low value-added activities such as harvesting and slaughtering rather than more profitable ones, for example, adding value through marketing and servicing. Prospects for industrial conversion were bleak; there were low rates of research and development expenditures, educational participation, and new business formation. Investment in training was low and the technological base was weak (Enderwick 1992). One major study concluded that New Zealand's "managers and employees lacked pressures and incentives to work, to invest and to develop skills" (Crocombe, Enright, and Porter 1991:155).

As an exporter of agricultural commodities, New Zealand was vulnerable to commodity booms followed by sharp declines. It could not sustain its position as a high-income country by continuing to restrict international trade. Macroeconomic policies were proving ineffective; the swings of the business cycle could not be dampened despite large budget deficits, controls on imports, and extensive foreign borrowing.

Economic planners believed that the nation should solve its problems through industrial restructuring, decentralization, deregulation, and a reliance on the operation of the free-market (Wooding 1993). Although there were conflicting views as to the specific causes of the economic crisis (Roper 1993), near the top of everyone's list of proposed solutions was labor-market reform. It was widely believed that "the full benefits of deregulation will only be achieved if it encompasses all three major sectors, monetary, goods and labour. Thus, labour market reform is a necessary condition for successful reform in the rest of the economy" (Enderwick 1992, 188).

In 1984, the government of the National Party was defeated in an election in which a key issue was its heavy foreign borrowing to support a budget deficit. The new Labour government began a series of economic reforms to free the private sector from the extensive controls that earlier administrations had placed on it. For instance, controls over the banking and finance sector were relaxed, making it easier for new banks to be formed, and equity in the state-owned Bank of New Zealand was sold. But efforts to reduce budget deficits were limited by the government's reluctance for political reasons to dismantle the expensive social-security network (Fraser and Wilson 1988). The contradictions of the reform effort were also apparent in the new labor legislation.

THE REVOLUTION IN LABOR LEGISLATION

The Industrial Conciliation and Arbitration Act of 1894 established a system of compulsory conciliation and arbitration that gave legal status to labor unions and made the results of their negotiations enforceable. The intent of the act, as expressed in its full title, was "to encourage the formation of industrial unions and associations and facilitate the settlement of industrial disputes by conciliation and arbitration" (Harbridge and Hince 1992b, 197).

The process of union registration enabled the state to promote and control union activity. Registered unions were given the right to organize specific groups of workers, to be recognized for negotiations, and to affect and enforce the terms of settlements (Harbridge and Moulder 1993). The price of this recognition was the restriction of the unions' right to strike and the employers' right to lockout.

An arbitration court resolved unsettled negotiations. Its jurisdiction extended to employers and employees not involved in initial negotiations, to nonunion as well as unionized workers. With the exception of the four-years period between 1984 and 1987, arbitration was compulsory in the sense that either the employer or union could force the other to the arbitration court for a settlement (Cowen 1993).[1]

Cowen (1993) argues that despite its initial intent to prevent disputes when bargaining was rejected or when negotiations broke down, the act actually undermined collective bargaining by reducing the incentive for parties to negotiate seriously. The government had expanded its role in defining the terms of awards and the availability of such intervention often became a crutch for negotiating parties. "Compulsory arbitration illustrates the point that government support for the structures of collective bargaining does not necessarily imply strong unions" (Cowen 1993, 71).

But it should also be kept in mind that, similar to the case of Australia discussed in the preceding chapter, New Zealand had been drifting away from a strictly compulsory arbitration system for some time. Under 1973 legislation, for instance, unions could negotiate agreements, which were subsequently extended to workers covered by awards (Boxall and Haynes

1992). During the recent term of the Labour government, from 1984 to 1990, compulsory arbitration was replaced by a voluntary form and the focus of negotiation, normally occupational, was moved to the industry and enterprise levels (Boxall and Deeks 1993; Harbridge 1993a). Employers also commonly paid above award rates when such were warranted by labor market conditions—in 1986 about 80 percent of employers did so (Harbridge and Rea 1992). Despite such signs of flexibility, however, the formal system of registration continued. Unions retained the right to exclusive representation and were able to append a clause to their settlements that compelled all the workers it covered to become union members (Harbridge 1993a).

Through the 1980s, proponents of labor law reform argued that national settlements and awards were inconsistent with employers' and workers' needs and preferences. The outdated, centralized system was not conducive to competition between unions over which workers to represent, or competition between employers over the wages and working conditions to offer (Cowen 1993). Occupational awards were negotiated centrally and, because one award strongly influenced the other, industries and firms were treated as if their circumstances were the same (Boxall and Deeks 1993). Critics added that compulsory unionism and blanket coverage, that is, the extension of a settlement to nonunion workers, discouraged employers and unions from fashioning terms which were specific to the workplace and which increased flexibility and productivity. "Employers could not arrive at accommodations with workers which reflected the state of their business and which allowed for growth. In effect, employers became convinced the whole apparatus of economic protection, accompanied by bargaining accommodation patrolled by the state, had become anachronistic" (Plowman and Street 1993, 94).

In 1984, the new Labour government promoted economic restructuring based on the operation of the free market. It initiated several important regulatory reforms, including the removal of exchange controls, the floating of the dollar, the partial deregulation of the capital markets, the reduction of tariffs, and greater scrutiny over the efficiency of state businesses (Cowen 1993). "The list of deregulatory measures introduced by the Labour government [was] staggering in its scope and in the rapidity of its enactment. No other OECD [Organization for Economic Development and Cooperation] economy [was] catapulted so quickly and intensely into structural adjustment" (Castle and Haworth 1993, 28).

But Labour's campaign for greater competitiveness was at odds with the basic premises and structures of the entrenched industrial relations system. The awards process, though no longer strictly compulsory, seemed incompatible with the need to raise productivity at the firm and workplace levels. Although the government did review the legislative foundations of union–management relations, this process was limited in scope. Its proposals, enacted in 1987, "were incremental rather than revolutionary" (Cowen 1993, 74).

The Labour Relations Act of 1987 continued compulsory unionism, but now it would be enforced by unions rather than employers. There were also minor modifications in procedures for determining union coverage. Enterprise bargaining was promoted and unions could opt out of awards by registering enterprise agreements. But the new law did not disturb the exclusive status of registered unions (Boxall 1990; Walsh and Ryan 1993). Because registration remained crucial to the unions' status, the act could manipulate registration to force the reform of union structure. It required that registered unions have at least 1,000 members. This will be discussed in detail later because of its tremendous impact on union mergers.

The 1987 legislation contrasted with Labour's broader strategy of economic reform through deregulation. In the debate within the Labour Party over economic policy, the "union strategists split . . . and enabled the endorsement of the economic policy, but ensured that union organization was strengthened rather than weakened" (Harbridge and Hince 1993, 226–27).[2] The unions retained their "legislative cocoon" (Harbridge and Honeybone 1995, 2): they kept legal status through registration and their exclusive bargaining rights and blanket-coverage provisions (Deeks 1990). Because the unions maintained traditional bargaining structures, they missed the opportunity to shift negotiations to the enterprise level.

Those employers favoring decentralized negotiations did not have the ability to opt out of awards. The awards had promoted multi-employer bargaining because they often included "blanket-coverage" provisions so employers had little to gain by negotiating individually. By the 1989/1990 bargaining round, 77 percent of employees under awards or registered agreements were covered by multi-employer arrangements (Harbridge, Honeybone, and Kiely 1994).

Employers complained that Labour was trying to reform the structure of bargaining while neglecting the core features of the labor relations law—compulsory union membership, exclusive union jurisdiction, and blanket coverage. The Labour Relations Act was sharply criticized in a campaign led by the New Zealand Business Roundtable, an organization of the chief executives of the largest companies and an ardent lobbyist for comprehensive deregulation. It argued that the retention of union structures and privileges blocked employers and their workers from engaging in direct negotiations, and that only such negotiations would lead to the higher productivity and lowered labor costs necessary for national competitiveness (Boxall 1990, 1993; Haworth 1993; Plowman and Street 1993).[3]

In the October 1990 election, the Labour government lost to the National Party. National had made labor law reform an election issue although it did not divulge the specific details of its proposal. "The National Party's 1990 election manifesto . . . portrayed the Labour Relations Act as constraining employers and employees from developing their own specific labour relations policies, and consequently as restricting growth in productivity, income and employment" (Walsh and Ryan 1993, 16).

Once in office, the new government promoted a labor policy based on voluntary unionism to make unions more responsive to their members; the ability of employers and employees to choose from an assortment of negotiating possibilities including legally binding, enforceable collective agreements; access to procedures for resolving negotiation and grievance disputes; and a minimum code of employment conditions to provide a safety net for the workers in the newly competitive environment (Walsh and Ryan 1993).

In December 1990, a labor relations bill was introduced into Parliament and passed after study, debate, and revision. When the resulting law, the Employment Contracts Act, took effect in May, it repealed the Labour Relations Act of 1987.[4] The Employment Contracts Act is a radical departure from the prior labor legislation. It focuses on the workers' freedom of association—their right to associate or not associate with their fellow workers for the purposes of advancing employment interests. But it also rejects a fundamental premise of the labor laws of industrialized nations, that is, the presumption of inequality of bargaining power between the employer and the individual employee, that employees are inherently in a weaker position, and that the law should ameliorate this imbalance (McAndrew 1992; Geare 1993).

The Employment Contracts Act greatly diminishes the unions' status. In the text, the term "employee organization" is used in place of "trade union." A "bargaining agent" is defined as a person rather than an organization. An employers' association described the new alternatives for representation in the following manner: in contract negotiations or any other disputed matter "an employee may select a union . . . as his or her representative, a friend, a church minister, a solicitor or any appropriate person. A young person might choose a parent'' (New Zealand Employers' Federation 1992, 3).

The legislation completely ends the unions' exclusive right to represent workers in bargaining and in processing grievances. Membership is purely voluntary. Workers cannot be pressured into becoming union members and union members cannot receive preference in employment. Unions can be prohibited by employers from approaching potential members at work. Union registration is ended and the Office of the Registrar of Unions is dissolved. Procedures for creating tripartite committee structures for consultation at the national level are repealed. The tribunals and awards system is dismantled.

Negotiations end in "employment contracts," a term that includes both collective agreements (previously called "agreements" or "awards") and individual agreements (previously called "contracts of service"). Workers and employers are free to select bargaining representatives and decide whether the contract will be individual or collective. Individual employment contracts do not have to be in writing unless the worker requests a written record of its content. These contracts can be negotiated at any time but may not be inconsistent with any applicable collective employment contracts. Collective contracts, on the other hand, can be negotiated between one or more employers and any or all of their employees. They need not be negotiated by unions; employers may negotiate with any authorized representatives of the employees or with the employees themselves.[5] Collective contracts, however, must be in writing and, if they cover 20 or more employees, they must be filed with the Secretary of Labour (Cowen 1993; Harbridge 1993a).[6]

The government considers the Employment Contracts Act crucial to increased productivity, sustained economic growth, and improved standards of living (Hince and Vranken 1991; Silverstone and Daldy 1993). The act is clearly biased against multi-employer bargaining, the predominant form at the time of passage, as well as collective bargaining in general. Its intent is the decollectivization of labor relations; even when there is collective bargaining, rights attach to individuals, not to organizations (McAndrews 1992). As Grills (1994, 100) describes it, the impact of the act is "to abolish the legal status of trade unions, to abolish the statutory assistance formerly given to the union as a bargaining agent in collective bargaining, and to diminish the role of the union as a representative of employees in disputes and personal grievance.''

Table 14 shows union membership increasing in the years up through 1989 and then falling sharply. Membership dropped prior to the passage of the Employment Contracts Act because some major awards and agreements were not renegotiated; employers anticipated that the National Party would deregulate the labor market after the election. Surveys by Harbridge and Hince (1994) revealed that there were 46,000 fewer union members when the Employment Contracts Act came into force in May 1991 than in September 1989. Within six months of its passage, union membership fell by about 90,000 members, almost 15 percent of the total, and there were 14 fewer unions. Within two years, membership was down 176,000 and there were 22 fewer unions.

Union density rates in New Zealand are not always comparable over time because they are derived from different sources and estimates of the labor force fluctuate widely. But the recent decline is unmistakable. Harbridge and Honeybone (1995) estimate that density fell from 44 percent in 1985 to 35 percent in 1991, soon after the passage of the Employment Contracts Act, and to 23 percent in December 1994.

Table 14. Unions and union membership in New Zealand, 1896–1994

Year	Number of registered unions[a]	Union membership (thousands)
1896	75	8
1900	133	14
1916	368	72
1928	403	104
1935	410	81
1936	487	185
1943	399	215
1950	370	268
1960	398	332
1970	353	378
1980	265	516
1987	232	570
1989	112	649
1991	66	514
1992	58	428
1993	67	409
1994	82	376

Sources: 1896–1991: Harbridge and Hince 1992a.
          1992–1994: Harbridge and Honeybone 1995.
[a]Registration was ended in 1991 by the Employment Contracts Act. Unions for 1991–1994 are not registered but rather responded to the private surveys conducted by Harbridge and Hince (1992a, 1994), and Harbridge and Honeybone (1995).

Two years after the act passed, collective-bargaining coverage had fallen by about 331,000 workers, about 45 percent, with the heaviest losses in agriculture, food and beverages, textiles and clothing, printing and paper, transportation and storage, retailing, restaurants and hotels, and mining. Losses were greatest in small single-plant companies, particularly those with less than 50 employees (Harbridge 1993c). By February 1993 there were 560,000 employees on *individual* employment contracts, up by 100,000 from a year earlier (Statistics New Zealand 1994). This figure comprises about 130,000 more workers than were under collective employment contracts.

Union losses slowed to 19,000 members in 1993 and 34,000 in 1994, compared to 86,000 the year before. This leveling off has been attributed to three factors: the bottoming out of the fall in multi-employer bargaining (few agreements remain to be scuttled); a return to collective bargaining by some employers who found that the costs of converting workers to individual bargaining were very high; and the possibility that earlier membership records were inflated but became more realistic when records were revised and consolidated after mergers (Harbridge 1994).

Under the Employment Contracts Act, enterprise bargaining spread as newly established bargaining agents opted for single-employer contracts and the New Zealand Employers Federation encouraged employers not to enter into multi-employer arrangements (Harbridge 1993b). Harbridge and Honeybone (1995, 7) found a "collapse of collective bargaining coverage" as the percentage of workers in multi-employer coverage fell from 77 percent during the 1989/1990 bargaining rounds to 20 percent during the 1994/1995 rounds. The number of workers under all types of collective agreements dropped from 721,000 during 1989/1990 to 366,000 during 1994/1995. Later, we will see that membership losses and the change in the locus of negotiations created new pressures for unions to merge.

New Zealand, which once had one of the most protected and regulated economies among industrialized countries, implemented some of the most radical, free-market reforms. It had been among the first countries to introduce a cradle-to-grave welfare state and it became the first to dismantle one ("The Mother of All Reformers" 1993). Presently, there is an economic recovery with significant reductions in inflation and unemployment, robust consumption, increased manufacturing production, and growth in export markets and foreign investment. Wage increases are down, the dollar is stronger, and business and consumer confidence are reported to be buoyant. There have been, however, some shortages of skilled workers, particularly in manufacturing and construction. Nonetheless, in 1994, the New Zealand economy was projected to be one of the fastest growing in the Organization for Economic Development and Cooperation.[7]

UNION REGISTRATION AND FRAGMENTATION

Registration perpetuated small, weak unions by enabling them to gain recognition from employers. The Industrial Conciliation and Arbitration Act of 1894 required that unions submit their rules (constitutions) to the registrar of trade unions. These documents had to show that a community of interest existed among potential members. As a result, membership rules often described specific occupations though enterprise or industrial coverage would also have been permissible. In order to eliminate inter-union competition, the registrar of unions was prohibited from registering more than one union with the same membership coverage. Prior to 1936, New Zealand was also divided administratively into eight geographic industrial districts and legislation prohibited the recognition of unions with members in more than a single district. Under such a system, unionism prospered but it was geographically fragmented and based primarily on occupations (Harbridge and Hince 1994).

Table 14 shows the extent of union fragmentation in New Zealand. The number of registered unions rose from 75 in 1896 to 133 in 1900 and 368 in 1916, the first two decades of the legislation prescribing registration, and peaked at 487 in 1936. The number of unions has since declined through mergers and disbandments. The most dramatic change occurred after the passage of legislation in 1987 that ended the registration of unions with fewer than 1,000 members—a 50-percent decline in the number of unions in two years, followed by another 50-percent decline over the next two years.

Though it was not compulsory, unions preferred registration because it established their jurisdictions and gave legal standing to their agreements with employers. Once registered, a union gained the right to represent all employees deemed by its rules to be "conveniently covered," and it could compel the employer to negotiate over these workers' wages and working conditions (Cowen 1993). As I mentioned earlier, a union could also have a membership clause included in its settlements that required workers covered by the settlement to join it. By 1990, nearly all the awards registered by the arbitration commission contained clauses requiring union membership.

Although registration brought members into the unions, it also weakened unions by reversing the process of organizing as practiced in most other countries. Harbridge (1993a, 33) observed that New Zealand's unions "gained recognition rights through legislation, undertook bargaining, and, upon reaching a settlement, enrolled workers who had little legal choice but to join the union concerned." Contrast this to the situation in North America, described in chapters 2 and 3, where unions must first persuade workers to join and be represented by them before they can legally compel employers to negotiate.

New Zealand's unions were structured to take advantage of statutory protections and thus became dependent on the registration/arbitration system. They lacked financial resources or staff for organizing and administering branches. Organizers visited worksites primarily to monitor and enforce award wages and conditions, and to process grievances. They only occasionally recruited new members (Oxenbridge 1996).[8] The unions survived by operating on a regional basis and representing their members on the narrow range of issues permitted by the awards process. They were preoccupied with procedural issues, and they tended to be run by administrators well-versed in the matters of the labor law and arbitration procedures rather than by activists and leaders of the rank-and-file (Harbridge and Honeybone 1995). Moreover, as the main labor federation, the New Zealand Council of Trade Unions (NZCTU), observed in 1988 the country's unions were:

> too small to have sufficient resources to take up wider issues [e.g., company investment decisions, national taxation and health policies]; too fragmented to develop vital unity; [and] not structured to be effective outside the narrow wages and conditions area. . . . What is clear is that unions will in the future need to be able to deliver an organisation throughout the country. Strength in pockets will no longer be enough (New Zealand Council of Trade Unions 1988, 5,15)

The registration system initially made it difficult for unions to expand by merging. Once registered on a local or district basis, unions could continue in perpetuity but could not expand through merger into other regions. In 1962, this restriction was relaxed; mergers could be carried out essentially by changing the merging unions' registration (*The New Zealand System* 1989).

Union fragmentation in New Zealand is now greatly reduced. Only about one-tenth of the unions with less than 1,000 members in 1985 were operating in 1993. At the same time, the concentration of union membership has increased; in 1985, 46 percent of union members belonged to the 12 unions with over 10,000 members each; in 1993, 71 percent of members were in the 11 unions of this size (Harbridge and Hince 1994). The restructuring of the labor movement occurred primarily through a wave of mergers induced by legislation.

The Merger Record

Since registration ended in 1991, there has been no official public record of unions and union membership in New Zealand. Harbridge and Hince (1994), however, have completed private surveys of unions and compiled a union directory. The list of mergers in appendix 5 is derived from union profiles in that directory. Table 15 shows the number of mergers since 1986, the earliest date for accurate and comprehensive figures from the` Harbridge and Hince (1994) directory. A huge merger wave is evident, rising through 1987 and 1988, reaching a crest of 66 mergers in 1989, then falling quickly over the next two years. Absorptions and affiliations were the primary merger form before, during, and after the merger wave, and comprised more than 80 percent of aggregate mergers.

Some prominent characteristics of recent mergers are evident in appendix 5. First, a few unions became centers of exceptionally intense and varied merger activity during the merger wave. For example, APEX took in

Table 15. Union mergers in New Zealand, 1986–1993

Year	Absorptions and affiliations	Amalgamations	Total
1986	3	1	4
1987	9	3	12
1988	16	5	21
1989	58	8	66
1990	18	4	22
1991	6	4	10
1992	2	1	3
1993	2	1	3
Total	114	27	141

Source: Appendix 5.

17 unions from 1988 to 1991 with members that included sales representatives, supervisors, and technicians. Places of employment ranged from wharfs to health-care institutions. The Amalgamated Engineering Union absorbed a jewelry workers' union in 1987, laundry workers', gold miners', and cement workers' unions in 1989, and draftspersons' and stoneworkers' unions in 1990.[9] The New Zealand Public Service Association absorbed several small health-care unions in 1989 and unions of local-government workers in 1993.

Second, some major unions were created by amalgamations. New Zealand's fourth-largest union, the Service Workers Union of Aotearoa, was formed in 1991 from the amalgamation of the 7 regional unions that it had previously represented in national negotiations. The seventh-largest union, the Communication and Energy Workers, was formed from the Electrical Workers Union and the Post Office Union in 1992. The eighth-largest union, FinSec (Financial Sector Union) emerged from the merger of the Insurance Trust and Life Agents with the Bank Officers in 1990.

As noted above, mergers in New Zealand often joined unions with quite different jurisdictions. For example, the Meatworkers has taken in the Saddlers, Collarmakers, Bagmakers, Sailmakers, Riggers, and Wholesale Oyster Workers. TradeSec (previously the Northern Furniture and Allied Industries Unions) absorbed the Northern Ship, Yacht and Boatbuilders, and the Painters, Glaziers, Signwriters and Stonemasons Union. Haworth (1993, 298) observed "this pattern [mergers of dissimilar unions] is not surprising in that it reflects the contingent nature of union alliances subject as they are to historical rivalries, interpersonal frictions, and regional diversity." On the other hand, about a third of the mergers in the late 1980s joined together unions in the same industry and another third were among those in similar occupations. Mergers did significantly reduce the number of unions and jurisdictional overlap in timber, longshoring, higher education, maritime, railways, health care, newspapers, footwear, food and beverages, and finance (Fuller 1989).

The Underlying Trends

THE 1,000-MEMBER RULE

The Labour Relations Act of 1987 sought to make unions viable institutions that could provide comprehensive, high-quality membership services and function without legislative props. Large size was equated with greater union effectiveness, and the way to create larger unions was simple and direct—raising the minimum size for union registration from 15 to 1,000 members. Nearly two-thirds of all unions fell below this threshold and faced the loss of registration if they could not expand within 12 months (Harbridge and Hince 1993).[10]

The number of smaller unions was greatly reduced as they searched for merger partners and quickly negotiated merger terms, usually absorptions and affiliations. The number of unions with fewer than 1,000 members fell from 135 in April 1988 (58 percent of all unions) to 69 (41 percent) in April 1989, and 19 unions (17 percent) in September 1989. By May 1991, there were only 4 unions with less than 1,000 members and their combined membership comprised less than one percent of total membership (Harbridge and Hince 1994). In the early 1990s, some unions that were forced to merge under the 1,000-member rule have reconstituted themselves, leaving the unions into which they had merged. This accounts for the 24 new unions that were formed in 1993 and 1994 (Harbridge and Honeybone 1995). But the vast majority of small unions, at least 80 percent, have continued in their mergers.

The merger wave of the latter 1980's occurred without substantial federation intervention. The New Zealand Council of Trade Unions (NZCTU) did not actively arrange mergers of small unions and it lacked the power to compel mergers. The federation did proclaim a need for more mergers to counter the effects of economic deregulation and the possibility of weakened representation through company-based unions. The formation of large, industry-based unions was encouraged to replace small occupational unions. The NZCTU also convened a series of industry-sector meetings to encourage mergers, a move compatible with the federation's belief that affiliated unions should resist employer pressure for negotiations at the enterprise level (New Zealand Council of Trade Unions 1988, 1992; Haworth 1993; Franks 1994).[11]

Aside from creating the prime reason for small unions to merge, the Labour Relations Act of 1987 simplified the merger process. Absorbing or affiliating unions could change constitutions to include the members of the smaller unions which have their registration canceled. In the case of an amalgamation, a new union could be registered in place of the merging unions, with the latter also having their registrations canceled. Such changes in the constitutions' membership rules were approved by votes of either the membership or delegates at a union conference (*The New Zealand System* 1989).[12] However, this fairly straightforward process of voting to change membership rules and amending registration proved to be short-lived. Union registration was ended with the passage of the Employment Contracts Act in 1991.

DECENTRALIZED BARGAINING

One of the objectives of the 1,000-member rule of the Labour Relations Act 1987 was to centralize union structure by merging unions and stopping or even reversing the spread of enterprise unionism. Not surprisingly, then, the 1,000-member rule was widely criticized by employers as an obstacle to the development of more flexible structures for representation at the workplace level (Walsh 1993). The Employment Contracts Act of 1991 discouraged multi-employer bargaining; there are no procedures for extending agreements to employers and strikes to support multi-employer bargaining are prohibited. A survey by McAndrew (1992) showed that in early 1991, 80 percent of employers were covered by national or nearly national awards. By mid-1992, 80 percent of respondents had contracts exclusive to their firms. Harbridge (1993d) also found that the enterprise agreements that replaced multi-employer agreements were genuine enterprise bargains, that is, they covered *all* unionized employees at the enterprise.

The restructuring of negotiations under the Employment Contracts Act made the unions' task far more demanding than ever before. The act made representation at the workplace more difficult for unions, and it ended registration and awards, previous sources of union status and influence.

A wide range of measures has been introduced to make it as difficult, and as expensive, and as cumbersome as possible to maintain effective union organization. These include the requirement to obtain individualized authorities for each separate aspect of representation (negotiation, administration and enforcement of contracts), to have separate, annual, pre-negotiating ratification meetings, lack of access to workplaces for recruitment and educational purposes and so on. When all of these obstacles have been overcome, there is no obligation on the employer to negotiate, and the employer can even put pressure on individuals to negotiate directly, even though they may have chosen to be represented by a union. (Douglas 1993, 197–198)

Such a sudden and complete change in worker representation can drain any union's assets and test the skills and perseverance of its officers and staff. To make matters even worse, however, most unions in New Zealand lack representative structures and qualified staff at the workplace level—the legacy of the centralized system of representation and compulsory membership. Moreover, the decentralization of negotiations means that union officers must be prepared to have the membership play a greater role in determining the content of agreements. This new role demands greater training in negotiations, contract language, and principles of work design for both officers and members (Boxall and Deeks 1993). The remaining smaller unions now find themselves lacking the economies of scale and industrywide structures needed to coordinate negotiations. Large unions must somehow involve a sometimes geographically remote membership in decision-making or face the possibility of losing them (Boxall and Hayes 1992).

The unions' survival is doubly threatened when the legislation that drives negotiations to the workplace level also eliminates the earlier source of union strength—compulsory union membership and blanket coverage. Membership losses have been severe, more than 40 percent since 1989, and a rebound seems highly unlikely. Even if there is a change in government, the return of the legislative props is highly improbable.

For those unions that were unaffected by the earlier 1,000-member rule, the vicissitudes of labor relations under the Employment Contracts Act are now reason enough to explore merger possibilities. Despite such motivation, few mergers occurred after 1991 (see table 15), most likely because the immediate merger potential had been spent in the adjustment to the 1,000-member rule four years earlier. Whether the Employment Contracts Act will eventually produce its own merger wave is uncertain. Will the remaining small unions successfully adapt to enterprise bargaining and the necessity for organizing, or will this be possible only after achieving economies of scale through mergers? Will union membership eventually stabilize, possibly reducing the motivation to merge? It is presently too early to see beyond the initial impact of the act on worker representation and union-membership levels.

The Employment Contracts Act has been criticized for going too far and overstepping the bounds of reform. Hince (1993) argues that there may have been a clear need for change but there was no unanimity regarding how much change was needed. The Employment Contracts Act "was by no means a consensus proposal—it was an imposed solution" (Hince 1993, 12). But the next legislation will probably be evolutionary and not shaped by extreme ideologies (Harbridge, Honeybone, and Kiely 1994). Rather, workers' rights to collective bargaining may be strengthened, perhaps by introducing a good-faith bargaining requirement.[13] The traditional legislative pillars of union strength—compulsory membership, exclusive jurisdiction, and blanket coverage—will not be resurrected (Boxall 1993; Clark 1993; Harbridge and Hince 1993; Uren 1993). And if the registration process reappears, the minimum-size threshold will be lowered, not raised.[14]

It may be some consolation to New Zealand's remaining unions to know that they are now more efficient representatives than their predecessors, more attuned to their membership, and less dependent on the state. Harbridge and Hince (1993, 233–34) observed: "A pattern of diminished aggregate union membership has developed, but unions have restructured, reorganized and are in a more competitive mode than before. Remaining unions are less likely to be simply a collection of workers artificially placed together by legislative compulsion and blanket award coverage."

Some unions, however, were in such a weakened condition that mergers could not save them and representation had to be abandoned. For example, the New Zealand Clerical Workers Union was formed by the amalgamation of four clerical unions in 1990, but its 20,000 members remained widely scattered, the result of the prior system of representation. In more than half of its workplaces, only a single worker was represented. The average workplace had three members. Its predecessor unions had survived in this condition because their awards cut across virtually all industry boundaries. With the advent of voluntary unionism, the clerical unions suffered severe membership losses, which continued after their merger. Its officers recognized the trend toward industrywide rather than occupationally-based unions and the absence of other clerical unions for further mergers. After a membership vote, they dissolved the Clerical Workers Union in 1991. The members was dispersed to 21 other unions on the basis of their industries (Franks 1994).

Ironically, the present union movement "in some ways looks more like meeting the objectives of the Labour Relations Act than those of the Employment Contracts Act" (Harbridge and Hince 1992a, 135). The Labour Relations Act tried to fortify the unions by compelling small unions to merge while encouraging large ones to form centers of merger activity. But the foundations of worker representation and union recognition were not significantly altered. One might argue that had the 1,000-member rule not been enacted, the merger wave of 1989 would only have been postponed, occurring in full force within a year or two after the passage of the Employment Contracts Act in 1991 with its radical change in the legal status of unions. But this is only speculation. What is certain is that the changes in union structure in New Zealand were swift and widespread and the instrument for these changes were union mergers.

CHAPTER 7

Conclusions: The Merger
Option in Hard Times

There is no scarcity of case studies of union mergers or analyses of merger trends over time, and numerous studies have already told us why unions merge and how they negotiate their merger agreements.[1] What we need are views of the broad sweep of union mergers in several countries— national profiles of merger activity during the hard times since 1980, which I developed in the preceding chapters. Though I did review a few individual mergers in detail, I did so to show landmark cases that foretold major trends (e.g., Unison as the prototype of the new British super-union) and to illustrate a concept or principle (e.g., the Typographical Union's [ITU] merger showing the long road to merger in the United States). In this concluding chapter, I briefly review the national profiles of union mergers and describe their common features.

National Profiles of Union Mergers

It is always tempting to compare the union merger record in different countries, but I believe that such a comparison reveals little. In an international comparison, the annual merger rate is a poor measure of the relative force of the motivation to merge or the barriers to merger. First, it is only logical that highly fragmented labor movements with many unions, such as Britain's and New Zealand's, would have more mergers than those with fewer unions, such as the United States' or Canada's. But even if merger frequency were adjusted by the number of unions, the results would be misleading because merger data are not comparable. The British figures are from the official lists of mergers registered at the certification office. The Australian mergers are derived from the votes conducted by the Australian electoral commission. Both include regional and single-company unions as well as national unions. The merger list for New Zealand is extracted from a privately compiled directory of unions, and the lists for the United States and Canada are from articles, news reports, and federation records. The New Zealand figures include many regional and enterprise-based unions along with national unions, but only national-union mergers are counted for the United States and Canada because information on affiliations is incomplete. Thus, merger activity for these two countries would be underestimated in a comparison.[2]

Although the five countries' merger records are not comparable, the forms of merger certainly are. The cases fall into the categories described in the chapter 1. With the exception of Australia, amalgamations are infrequent, comprising only 11 percent of the mergers in the United States, 17 percent in Canada, 14 percent in Britain, and 19 percent in New Zealand. As I mentioned in the preceding chapters, this low rate is due to the relative difficulty of amalgamating, that is, forming new unions by combining two or more of roughly equal size. Absorptions and affiliations are easier; small unions become parts of larger ones, with the latter usually undergoing little change. Amalgamations are fairly common in Australia, however, comprising 48 percent of mergers, because the labor federation (the Australian Council of Trade Unions [ACTU]) assists and pressures unions in the same or related industries to merge with each other. There has also been no shortage of amalgamation partners because the narrow scope of tribunal awards assured the presence of several unions in each industry.

We also saw illustrations of the varied degrees of integration discussed in the first chapter. Amalgamations occasionally create semi-autonomous sections or divisions; this is evident in the British Amalgamated Engineering and Electrical Union (AEEU), a merger that was quickly negotiated and agreed to before arrangements for greater integration could be settled. Some of New Zealand's smallest unions, driven to merge by the 1,000-member rule, amalgamated into "umbrella" organizations in which they enjoyed considerable autonomy but could still claim to exceed the minimum-size threshold. Most often, however, amalgamations require high degrees of integration after brief transitional periods. For example, in the merger forming the Canadian Communications, Energy and Paperworkers Union (CEP), divisions were not created and duplicate officers' positions were only temporary. The merger committees believed that a high degree of integration was needed to avoid the factionalism that could result from the officers' and members' continued close identity with their prior unions.

Absorptions and affiliations usually had low degrees of integration, with the smaller unions becoming semi-autonomous sections of larger ones. Sections generally elect their own officers, hire staff, hold conventions or policy meetings, and set bargaining priorities. In the United States, for instance, we saw this pattern in the Service Employees' affiliations and the absorptions of the ITU and the National Union of Hospital and Health Care Employees. In Australia, the loose integration of unions after the merger wave of 1991 to 1992 caused some critics to doubt whether more efficient unions had been created and if the federation's plan for structural reform could actually work.

Unions amalgamated with each other to expand their jurisdictions and enhance growth potential and institutional stability. Or they joined with other unions in the same or neighboring jurisdictions to reduce organizing rivalry and membership losses, and to present a unified bargaining front against employers. Absorptions and affiliations, on the other hand, were mostly reactions by the smaller unions to severe membership losses or a clear inability to grow, as well as the lack of economies of scale in their operations. Larger unions often used these mergers to avoid the high costs and low gains associated with conventional membership recruitment at workplaces.

There is far more to recent union mergers, however, than the general patterns described above. When we examine national profiles of merger activity, we see that each has a distinct character that evolved from the broader context of the country's industrial relations system.

In the United States, the crisis of the labor movement and the growing importance of the nonunion sector forced unions to turn to mergers for adaptation and survival. Since the early 1980s, union membership fell sharply, employer opposition intensified during negotiations and organizing, and the unions' bargaining and political power were greatly diminished. With little chance of the membership gains sufficient to counter losses, American unions showed a heightened interest in the merger option. This trend will undoubtedly continue as the chances fade for laws that make organizing easier and as union officers hear of the benefits of merging during the high profile negotiations for the amalgamation of the

Auto Workers, Steelworkers, and Machinists. A few unions are also using affiliations as key elements in their growth strategies, a sign of the high costs and low yields of traditional organizing as well as the difficult position of smaller unions. But, as the cases of the printers' and hospital workers' unions demonstrate, merging remains exceedingly difficult in the United States in the absence of proactive federation policies and legislation to resolve members' and officers' opposition.

Canadian unions are on the verge of a merger wave. Although most unions have been resilient during the recent hard times, rejecting concession bargaining and countering membership losses with new recruits, growth potential is clearly limited in both the private and public sectors. Moreover, employer opposition is rising (though it is not nearly comparable to that in the United States), political influence is declining, legislation friendly to unions is being rescinded, and employment continues to shift to lesser unionized sectors.

The confluence of three historic trends in Canada lowers merger barriers and raises the motivation to merge. I illustrated these trends with three landmark mergers. First, the absorption of the fishermens' local into the Canadian Auto Workers shows the declining influence of international unions and tremendous new potential for mergers. International unions can no longer block the mergers of their Canadian sections, and these sections become attractive merger partners for the national unions. Second, mergers can be by-products of the consolidation of bargaining units. The merger of the postal unions shows the forced merger at its worst; this long and bitter contest may convince unions in narrow bargaining units to merge on their own and preempt adverse labor-board decisions. Finally, the amalgamation that created the CEP in 1992 signals an important amalgamation trend—the creation of super-unions with exceptionally diverse memberships and policies of expanding through mergers. A wave of mergers over the next decade will accelerate the decline of the international unions, incite new movements for Canadian-section autonomy, and lead to competition between large, aggressive unions such as the CAW and CEP that act as merger centers.

I find it remarkable how little the aggregate data can tell us about the importance of union mergers in Great Britain. Despite numerous reports of "merger mania" sweeping that country, the recent British merger pace is erratic and unexceptional. The climate of labor relations would have us expect far more. Since 1980, union membership and density are declining sharply, hostile governments seek to curb the unions' power, multi-unionism (too many unions at individual workplaces) and union fragmentation (too many small unions) remain chronic problems, and union resources are strained by the new demands of membership recruitment and decentralized negotiations. Employment in the core of the unions' strength—manufacturing and government services—is shrinking, mostly because of foreign competition and privatization, respectively. Still, there has been no merger wave.

But the underlying patterns of merger activity show that mergers continued to play an important role in Britain. Mergers are among the pivotal industrial relations events of the 1980s and 1990s. The merger forming the AEEU threatened to split the Trades Union Congress (TUC), a three-union amalgamation created Unison, the first new super-union, and absorptions and affiliations built new general unions, such as the General, Municipal, Boilermakers, and partially offset membership losses in older ones, such as the Transport and General Workers Union (TGWU).

More so than any other country, Britain has a tradition of union mergers. Mergers are the building blocks of the largest and most powerful unions and the customary way for declining regional unions to end their independent existence. Union officers and members do not see mergers as radical restructuring but rather as natural and perhaps inevitable steps in the evolution of their country's unions.

The British law of union mergers simplifies and standardizes the merger approval process and, as I argued, facilitates mergers by channeling and resolving members' and officers' opposition quickly and to finality. The TUC, like labor federations in the United States and Canada, mildly encourages mergers and mediates stalled merger negotiations, but it is careful not to intrude too deeply in internal union affairs by proposing specific mergers or criticizing individual unions for not merging. Nonetheless, the merger tradition and merger-friendly legislation make merging a top option for British unions in hard times.

Union mergers in Australia have been nothing short of phenomenal. As reactions to public policy and federation pressures, mergers have reshaped the labor movement in a few years. The national system of wage fixation based on tribunal awards created an exceptionally fragmented labor movement, yet one in which unions were secure as representatives. The extraordinary merger wave in 1991 and 1992, about a tenfold increase in the number of mergers, was crucial to the government's and the ACTU's programs to reduce union fragmentation, reform union structure, and revitalize the labor movement to operate in a more competitive economy. In bold contrast to the neutrality of labor federations in the United States, Canada, and Britain, the ACTU aggressively promotes mergers to create broader-based unions. The ACTU had become exceptionally powerful through its role in the national awards system and the negotiation of accords with the federal government. The structural reform of the fragmented labor movement is central to the federation's program of strategic unionism and the continued relevance of unions into the next century.

A unique feature of Australian union mergers is their sequential character. Series of mergers join unions in the same or related jurisdictions, quickly forming new unions through complex mixes of amalgamations and absorptions. From 1989 to 1993, 17 industrywide and multicraft unions were created from the mergers of 110 unions.

In New Zealand, a huge wave of union mergers was a prelude to the sudden, radical transformation of the industrial relations system. The awards system created a secure but highly fragmented union movement (a process and outcome quite similar to that in Australia). The Labour government promoted mergers, believing that outmoded union structures stood in the way of greater productivity, lower labor costs, and national competitiveness. Its stated intent was to create "viable" unions that could function after the removal of the legislative props of compulsory membership, perpetual representational status, and the extension of settlements to nonunion workers. The 1,000-member rule, the new minimum-size threshold for union registration imposed by the Labour Relations Act of 1987, sent a clear signal to the smallest unions that they must grow, merge, or perish. What followed was a merger wave, over 100 mergers from 1988 to 1990, and the end to 90 percent of unions with fewer than 1,000 members. But a government supportive of unions was soon followed by one that was antagonistic, and the Employment Contracts Act of 1991 radically changed labor relations and the status of unions as worker representatives. The newlymerged unions must now deal with serious membership declines and the sudden, sweeping decentralization of negotiations.

Common Features of Union Mergers

The preceding chapters show how features of the broader context of labor relations, whether they are evolving systems of worker representation and promerger laws in Australia and New Zealand or the decline of international unionism in Canada, affect the motivation and the barriers to merger. We saw that merger waves were not generated by a sudden, mass recognition of the benefits of mergers but rather, depending on the nation, by legislation, federation policies and programs, groups of unions newly amenable to mergers, the improbability of growth through traditional organizing, and so on. Moreover, the choice between absorption and amalgamation is not only affected by the severity of the hard times but by the availability of merger partners (e.g., absorptions of the many small, regional, or specialized unions in Britain), federation policies (e.g., the pressure to amalgamate unions in similar industries in Australia), and laws directed at reshaping union movements (e.g., the minimum-size thresholds in Australia and New Zealand).

By now its should be apparent that the chapters are arranged in order of the intensity of merger activity—heightened interest in the United States, the brink of a merger wave in Canada, the continuation of the merger tradition in Britain, the quick and complex sequences of mergers for major structural reform in Australia, and the enormous merger wave induced by legislation in New Zealand. Despite this variation, I see some common features of union mergers in the five countries.

THE IMPACT OF MERGER ON UNION MEMBERS

Although it is quite understandable that scholars and legislators would feel comfortable with some universal principles of how mergers affect union members (e.g., Fink 1987; House of Commons 1990), this is an area where generalizations are best avoided. In each of the selected countries, there were mergers that had little if any impact on members. In large absorbing or affiliating unions, many members may not even be aware that mergers occurred, particularly if locals are not required to combine. They are frequently exempted by law or union policy from voting on affiliations and absorptions because these mergers have a minimal impact on representation and union governance.

Members of a smaller merging union may see the benefits of large and expert staffs and financial assistance during strikes and organizing campaigns, but there may be little impact beyond this if the merger calls for low degrees of integration. As I mentioned in chapter 1 and briefly emphasized again early in this chapter, this is a common condition of absorptions and affiliations. Smaller unions may simply continue their usual governing and administrative practices after mergers, perhaps even keeping their own constitutions, headquarters, and newspapers. Typical is the situation described in a brochure promoting the absorption of the Newspaper Guild into the Communications Workers in the United States in 1995: "We [the Newspaper Guild] maintain control of our finances, governance, policies and institutions. There is no question that some things would be different, but our union would still be the Newspaper Guild, it would just have an extra set of initials" (The Newspaper Guild/Communications Workers of America 1995, 2).

At the other extreme, we have seen some mergers whose impact is substantial and readily felt by the members. In the United States, for instance, organizing raids against unaffiliated state employees' unions ended when they joined with AFL-CIO unions; mergers into affiliates of the British TUC and Canadian Labour Congress (CLC) had a similar effect. The dues of the American ITU's members were lowered after it was absorbed by the Communications Workers. In Canada, members of the Letter Carriers Union found most aspects of union governance changed after their union was compelled to merge into the Canadian Union of Postal Workers. Members of Australian unions saw mergers directly affect the strength of representation when there were also changes in their unions' designation as "principal," "significant," or "other" union.

I also find it difficult to make sweeping statements about the impact of mergers on union democracy—the responsiveness of union officers to their members and the extent of meaningful membership participation in union decision-making. Brooks and Gamm (1976) argue that officers often put their interests first when negotiating mergers and try to find ways to increase their authority and perpetuate their terms in office. They might achieve these aims by having officers of the merged union elected by convention delegates rather than by membership ballots, increasing the terms of office, or converting vice-president-at-large positions into regional ones, thus reducing the chances that a challenger to an incumbent president will have national support. Although this may have happened in some mergers, I would argue that far more often political opposition coalesces when officers try to change election procedures, the duties of executive-council members, or the division of authority between the national and local unions (Chaison 1986). We have seen how political opponents lose little time building their election platforms around appeals for no merger, better mergers terms, or merger with another union. There is no evidence that union officers, in general, have a free hand to use merger to increase their power or that union members are unaware or unconcerned about merger terms and their implications.

It is also sometimes assumed that mergers stifle membership participation because they create large unions with "a bigger, tighter bureaucracy with less of a role for the rank and file" (Moody 1995:14). But such charges are made without an appreciation of how often autonomy is preserved for absorbed and affiliating unions, and how amalgamating unions grant power to industry and regional divisions in order to win the members' approval of the merger agreement. Recall, for instance, that the Service Employees in the United States successfully expanded through absorptions and affiliations, allowing smaller unions to retain substantial authority in governance and bargaining, and that the large British general unions were built through amalgamations and subsequent absorptions (e.g., the TGWU or the GMB) and which often resemble federations because so much decision-making resides in regional and industry sections. Such strategies for union growth at least partially avoid the negative features of large size because of the high degree of decentralization necessary to gain membership approval of the merger terms and to attract future merger partners.

THE BIAS AGAINST SMALL UNIONS

Advocates of union mergers are almost universally biased against small unions, believing them to be ineffectual anachronisms. The most blatant resistance is found in Australia and New Zealand where public policy, in the form of minimum-size requirements, equates the creation of bigger unions with the reform of union structure, the furtherance of the public interest, and the pursuit of national competitiveness. In the United States, Canada, and Great Britain, small unions have not been directly challenged, but merger proponents in federations and large unions seldom miss opportunities to point out how small unions lack economies of scale in their operations, that is, have too few members to pay for and utilize specialized union services and expert staff. They also claim that small unions are financially troubled and unable to support organizing, strike benefits, research and education programs (Chaison 1995).

Voices are seldom raised in defense of small unions; their case seems to be made mostly by Australian opponents of the ACTU's plan for restructuring the labor movement (Way 1993) and by British union officers concerned about preserving their small, regional organizations ("Small Unions" 1992). I believe we should refrain romanticizing about small unions as the ideal workers' collectives, but we should also not exaggerate their deficiencies. The effects of union size are not always as obvious as merger proponents claim, which provides an opportunity for a lively and informed debate.

A good case can be made that small size is not problematic for unions that negotiate only a few collective agreements, or that represent specialized groups of workers or those in narrow geographic areas. These include enterprise-based unions at larger companies, national unions of performing artists, professional athletes, and airline pilots; and state, provincial, and citywide unions of public employees. Officers of smaller unions also claim that their organizations maintain closer contact with members, respond more quickly to their needs, and have a greater awareness of company and community problems. I dealt with these points in greater detail in earlier chapters, particularly the review of mergers in Britain, where there remain several small, highly specialized and regional unions.

This is not the place to enter the union size/effectiveness debate. But I do wish to emphasize that a common feature of the context of mergers in the five countries is an explicit bias against small unions. Federations exhort small unions to merge, legislators inveigh against the costs of union fragmentation, and mergers are promoted to strengthen small unions by making them parts of larger ones. Absent is an appraisal of the advantages of small union size under the emerging systems of decentralized collective bargaining and the impact of merger on the small unions' members.[3]

RATIONALIZING UNION JURISDICTIONS

Underlying the recent mergers in the five countries is a tension between the goals of rationalizing jurisdictions and diversifying membership. Rationalizing union jurisdiction entails reducing the overlap between unions' organizing territories, usually by creating industrywide unions. Proponents of rationalization allege that mergers between unions whose members are in the same or related industries reduce union rivalry in organizing and bargaining, increase union awareness of and concern for industry conditions, and instill a sense of solidarity among the union's members (Chaison 1995).

There have been moves to reduce jurisdictional overlap through mergers in each of five countries. These range from the AFL-CIO's proposed policy (never formally enforced) of recognizing only mergers of affiliates that share communities of interest, to the relaxation of merger-balloting requirements in Australia when unions operate in the same industries or occupations.

I find the notion that a nation's labor movement should be a family of unions with well-defined, distinct jurisdictions to be at odds with reality. In each of the selected countries, there is an accelerating trend toward membership diversity. Most large, growing unions recruit members well outside of their traditional jurisdictions. Absorptions and affiliations frequently join dissimilar unions; in some instances (e.g., CEP in Canada and GMB in Britain), merging unions sought greater membership diversity to prevent destabilizing membership losses and to attract future merger partners.

On the one hand, we have structural reformers (e.g., federation officers and legislators in Australia) who envision the eventual formation through merger of compact labor movements with broad but clear jurisdictional boundaries. On the other hand, we have the typical union officers and members, accepting or rejecting mergers because of specific terms and with little regard to schemes for reform. It is the interests of the officers and members that determine which unions will merge. Strauss (1993, 49) has argued that "in practice, whether and with whom a merger takes place has frequently been motivated more by internal political factors than by long-run, strategic economic needs. Thus, union structure is determined more by past history than by future needs, by the need to integrate pension plans or the career ladders of top officers than by collective bargaining requirements." We can add to this argument the fact that jurisdiction also carries little weight with officers and members, particularly if their union already has a heterogeneous membership due to opportunistic organizing and earlier mergers.

Because officers and members have the final say on whether a merger makes sense, the drift toward diversity and the blurring of jurisdictional boundaries overshadows plans for rationalization. For instance, the ACTU's plan for industrywide unionism cannot reverse the membership diversity of many Australian unions nor stop mergers from creating multi-craft and multi-industry unions as well as industrywide ones. This brings us to another common feature of mergers—the extent to which they are essentially voluntary arrangements.

THE VOLUNTARY NATURE OF MERGERS

The voluntary nature of mergers is so obvious that it is often forgotten, particularly by merger advocates in legislatures or academia when they discuss the need to reform union structure. As I emphasized above, the decision of whether to merge and with whom to merge is made by, and only by, union officers and members.

The voluntary nature of mergers is sacrosanct in the five countries. Governments may alter balloting requirements to encourage mergers among unions in similar jurisdictions or between very small and large ones. Labor boards, courts or government officials may block mergers that are inappropriately negotiated or approved. Minimum-size thresholds for registration can threaten the legal status of unions if they do not merge or suddenly grow. But the ultimate decision of when, how, and with whom to merge remains within the union. Even the most extreme case of compulsion—the forced merger of the Canadian postal unions—had its voluntary side; the unions were free at first to negotiate merger terms, and failing that, their combined membership was free to choose a single representative.

The voluntary nature of union mergers explains the difficult role of labor federations. As I noted earlier, federations must balance their encouragement of mergers with their concern for not intruding, or even appearing to intrude, in affiliates' internal affairs. But federation officers also know that there are times they cannot avoid direct involvement in mergers. Expelled unions cannot be allowed to re-enter federations through mergers, coverage under federation no-raid agreements cannot be "sold" by affiliates through superficial mergers, and disputes between affiliates over mergers must somehow be resolved. The AFL-CIO had no choice but to oppose the ITU–Teamster merger and to mediate the dispute over the dual merger of the health-care union; the TUC had to resolve its affiliates' objections to the AEEU merger; and the CLC could not sidestep the dispute between the Canadian Auto Workers and the United Food and Commercial Workers. In the end, however, the most that a federation can do is threaten sanctions (expulsion, suspension, or withdrawal of services) and proclaim the desired course of action (do not merge or merge with another union). It remains for the unions' officers and members to weigh the cost and benefits of merger, to do what they feel is best, and to face the consequences if the federation disapproves.

Finally, the voluntary nature of mergers imposes limitations on the labor law. We saw how the law has been be used to block or delay mergers (the United States), to facilitate mergers by resolving opposition and identifying the members' choice (Britain), and to generate merger waves involving small unions (New Zealand).[4] Despite the variety of legal approaches, the decision to merge remains voluntary. Take an extreme case. The 1,000-

member rule in New Zealand and the 1,000-member and 10,000-member rules in Australia forced smaller unions to grow, merge or perish. But officers and members could still choose from among these alternatives, select a likely merger partner, and negotiate merger terms. Minimum-size thresholds can create a strong motivation to merge but they cannot require that unions merge, much less merge with unions in similar jurisdictions.

THE LIMITATIONS OF UNION MERGERS

In each country, mergers were typically unable to resolve the fundamental problems that caused them. Mergers were adaptations to the hard times, not antidotes. Neither amalgamations, absorptions, nor affiliations could reverse the spread of domestic or foreign nonunion competition or regain the union jobs lost to that competition. British union mergers could not change the policies of hostile governments or the minds of employers who decide not to extend union recognition in their new plants. In the United States, mergers could not convince employers to halt and reverse their retreat from collective bargaining or to relax their intense opposition during organizing campaigns. Mergers in New Zealand and Australia may have helped unions survive minimum size requirements and adapt to decentralized negotiations, but they will not return them to the security of the centralized awards systems or multi-employer bargaining.

We should keep in mind, however, that union mergers were never intended to end the hard times. Quite often, mergers were stop-gap measures, ways to forestall membership losses and create the possibility of future organizing and renewed influence. For many of the absorbed and affiliating unions, merger was not selected from an extensive list of options; it was the least costly, quickest alternative to slow decline, eventual disbandment, and the loss of employment for union officers and representation for members. For larger unions, merging meant having a better chance of weathering the hard times, perhaps by gaining enough workers to offset attrition, and maintaining effective, solvent organizations for the days when circumstances improve.

Union mergers have undeniable limitations and can do little to change the broader context that produce them. Merger advocates may have exaggerated the deficiencies of small unions as well as the ability of mergers to rationalize union structure. It is even difficult to reach general conclusions about the impact of mergers on union members. But we must not let this diminish the importance of union mergers. In our national profiles, we saw that mergers create vital new unions, continue representation for members of declining unions, and prepare entire labor movements for radical transformations of labor relations. After our view of mergers from the five countries, there can be no doubt that merging has become synonymous with the evolution of unions; that at the start of the next century, the largest, most powerful, and fastest growing unions will have been created and fortified by union mergers.

APPENDIX 1

Union Mergers in the United States, 1980–1994

1980

International Jewelry Workers Union	*into*	Service Employees International Union
Barbers and Beauticians and Allied Industries International Association	*into*	United Food and Commercial Workers
The American Railway and Airway Supervisors Association	*into*	Brotherhood of Railway, Airline and Steamship Clerks
Granite Cutters International Association	*into*	Tile, Marble and Terrazzo Finishers and Shopmen International Union
Inland Boatmen's Union of the Pacific	*into*	International Longshoremen's and Warehousemen's Union

1981

American Radio Association	*into*	International Organization of Masters, Mates and Pilots
United Retail Workers Union	*into*	United Food and Commercial Workers

1982

United Hatters, Cap and Millinery Workers International Union	*into*	Amalgamated Clothing and Textile Workers Union
International Brotherhood of Pottery and Allied Workers	*into*	Glass Bottle Blowers
Aluminum, Brick and Clay Workers International Union *and* United Glass and Ceramic Workers	*to form*	Aluminum, Brick and Glass Workers International Union

International Production, Service and Sales Union	*into*	Hotel and Restaurant Employees International Union
National Association of Government Employees	*into*	Service Employees International Union

1983

Insurance Workers International Union	*into*	United Food and Commercial Workers
Graphics Arts International Union *and* International Printing and Graphic Communications Union	*to form*	Graphic Communications International Union
Western Railway Supervisors Association	*into*	Brotherhood of Railway, Airline and Steamship Clerks
National Association of Government Inspectors and Quality Assurance Personnel	*into*	American Federation of Government Employees

1984

United Cement, Lime and Gypsum Workers	*into*	International Brotherhood of Boiler Makers

1985

National Industrial Union	*into*	International Brotherhood of Teamsters
Upholsterers International Union	*into*	United Steelworkers of America
Railroad Yardmasters of America	*into*	United Transportation Union

1986

National Association of Planners, Estimators, and Progressmen	*into*	Professional and Technical Engineers
United Telegraph Workers	*into*	Communications Workers of America
Brotherhood of Railway Carmen	*into*	Brotherhood of Railway, Airline and Steamship Clerks

1987

United Furniture Workers of America	*into*	International Union of Electronic, Electrical, Technical, Salaried and Machine Workers
International Typographical Union	*into*	Communications Workers of America
Screen Extras Guild	*into*	International Brotherhood of Teamsters
Professional Flight Attendants *and* American Flight Attendants Association	*to form*	Association of Flight Attendants International

Die Sinkers' Conference	*into*	International Association of Machinists

1988

Glass, Pottery, and Plastics Workers Union *and* International Molders and Allied Workers	*to form*	Glass, Molders, Pottery, Plastics and Allied Workers
Industrial Union of Marine and Shipbuilding Workers of America	*into*	International Association of Machinists
Tile, Marble and Terrazzo Finishers, Shopworkers and Granite Cutters	*into*	United Brotherhood of Carpenters

1989

District 1, Marine Engineers Beneficial Association	*into*	National Maritime Union
National Union of Hospital and Health Care Employees	*into*	Service Employee International Union and American Federation of State, County and Municipal Employees
National Brotherhood of Packinghouse and Industrial Workers	*into*	United Food and Commercial Workers
Insurance Workers of America	*into*	Insurance Workers International Union

1991

Independent Food Handlers and Warehouse Employees	*into*	United Food and Commercial Workers
American Train Dispatchers Association	*into*	Brotherhood of Locomotive Engineers
National Writers Union	*into*	United Automobile Workers
Independent Workers of North America	*into*	United Paperworkers International Union
Pattern Makers' League of North America	*into*	International Association of Machinists

1992

Leather Workers International Union	*into*	Office and Professional Employees International Union
Coopers International Union	*into*	Glass, Molders, Pottery, Plastics and Allied Workers Union
International Association of Sideographers	*into*	International Association of Machinists
National Association of Broadcast Employees and Technicians	*into*	Communications Workers of America
Society of Engineering Office Workers	*into*	United Automobile Workers

1993

International Union of Life Insurance Agents	*into*	United Food and Commercial Workers
Retail, Wholesale and Department Store Union	*into*	United Food and Commercial Workers
Union of Technical and Professional Employees	*into*	United Electrical Workers
National Industrial Workers Union	*into*	United Electrical Workers
Allied Industrial Workers	*into*	United Paperworkers International Union
United Service Workers of America	*into*	Service Employees International Union

1994

International Woodworkers of America	*into*	International Association of Machinists
Association of Western Pulp and Paper Workers	*into*	United Brotherhood of Carpenters
United Garment Workers of America	*into*	United Food and Commercial Workers
Stove, Furniture and Allied Appliance Workers	*into*	Brotherhood of Boilermakers, Iron Ship Builders, Blacksmiths, Forgers and Helpers
International Brotherhood of Firemen and Oilers	*into*	Service Employees International Union

Sources: Adams 1984; Williamson 1995.
Note: The list does not include mergers involving local, regional, single-plant, and single-company unions.

APPENDIX 2

Union Mergers in
Canada, 1980–1993

1980

Canadian Allied Manufacturers Wholesale and Retail Union	*into*	United Food and Commercial Workers Union
Canadian Chemical Workers Union *and* Oil, Chemical and Atomic Workers Union[a] *and* several Quebec-based independent chemical-union locals directly chartered by Quebec Federation of Labour	*to form*	Energy and Chemical Workers Union
International Jewelry Workers Union	*into*	Service Employees International Union

1982

Institution Employees Union	*into*	Manitoba Government Employees Association
National Union of Independent Gas Workers	*into*	Energy and Chemical Workers Union
United Hatters, Cap and Millinery Workers	*into*	Amalgamated Clothing and Textile Workers Union

1983

Graphic Arts International Union *and* International Printing and Graphic Communications Union	*to form*	Graphic Communications International Union

1984

International Union of Electrical,	*to form*	Communications, Electronic, Elec-

Radio and Machine Workers[a] *and* Communications Workers of Canada

United Cement, Lime, Gypsum and Allied Workers	*into*	trical, Technical and Salaried Workers of Canada International Brotherhood of Boilermakers, Iron Ship Builders, Blacksmiths, Forgers and Helpers
Canadian Union of Restaurant and Related Employees	*into*	Hotel and Restaurant Employees and Bartenders International Union

1985

Canadian Union of Industrial Employees	*into*	International Brotherhood of Teamsters
Quebec Federation of Professionals in Educational Services *and* Union of Professionals of the Quebec School System	*to form*	Federation of Quebec School Commissions Professional Employees' Union

1986

Canadian Air Line Employees Association	*into*	Canadian Auto Workers
Health Sciences Association of British Columbia	*into*	National Union of Provincial Government Employees
National Council of Canadian Labour	*into*	Canadian Brotherhood of Railway, Transport and General Workers
Upholsterers International Union of North America	*into*	United Steelworkers of America
Canadian Air Line Flight Attendants	*into*	Canadian Union of Public Employees
Canadian Union of United Brewery, Flour, Cereal, Soft Drink and Distillery Workers	*into*	United Food and Commercial Workers Union
New Brunswick Association of Professional Public Employees	*into*	Professional Institute of the Public Service of Canada

1988

Glass, Pottery and Plastics Workers *and* International Molders and Allied Workers Union	*to form*	Glass, Molders, Pottery, Plastics and Allied Workers
International Air Line Employees Association	*into*	Transportation Communication International Union
Food and Service Workers of Canada	*into*	Canadian Association of Industrial, Mechanical and Allied Workers
Federation of United Nurses *and* Federation of Quebec Professional Unions of Nurses *and* Federation of Quebec Nurses	*to form*	Quebec Federation of Nurses
Canadian Association of Passenger	*into*	Canadian Auto Workers

Agents		
Organization of Professional Engineers Employed by the Province of Manitoba	*into*	Professional Institute of the Public Service
Quebec Union of Health Professionals and Technicians	*into*	Centrale des enseignement du Québec
Fishermen, Food and Allied Workers	*into*	Canadian Auto Workers
Great Lakes Fishermen and Allied Workers Union	*into*	Canadian Auto Workers
Letter Carriers Union of Canada	*into*	Canadian Union of Postal Workers

1990

Canadian Seafood and Allied Workers Union	*into*	Canadian Auto Workers
Canadian Signal and Communications Union	*into*	International Brotherhood of Electrical Workers
Quebec Liquor Board Employees Union	*into*	Canadian Union of Public Employees
Ontario Catholic Occasional Teachers Association	*into*	Ontario English Catholic Teachers Association
Telephone Employees Union	*into*	Atlantic Communication and Technical Workers Union

1991

Federation of Provincial School Authority Teachers	*into*	Ontario Secondary School Teachers Federation
United Telegraph Workers	*into*	Communications Workers of America
Air Crew Association of Canada	*into*	Canadian Air Line Pilots Association
Brotherhood of Railway Carmen of Canada	*into*	Canadian Auto Workers

1992

United Electrical, Radio and Machine Workers of Canada	*into*	Canadian Auto Workers
Canadian Association of Industrial, Mechanical and Allied Workers	*into*	Canadian Auto Workers
Canadian Textile and Chemical Union	*into*	Canadian Auto Workers
Pattern Makers' League of North America	*into*	International Association of Machinists and Aerospace Workers
International Leather Goods, Plastics and Novelty Workers Union	*into*	International Brotherhood of Teamsters
United Headwear, Optical and Allied Workers Union of Canada	*into*	International Brotherhood of Teamsters

| Association of University and College Employees | *into* | Canadian Union of Public Employees |
| Canadian Paperworkers Union *and* Communications and Electrical Workers *and* Energy and Chemical Workers Union | *to form* | Communications, Energy and Paperworkers Union of Canada |

1993

Federation of University Professors and Lecturers	*into*	Quebec Federation of University Professors
Alberta Hospital Employees Union	*into*	Canadian Union of Public Employees
Retail, Wholesale and Department Store Union[a]	*into*	United Steelworkers of America

Source: Kumar and Coates 1991; Labour Canada various years.
Note: The list excludes single-plant, single-company, and municipal employee associations.
[a] Canadian section of international union.

APPENDIX 3

Union Mergers in Great Britain, 1980–1993

1980

Yorkshire Society of Textile Craftsmen	*into*	National Union of Dyers, Bleachers and Textile Workers
Huddersfield and District Healders and Twisters Trade and Friendly Society	*into*	National Union of Dyers, Bleachers and Textile Workers
National Union of Social Workers	*into*	British Union of Social Workers
Telephone Contract Officers Association	*into*	Association of Scientific, Technical and Managerial Staffs
Australia and New Zealand Banking Group Ltd London Staff Association	*into*	Association of Scientific, Technical and Managerial Staffs
Britannic Assurance Chief Office Staff Association	*into*	Association of Scientific, Technical and Managerial Staffs
United Kingdom Association of Professional Engineers	*into*	Electrical, Electronic, Telecommunication and Plumbing Union
Telecommunications Staff Association	*into*	Electrical, Electronic, Telecommunication and Plumbing Union
Steel Industry Management Association	*into*	Electrical, Electronic, Telecommunication and Plumbing Union
National Woolsorters Society	*into*	Association of Professional, Executive, Clerical and Computer Staff [APEX]
Nottingham and District Dyers and Bleachers Association	*into*	National Union of Hosiery and Knitwear Workers
Amalgamated Textile Workers Union—Oldham AWA Division	*into*	Oldham Provincial Union of Textile and Allied Workers

Barclays Group Staff Association *and* Lloyds Bank Group Staff Association *and* National Westminster Staff Association	*to form*	Clearing Bank Union

1981

The Accrington, Church and Oswaldtwistle Weavers', Winders' and Warper's, etc., Association	*into*	Northern Textile and Allied Workers' Union
National Union of Gold, Silver and Allied Trades	*into*	Amalgamated Union of Engineering Workers—Technical, Administrative and Supervisory Section
Hawker Siddeley Power Engineering Limited Engineers Association	*into*	Engineers' and Managers' Association
Eagle Star Staff Association	*into*	The Banking, Insurance and Finance Union

1982

National Union of Dyers, Bleachers and Textile Workers	*into*	Transport and General Workers Union
National Union of Insurance Workers—Royal Liver and Composite Section	*into*	The Banking, Insurance and Finance Union
National Union of Agricultural and Allied Workers	*into*	Transport and General Workers Union
National Amalgamated Stevedores and Dockers	*into*	Transport and General Workers Union
British Transport Officers Guild	*into*	Electrical, Electronic, Telecommunication and Plumbing Union
Amalgamated Society of Journeymen Felt Hatters and Allied Workers of Great Britain	*into*	National Union of Tailors and Garment Workers
Amalgamated Felt Hat Trimmers, Wool Formers and Allied Workers Association	*into*	National Union of Tailors and Garment Workers
Association of Government Supervisors and Radio Officers	*into*	Institution of Professional Civil Servants
National Graphical Association *and* Society of Lithographic Artists, Designers, Engravers and Process-Workers	*to form*	National Graphical Association
National Society of Operative Printers, Graphical and Media Personnel	*into*	Society of Graphical and Allied Trades
Bolton and District Union of Textile and Allied Workers *and* Bolton and District Power Loom Weavers,	*to form*	North West Lancashire, Durham and Cumbria Textile Workers Union

Winders, Warpers, Loom Sweepers
and Ancillary Workers Association
and North Lancashire and Cumbria
Textile Workers Association *and*
Amalgamated Textile Trades
Union—Wigan Chorley and Skelm-
ersdale District

National Union of General and Municipal Workers *and* Amalgamated Society of Boilermakers, Shipwrights, Blacksmiths and Structural Workers	*to form*	General, Municipal, Boilermakers and Allied Trades Union

1983

The British Fire Service Federation	*into*	National Association of Fire Officers
Youth Hostels Association Staff Association	*into*	Association of Scientific, Technical and Managerial Staffs
The British Roll Turners Trade Society	*into*	Amalgamated Union of Engineering Workers—Engineering Section
The National Association of Executives, Managers and Staffs	*into*	National Association of Theatrical, Television and Kine Employees
The National Society of Brushmakers and General Workers	*into*	Furniture, Timber and Allied Trades Union
The Scottish Lace and Textile Workers Union	*into*	General, Municipal, Boilermakers and Allied Trades Union
Association of Management and Professional Staffs	*into*	Electrical, Electronic, Telecommunication and Plumbing Union
National Union of Sheet Metal Workers, Coppersmiths and Heating and Domestic Engineers	*into*	Amalgamated Union of Engineering Workers—Technical Administrative and Supervisory Section
The Burnley Building Society Staff Association *and* Provincial Building Society Staff Association	*to form*	National and Provincial Building Society Staff Association

1984

National Union of Textile and Allied Workers—Rochdale Districts	*into*	Amalgamated Textile Workers Union—Central Lancashire and Calderdale
Rolls-Royce Management Association	*into*	Electrical, Electronic, Telecommunication and Plumbing Union
Cosesa	*into*	Association of Scientific, Technical and Managerial Staffs
Chelsea Building Society Staff Association	*into*	Banking, Insurance and Finance Union
Coventry Building Society Staff Association	*into*	Banking, Insurance and Finance Union

Northern Textile and Allied Workers Union	*into*	Transport and General Workers Union
Burnley, Nelson, Rossendale and District Textile Workers Union	*into*	Transport and General Workers Union
Sheffield Sawmakers Protection Society	*into*	Transport and General Workers Union
Association for Adult and Continuing Education	*into*	National Association of Teachers in Further and Higher Education
Bolton and District Power Loom Overlookers Association	*into*	United Association of Power Loom Overlookers
Amalgamated Union of Engineering Workers—Foundry Section	*into*	Amalgamated Union of Engineering Workers—Engineering Foundry and Construction Section
Amalgamated Union of Engineering Workers—Constructional Section	*into*	Amalgamated Union of Engineering Workers—Engineering Foundry and Construction Section
Association of Patternmakers and Allied Craftsmen	*into*	Amalgamated Union of Engineering Workers—Technical Administrative and Supervisory Section
National Union of Insurance Workers—Prudential Section	*into*	National Union of Insurance Workers
National Union of Insurance Workers—Royal London Section	*into*	National Union of Insurance Workers
Liverpool Victoria Section of the National Union of Insurance Workers	*into*	National Union of Insurance Workers
Association of Broadcasting and Allied Staffs *and* National Association of Theatrical, Television and Kine Employees	*to form*	Entertainment Trades Alliance
Cadbury Limited Representatives Association *and* Cadbury Typhoo Representatives Association *and* Schweppes Limited Representatives Association *and* Jayes Representatives Association	*to form*	Cadbury Schweppes Representative Association

1985

National Union of Mineworkers—Nottingham Area *and* National Union of Mineworkers—South Derbyshire Area *and* Colliery Trades and Allied Workers Association	*to form*	Union of Democratic Mineworkers
National Union of Blast-Furnacemen, Ore Miners, Coke Workers and Kindred Trades	*into*	Iron and Steel Trades Confederation

Clerical and Secretarial Staffs Association of the University of Liverpool	*into*	Association of Scientific, Technical and Managerial Staffs
Bank of New Zealand London Staff Association	*into*	Association of Scientific, Technical and Managerial Staffs
Squibb UK Staff Association	*into*	Association of Professional, Executive, Clerical and Computer Staff
Radio and Electronic Officers Union	*into*	Merchant Navy and Airline Officers Association
Mercantile Marine Service Association	*into*	Merchant Navy and Airline Officers Association
Association of Lecturers in Scottish Central Institutions	*into*	Educational Institute of Scotland
Royal College of Nurses Staff Association	*into*	Association of Professional, Executive, Clerical and Computer Staff
Grindlays Staff Association	*into*	Association of Scientific, Technical and Managerial Staffs
National Society of Metal Mechanics	*into*	Amalgamated Union of Engineering Workers—Technical Administrative and Supervisory Section

1986

Association of Official Architects	*into*	Federation of Managerial and Professional Officers Unions
Association of Education Officers	*into*	Federation of Managerial and Professional Officers Unions
Association of Local Authority Chief Architects	*into*	Federation of Managerial and Professional Officers Unions
Association of Local Government Lawyers	*into*	Federation of Managerial and Professional Officers Unions
Association of Local Government Personnel Officers	*into*	Federation of Managerial and Professional Officers Unions
Association of Local Government Supplies Officers	*into*	Federation of Managerial and Professional Officers Unions
Association of Passenger Transport Executives and Managers	*into*	Federation of Managerial and Professional Officers Unions
Association of Planning Officers	*into*	Federation of Managerial and Professional Officers Unions
Association of Public Service Professional Engineers	*into*	Federation of Managerial and Professional Officers Unions
Guild of Directors of Social Services	*into*	Federation of Managerial and Professional Officers Unions
Guild of Local Authority Valuers and Estate Surveyors	*into*	Federation of Managerial and Professional Officers Unions
Guild of Water Service Senior Officers	*into*	Federation of Managerial and Professional Officers Unions

National Association of Chief Environmental Health Officers	*into*	Federation of Managerial and Professional Officers Unions
National Association of Chief Housing Officers	*into*	Federation of Managerial and Professional Officers Unions
National Union of Chief Leisure Officers	*into*	Federation of Managerial and Professional Officers Unions
National Union of Local Authority Secretaries	*into*	Federation of Managerial and Professional Officers Unions
Society of Chief Trading Standards Officers	*into*	Federation of Managerial and Professional Officers Unions
Society of Metropolitan and County Chief Librarians	*into*	Federation of Managerial and Professional Officers Unions
Society of Public Analysts and Other Official Analysts	*into*	Federation of Managerial and Professional Officers Unions
Sun Alliance and London Staff Association	*into*	Association of Scientific, Technical and Managerial Staffs
Amalgamated Textile Warehouse Operatives—Bolton & District Branch	*into*	General, Municipal, Boilermakers and Allied Trades Union
Amalgamated Textile Warehouse Operatives (Hyde & District Branch)	*into*	General, Municipal, Boilermakers and Allied Trades Union
Amalgamated Textile Workers Union	*into*	General, Municipal, Boilermakers and Allied Trades Union
Amalgamated Textile Workers Union (Central Lancashire and Calderdale)	*into*	General, Municipal, Boilermakers and Allied Trades Union
Amalgamated Textile Workers Union (Southern Area)	*into*	General, Municipal, Boilermakers and Allied Trades Union
Amalgamated Textile Workers Union—Staff Section	*into*	General, Municipal, Boilermakers and Allied Trades Union
Blackburn and District Weavers, Winders and Warpers Association	*into*	General, Municipal, Boilermakers and Allied Trades Union
Colne and Craven Textile Workers Association	*into*	General, Municipal, Boilermakers and Allied Trades Union
North West Lancashire, Durham and Cumbria Textile Workers Union	*into*	General, Municipal, Boilermakers and Allied Trades Union
Oldham Provincial Union of Textile and Allied Workers	*into*	General, Municipal, Boilermakers and Allied Trades Union
Cotton, Rayon and Allied Fibres Tape Sizers Association	*into*	Nelson and District Association of Preparatory Workers
Tobacco Workers Union	*into*	Amalgamated Union of Engineering Workers—Technical Administrative and Supervisory Section

1987

Thames Water Staff Association	*into*	National and Local Government Officers Association

Bank of England Staff Organization	*into*	Banking Insurance and Finance Union
Amalgamated Union of Asphalt Workers	*into*	Transport and General Workers Union
National Tile, Faience and Mosaic Fixers Society	*into*	Transport and General Workers Union
Society of Civil and Public Servants *and* Civil Service Union	*to form*	National Union of Civil and Public Servants

1988

Amalgamated Union of Engineering Workers—Technical Administrative and Supervisory Section *and* Association of Scientific, Technical and Managerial Staffs	*to form*	Manufacturing, Science and Finance Union
Alliance Building Society Staff Association *and* Leicester Building Society Staff Association	*to form*	Alliance and Leicester Building Society Staff Association
United Friendly Assistant Managers Association	*into*	United Friendly Divisional and District Managers
Association of Lecturers in Colleges of Education in Scotland	*into*	Educational Institute of Scotland
United Friendly Field Management Association	*into*	Manufacturing, Science and Finance Union
Imperial Supervisors Association	*into*	Manufacturing, Science and Finance Union
Greater London Staff Association	*into*	General, Municipal, Boilermakers and Allied Trades Union
Preston and Districts Powerloom Overlookers Association	*into*	Blackburn and District Amalgamated Powerloom Overlookers Association
Church of England Children's Society Staff Association	*into*	Manufacturing, Science and Finance Union
Association of Her Majesty's Inspectors of Taxes	*into*	Association of First Division Civil Servants
Gateway Building Society Staff Association	*into*	Woolwich Independent Staff Association

1989

General, Municipal, Boilermakers and Allied Trades Union *and* Association of Professional, Executive, Clerical and Computer Staff	*to form*	General, Municipal, Boilermakers [GMB]
Imperial Group Staff Association	*into*	Manufacturing, Science and Finance Union
Association of Scottish Local Government Directors of Personnel	*into*	Federated Union of Management and Professional Officers

Northern Rock Building Society Staff Association	*into*	Banking Insurance and Finance Union
Association of British Professional Divers	*into*	Electrical, Electronic, Telecommunication and Plumbing Union
Ministry of Defence Staff Association	*into*	Electrical, Electronic, Telecommunication and Plumbing Union
Springfield Foremans Association	*into*	Electrical, Electronic, Telecommunication and Plumbing Union
Nelson and District Power Loom Overlookers Society	*into*	Electrical, Electronic, Telecommunication and Plumbing Union
Greater London Senior Staff Guild	*into*	Federated Union of Management and Professional Officers
National Association of Senior Probation Officers	*into*	Electrical, Electronic, Telecommunication and Plumbing Union

1990

Nationwide Building Society Staff Association *and* Anglia Building Society Staff Association	*to form*	Nationwide Anglia Building Society Staff Association
National Union of Railwaymen and National Union of Seamen	*to form*	National Union of Rail, Maritime and Transport Workers
National Union of Hosiery and Knitwear Workers *and* National Union of the Footwear Leather and Allied Trades	*to form*	National Union of Knitwear, Footwear and Apparel Trades
Nationally Integrated Caring Employees	*into*	Electrical, Electronic, Telecommunication and Plumbing Union
National Union of Labour Organizers	*into*	GMB
Law Society Legal Aid Staff Association	*into*	GMB
North of England Building Society Staff Association	*into*	Banking, Insurance and Finance Union
Health Visitors Association	*into*	Manufacturing, Science and Finance Union
National Association of Fire Officers	*into*	Electrical, Electronic, Telecommunication and Plumbing Union
Prison Service Union	*into*	Electrical, Electronic, Telecommunication and Plumbing Union
Association of Agricultural Education Staffs	*into*	National Association of Teachers in Further and Higher Education
National Unilever Managers Association	*into*	Institution of Professionals Managers and Specialists
Institute of Journalists (Trade Union)	*into*	Electrical, Electronic, Telecommunication and Plumbing Union

Television and Film Production Employees Association	*into*	Electrical, Electronic, Telecommunication and Plumbing Union
Haslingden and District Power-Loom Overlookers Society	*into*	Electrical, Electronic, Telecommunication and Plumbing Union
National Association of Power-Loom Overlookers	*into*	Electrical, Electronic, Telecommunication and Plumbing Union

1991

Association of Cinematograph, Television and Allied Technicians *and* Broadcasting and Entertainment Trades Alliance	*to form*	Broadcasting Entertainment and Cinematograph Technicians Union
Society of Graphical and Allied Trades *and* National Graphical Association	*to form*	Graphical, Paper and Media Union
National Association of Collier Overmen, Deputies and Shotfirers (Staffordshire Area)	*into*	National Association of Colliery Overmen, Deputies and Shotfirers Midland Area
National Union of Tailors and Garment Workers	*into*	GMB
PMB Staff Association	*into*	Institution of Professionals, Managers and Specialists
Wire Workers Union	*into*	Iron and Steel Trades Confederation
Australian Mutual Provident Society Staff Association	*into*	Manufacturing, Science and Finance Union
Colne and District Power Loom Overlookers Association	*into*	Electrical, Electronic, Telecommunication and Plumbing Union

1992

British Cement Staffs Association	*into*	Electrical, Electronic, Telecommunication and Plumbing Union
Association of National Health Service Officers	*into*	National and Local Government Officers
Town and Country Building Society Staff Association	*into*	Woolwich Independent Staff Association
Amalgamated Engineering Union *and* Electrical, Electronic, Telecommunication and Plumbing Union	*to form*	Amalgamated Engineering and Electrical Union

1993

Yorkshire Association of Power Loom Overlookers	*into*	Transport and General Workers Union
Association of Staff of Probation and Bail Hostels	*into*	Amalgamated Engineering and Electrical Union
Association of Preparatory Workers	*into*	Amalgamated Engineering and Electrical Union

A. Monk and Company Staff Association	*into*	Amalgamated Engineering and Electrical Union
National Association of Colliery Overmen, Deputies and Shot-firers—North Western Area	*into*	National Association of Colliery Overmen, Deputies and Shot-firers—Yorkshire Area
Hospital Physicists Association	*into*	Manufacturing, Science and Finance Union
Lancashire Box, Packing Case and General Woodworkers Friendly Relief, Sick, Superannuation, and Burial Society	*into*	Transport and General Workers Union
Furniture, Timber and Allied Trades Union	*into*	GMB
National Union of Scalemakers	*into*	Manufacturing, Science and Finance Union
National and Local Government Officers Association *and* National Union of Public Employees *and* Confederation of Health Service Employees	*to form*	Unison—The Public Service Union

Source: Certification Office for Trade Unions and Employers' Associations various years.

Union Mergers in Australia, 1980–1994

1982

Marine Cooks, Bakers and Butchers' Association	*into*	Seamen's Union of Australia
Federated Moulders' (Metals) Union of Australia	*into*	Amalgamated Metal Workers and Shipwrights Union

1984

Federated Felt Hatting and Allied Trades Employees Association	*into*	Australian Textile Workers Union

1985

Federated Photo Engravers, Photolithographers, and Photogravure Employees	*into*	Printing and Kindred Industries Union

1986

Australian Public Service Artisans Association	*into*	Association of Draughting Supervisory and Technical Employees
Australian Textile Workers Union *and* Australian Boot Trade Employees Federation	*to form*	Amalgamated Footwear and Textile Workers Union of Australia
Motor Transport and Chauffeurs Association	*into*	Transport Workers Union

1987

Victorian Operative Bricklayers Society *and* Victorian Plaster Industry	*to form*	Victorian State Building Trades Union

Workers Union *and* Victorian Plasterers Society

| Australian Telephone and Phonograms Officers' Association *and* Australian Telecommunication Employees Association | *to form* | Australian Telecommunications Employees Association/Australian Telephone and Phonogram Officers' Association |

1988

Federated Marine Stewards and Pantrymen's Association of Australia	*into*	Seamen's Union of Australia
Manufacturing Grocers' Employees Federation of Australia *and* Federated Millers and Mill Employees Association of Australia	*to form*	Federated Millers and Manufacturing Grocers Employees Association of Australasia
Undertakers' Assistants and Cemetery Employees Union	*into*	Australian Workers Union
Federated Storemen and Packers Union of Australia *and* Federated Rubber and Allied Workers Union of Australia	*to form*	National Union of Storeworkers, Packers, Rubber and Allied Workers (National Union of Workers)

1989

Royal Australian Nursing Federation *and* New South Wales Nurses Association	*to form*	Australian Nursing Federation
Administrative and Clerical Officers Association *and* Australian Public Service Association *and* ABC Staff Union	*to form*	Australian Public Sector and Broadcasting Union
Australian Universities Industrial Association *and* Australian Advanced Education Industrial Association	*to form*	Australian Universities Industrial Association
Australasian Coal and Shale Employees Federation *and* Federated Mining Mechanics Association	*to form*	United Mineworkers Federation of Australia
Professional Officers (State Public Services and Instrumentalities) Association	*into*	State Public Services Federation

1990

| Union of Postal Clerks and Telegraphists | *into* | Australian Postal and Telecommunications Union |
| Australian Timber Workers Union *and* Pulp and Paper Workers Federation | *to form* | Australian Timber and Allied Industries Union |

Amalgamated Metal Workers' Union *and* Association of Draughting, Supervisory and Technical Employees	*to form*	Metals and Engineering Workers' Union

1991

Hospital Employees' Federation *and* Health and Research Employees' Association	*to form*	Health Services Union of Australia
Meat Inspectors' Association	*into*	Australian Public Sector, Professional and Broadcasting Union
Association of Professional Engineers *and* Association of Professional Scientists	*to form*	Association of Professional Engineers and Scientists of Australia
National Union of Storeworkers, Packers, Rubber and Allied Workers *and* United Sales Representatives and Commercial Travellers' Guild *and* Commonwealth Foremen's Association	*to form*	National Union of Workers
Mannequins and Model Guild	*into*	Shop, Distributive and Allied Employees Association
Australian Hairdressers, Wigmakers and Hairworkers Employees Federation	*into*	Shop, Distributive and Allied Employees Association
Australian Foremen Stevedores Association	*into*	Waterside Workers Federation
ACT Teachers Federation	*into*	Australian Teachers Union
NT Teachers Federation	*into*	Australian Teachers Union
Professional Divers Association of Australasia	*into*	Seamen's Union of Australia
Repatriation Department Medical Officers Association	*into*	Commonwealth Medical Officers Association
External Plant Officers Association *and* Telecommunication Technical Officers Association	*to form*	Telecommunications Officers Association
Federated Ironworkers' Association of Australia *and* Australasia Society of Engineers	*to form*	Federation of Industrial Manufacturing and Engineering Employees
Australian Insurance Employees Union *and* Australian Bank Employees Union and AMP Society Staff Association *and* Trustee Companies' Officers Association *and* Wool Brokers Staffs Association	*to form*	Finance Sector Union of Australia
Municipal Officers Association *and* Australian Transport Officers Feder-	*to form*	Australian Municipal, Transport, Energy, Water, Ports, Community and

ation *and* Technical Service Guild		Information Services Union (Australian Services Union)
Building Workers Industrial Union [BWIU] *and* Australian Timber and Allied Industries Union [ATAIU]	*to form*	ATAIU and BWIU Amalgamated Union
Federated Ironworkers' Association *and* Australasian Society of Engineers	*to form*	Federation of Industrial, Manufacturing and Engineering Employees
Amalgamated Footwear and Textile Workers' Union *and* Clothing and Allied Trades Union	*to form*	Textile, Clothing and Footwear Union of Australia
Northern Territory Independent Schools Staff Association	*into*	Independent Teachers Federation
Slaters, Tilers and Roofing Industry Union of Victoria	*into*	Victorian State Building Trades Union
Australian Government Lawyers Association	*into*	Professional Officers Association
Australian Postmasters Association	*into*	Australian Postal and Telecommunications Union
Amalgamated Society of Carpenters and Joiners	*into*	Federation of Industrial, Manufacturing and Engineering Employees
Australian Brushworkers' Union	*into*	Federation of Industrial, Manufacturing and Engineering Employees
Australian Rope and Cordage Workers Union	*into*	Federation of Industrial, Manufacturing and Engineering Employees
Australian Commercial and Industrial Artists Association	*into*	Australian Journalists Association
Australian Public Sector and Broadcasting Union, *and* Professional Officers Association	*to form*	Australian Public Sector, Professional and Broadcasting Union
ATAIU and BWIU (Building Workers Union of Australia) Amalgamated Union *and* United Mineworkers Federation	*to form*	Construction, Forestry and Mining Employees Union
Federated Millers and Manufacturing Grocers' Employees Association	*into*	National Union of Workers
Federated Cold Storage and Meat Preserving Employees Union	*into*	National Union of Workers
Victorian Printers Operative Union	*into*	Printing and Kindred Industries Union

1992

Postal Supervisory Officers Association	*into*	Australian Postal and Telecommunications Union

Federated Miscellaneous Workers Union *and* Federated Liquor and Allied Industries Union	*to form*	Australian Liquor, Hospitality and Miscellaneous Workers Union
Australian Postal and Telecommunications Union *and* Australian Telecommunications Employees' Association/Australian Telephone and Phonogram Officers' Association	*to form*	Communication Workers Union of Australia
Actors Equity *and* Australian Journalists Association *and* Australian Theatrical and Amusement Employees Association	*to form*	Media, Entertainment and Arts Alliance
CSIRO [Commonwealth Scientific and Industrial Research Organization] Technical Officers Association *and* CSIRO Technical Association	*to form*	CSIRO Staff Association
Australian Flight Attendants' Association *and* Australian International Cabin Crew Association	*to form*	Flight Attendants Association
Australian Social Welfare Union	*into*	Australian Services Union
Australian Shipping and Travel Officers Association	*into*	Australian Services Union
West Australian Railway Officers Association	*into*	Australian Services Union
Clothing and Allied Trades Federation	*into*	Textile, Clothing and Footwear Union of Australia
Food Preservers Union *and* Confectionery Workers Union	*to form*	Confectionery Workers and Food Preservers Union
University Library Officers Association	*into*	State Public Services Federation
Construction, Forestry and Mining Employees Union *and* Federated Engine Drivers and Firemen's Association *and* Operative Plasterers' and Plaster Workers' Federation	*to form*	Construction, Forestry, Mining and Energy Union
Australian Public Sector, Professional and Broadcasting Union, *and* Professional Radio and Electronics Institute	*to form*	Public Sector, Professional, Technical, Communications, Aviation and Broadcasting Union
Australian Glass Workers Union	*into*	Federation of Industrial, Manufacturing and Engineering Employees
Metal and Engineering Workers Union *and* Vehicle Builders Union	*to form*	Automotive, Metal and Engineering Workers Union
Electrical Trades Union of Australia	*to form*	Electrical, Electronic, Plumbing and

and Plumbers and Gasfitters Employees' Union of Australia | | Allied Workers Union of Australia

Merchant Service Guild of Australia *and* Australian Stevedoring Supervisors Association | *to form* | Australian Maritime Officers Union

Construction Forestry and Mining Employees Union *and* Victorian State Building Trades Union *and* Operative Painters and Decorators Union of Australia *and* Federated Furnishing Trades Society of Australasia | *to form* | Construction, Forestry, Mining and Energy Union

Public Sector, Professional, Technical, Communications, Aviation and Broadcasting Union *and* CSIRO Staff Association | *to form* | Public Sector, Professional, Scientific Research, Technical, Communications, Aviation and Broadcasting Union

Federated Clerks Union of Australia *and* Federated Municipal and Shire Council Employees Union of Australia *and* Australian Municipal, Transport, Energy, Water, Ports, Community and Information Services Union | *to form* | Australian Municipal, Administrative, Clerical and Services Union

1993

Seamen's Union of Australia *and* Waterside Workers' Federation of Australia | *to form* | The Maritime Union of Australia

Telecommunications Officers Association | *into* | Communication Workers Union of Australia

Australian Workers Union [AWU] *and* Federation of Industrial, Manufacturing and Engineering Employees [FIME] | *to form* | AWU-FIME Amalgamated Union

Pastrycooks, Bakers, Biscuitmakers and Allied Trades Union | *into* | Australian Liquor, Hospitality and Miscellaneous Workers Union

Automotive, Metals and Engineering Union *and* Confectionery Workers and Food Preservers Union of Australia | *to form* | Automotive, Food, Metals and Engineering Union

Totalisator Employees' Association of Victoria | *into* | Australian Municipal, Administrative, Clerical and Services Union

Association of Professional Engineers and Scientists, Australia *and* Senior Managers Association (Postal and Communications Commissions) | *to form* | Association of Professional Engineers, Scientists and Managers, Australia *and* Australian Broadcasting Commission Senior Officers' Association

Commonwealth Bank Officers of Australia	*into*	Finance Sector Union of Australia

1994

Public Sector, Professional, Scientific Research, Technical, Communications Aviation and Broadcasting Union *and* State Public Services Federation	*to form*	CPSU, the Community and Public Sector Union
Electrical, Electronic, Plumbing and Allied Workers Union of Australia *and* Communications Workers Union of Australia	*to form*	Communications, Electrical, Electronic, Energy, Information, Postal, Plumbing and Allied Services Union of Australia [known as CEPU]
Ambulance Employees Association of Victoria	*into*	Australian Liquor, Hospitality and Miscellaneous Workers Union
Bakery Employees' and Salesmens' Federation of Australia	*into*	Australian Liquor, Hospitality and Miscellaneous Workers Union
Automotive, Food, Metals and Engineering Union *and* Printing and Kindred Industries Union	*to form*	Automotive, Food, Metals, Engineering, Printing and Kindred Industries Union

Source: Creighton, Ford, and Mitchell 1993; "Meet Australia's Super Unions" 1993; Kerslake 1995.

Note: The list includes mergers in which at least one union is federally registered. Amalgamations were distinguished from absorptions and affiliations on the basis of name changes of registered unions (i.e., names of absorbing unions were not changed).

APPENDIX 5

Union Mergers in New Zealand, 1986–1993[a]

1986

Nelson Liftmen, Cleaners and Caretakers	*into*	Wellington and Taranaki Caretakers, Cleaners and Lift Attendants and Watchmen
Auckland Paint and Varnish Manufacturers Employees *and* Auckland Drug, Chemical and Related Products Factories Employees	*to form*	Auckland Chemical, Paint, Varnish, Drug, Ink Manufacturers and Related Products Factories Employees Union
Gisborne Road Transport & Motor & Horse Drivers and Their Assistants	*into*	Northern Drivers
Canterbury and Westland Stores, Packing and Warehouse	*into*	Southern Distributors and General Workers

1987

Wellington Abattoir Employees	*into*	United Food and Chemical Workers
Otago & Southland Food, Drug & Chemical Manufacturing & Flourmilling Related Trades Employees	*into*	United Food and Chemical Workers
Wellington, Nelson, Canterbury, Otago & Southland Jewellers, Watchmakers & Related Trades	*into*	New Zealand Amalgamated Engineering Union
Otago and Southland Laundry Employees *and* Otago Hotel, Hospital, etc. Union	*to form*	Otago Hotel, etc. and Otago and Southland Laundry IUW [Industrial Union of Workers]
Otago and Southland Oyster Openers and Other Depot Employees	*into*	United Food and Chemical Workers

Greymouth Clerical and Office Staff Employees *and* Canterbury Clerical Workers	*to form*	Canterbury/Westland Clerical Workers Union
Wellington District Rubber Workers	*into*	New Zealand Rubber Workers
Canterbury District Rubber Workers	*into*	New Zealand Rubber Workers
Auckland and Gisborne Amalgamated Society of Shop Employees and Related Trades	*into*	Northern Distribution Workers and Hawkes Bay Province Stores, Packing and Warehouse Workers
New Zealand Shop Employees & Related Trades *and* Wellington Drivers	*to form*	Central Distribution Union
Farm Workers Association	*into*	New Zealand Workers Union
Canterbury and Westland Storeworkers Division of the Distribution and General Workers Union	*into*	New Zealand Amalgamated Engineering Union

1988

Auckland District Boilermakers, Structural Metal Fabricators and Assemblers, Metal Ship and Bridge Builders	*into*	New Zealand Shipwrights, Boatbuilders
Canterbury Boilermakers, Structural Metal Fabricators and Assemblers, Metal Ship and Bridge Builders	*into*	New Zealand Shipwrights, Boatbuilders
United Boilermakers, Iron and Steel Shipbuilders of Otago	*into*	New Zealand Shipwrights, Boatbuilders
Portland Cement Works Employees	*into*	New Zealand Labourers Union
South Island Fire Brigades Employees *and* Northern and Central Region Fire Brigade Unions *and* New Zealand Executive Fire Officers Society	*to form*	New Zealand Professional Firefighters Union
Wellington, Taranaki, Marlborough and Nelson Laundry Workers, Dyers and Dry Cleaners *and* Wellington and Taranaki Clothing and Related Trades Union	*to form*	Central Districts Clothing, Laundry and Allied Industries
Northern Legal Employees *and* Northern Clerical Union	*to form*	Northern Clerical and Legal Employees Administrative and Related Workers Union
Taranaki Legal Employees	*into*	New Zealand Insurance Trust and Life Agents
Canterbury Local Bodies Officers *and* Dunedin Local Bodies Officers	*to form*	Southern Local Government Officers Union
Northern Optical Dispensers and Technicians Association Employees	*into*	Auckland Chemical, Paint, etc. Employees Industrial Union of Workers

Canterbury, Westland, Nelson and Marlborough Clothing and Related Trades *and* Otago and Southland Clothing and Related Trades	*to form*	South Island Clothing and Related Trades Union
Wellington and Taranaki Clothing and Related Trades *and* Central District Clothing, Laundry and Allied IUOW	*to form*	Wellington, Taranaki, Marlborough and Nelson Laundry Workers, Dyers and Drycleaners, IUOW
Wellington, Taranaki, Canterbury, Otago and Southland Cool Stores and Cold Stores Employees	*into*	New Zealand Storeworkers, Packers, and Warehouse Employees
New Zealand Dairy Factory Managers	*into*	APEX [Association of Professional, Executive, Clerical and Computer Staffs]
Auckland Provincial Dairy Chemists	*into*	APEX
New Zealand Commercial Travelers and Sales Representatives	*into*	APEX
Auckland Carriers Wharf Foremen	*into*	APEX
Lyttleton Waterfront Workers *and* Mt. Maunganui and Tauranga Waterside Workers *and* Napier Waterfront Workers *and* Nelson Waterfront Workers *and* New Plymouth Waterfront Workers *and* Onehunga Manakau Waterside Workers *and* Picton Waterfront Workers *and* Port Chalmers Waterfront Workers *and* Timaru Waterfront Workers *and* Whangarei Waterside Workers *and* Wellington Amalgamated	*to form*	New Zealand Waterfront Workers Union
Northern Industrial District Optical Dispensers and Technicians Association	*into*	Auckland Chemical Workers
Northern Industrial District Medical Laboratory Assistants	*into*	Auckland Chemical Workers
South Island Fire Brigades Employees *and* Northern Fire Brigades Employees *and* Central Regions Fire Brigades Employees *and* New Zealand Executive Fire Officers Society	*to form*	New Zealand Professional Firefighters Union

1989

Federated Cooks and Stewards of New Zealand and New Zealand Seamens' Union *and* North Shore Ferry	*to form*	New Zealand Seafarers Union

Employees

Hawkes Bay and Wairarapa Accountants Employees *and* Nelson Public Accounts Employees *and* Wellington Chartered Accountants *and* Christchurch Accountants and Sharebrokers Employees	*to form*	Canterbury Accountants, Sharebrokers and Hawkes Bay, Wairarapa, Wellington and Nelson Accountants Employees Union
Actors Variety and Performing Artists Equity of New Zealand	*into*	New Zealand Performance and Entertainment Union
New Zealand Sales Advertising Representatives Guild	*into*	APEX
Auckland Asbestos, Cement and Cellulose Fibre Cement Products Workers	*into*	New Zealand Engineers Union
Reserve Bank of New Zealand Officers	*into*	FinSec (Financial Sector Union)
New Zealand Tobacco Workers	*into*	New Zealand Workers Union
Northern Butchers, Grocers, Smallgoods and Bacon Factory Employees	*into*	Northern Distribution Union
Northern Chemical Fertiliser Workers	*into*	New Zealand Food Processing Union
Canterbury United Flour Mill Employees	*into*	Canterbury Westland Furniture Union
Auckland Operative Footwear Society *and* Wellington and Taranaki Footwear Operatives *and* Canterbury, Westland, Nelson and Marlborough Footwear Operatives *and* Otago-Southland Footwear Operatives	*to form*	New Zealand Footwear Workers Union
Canterbury Frozen Meat Co.'s Foremen and Board Walkers	*into*	APEX
Wellington, Taranaki, Nelson and Marlborough Federated Furniture and Related Trades *and* Canterbury and Westland Federated Furniture and Related Trades *and* Otago and Southland Federated Furniture and Related Trades	*to form*	New Zealand Furniture and Allied Industries Union
Otago and Southland Gas Works and Related Trades Employees	*into*	New Zealand Labourers
Westland Gold Dredge and Alluvial Gold Mines Employees	*into*	New Zealand Engineering Union
Taranaki Natural Gut Strings Workers	*into*	United Food and Chemical Workers
Marlborough Hotel, Hospital, Res-	*into*	Nelson/Marlborough Distribution

taurant and Related Trade Employees		Workers Union
Wellington, Taranaki, etc. Ice Cream and Related Products	*into*	New Zealand Dairy Workers Union
Auckland, Wellington, etc. Southland Iron and Brass Moulders	*into*	New Zealand Shipwrights, Boatbuilders
Westland Laundry Workers, Dry Cleaners and Depot Hands	*into*	New Zealand Engineering Union
Canterbury Laundry Workers, Dry Cleaners and Depot Hands	*into*	Southern Distribution Union
New Zealand Painters and Decorators, Glaziers and Signwriters	*into*	New Zealand Stonemasons
New Zealand Commercial Pilots and Flight Instructors Association	*into*	New Zealand Airline Pilots Association
Agricultural Pilots Association of New Zealand	*into*	New Zealand Airline Pilots Association
South Island Motion Picture Projectionists	*into*	New Zealand Performance and Entertainment Union
Canterbury and Wellington Dental Assistants	*into*	New Zealand Distribution and General Workers Union
Dunedin City Council and The Dunedin Drainage and Sewerage and Drainage Board Inspectors and Officials	*into*	Southern Local Government Officers Union
Hawkes Bay Road Transport and Motor and Horse Drivers and Their Assistants	*into*	Northern Distribution Workers Union
Blenheim Road Transport and Motor and Horse Drivers and Their Assistants	*into*	Nelson–Marlborough Distribution Union
Nelson Road Transport and Motor and Horse Drivers and Their Assistants	*into*	Nelson–Marlborough Distribution Union
Otago Road Transport and Motor and Horse Drivers and Their Assistants *and* Southland Drivers	*to form*	Southern Drivers Union
Auckland Rope and Twine Workers	*into*	New Zealand Woolen Mills Union
Dunedin Rope and Twine Spinners	*into*	New Zealand Woolen Mills Union
New Zealand (except Northern) Rubber Workers	*into*	New Zealand Workers Union
New Zealand (except Northern, Westland) Saddlers, etc.	*into*	New Zealand Store and Warehouse Employees Union
New Zealand Shipping Officers	*into*	Merchant Service Guild
Blenheim Amalgamated Shop Assistants and Related Trades	*into*	Nelson–Marlborough Distribution Workers Union
Otago and Southland Amalgamated	*into*	Distribution and General Workers

Society of Shop Assistants		Union
Auckland Stage Employees	*into*	New Zealand Performance and Entertainment Union
New Zealand Foreman Stevedores, Timekeepers and Permanent Hands	*into*	Merchant Service Guild
New Zealand Stone Masons	*into*	New Zealand (except Hawkes Bay, Wanganui etc.) Painters and Decorators etc.
Auckland Sugar Works Employees	*into*	Northern Distribution Union
Auckland Sugar Manufacturing Industry Technical and Engineering Staff and Office Employees	*into*	APEX
Ford Motor Co. Supervisors, Salaried Engineers and Other Technical Staff	*into*	APEX
General Motors Co. Motor Vehicle Assembly Plants Supervisors and Foremen	*into*	APEX
Northern Integrated Pulp, Paper, Timber and Forest Product Managers, Supervisors and Executive Officers	*into*	APEX
Northern Theatrical and Places of Amusement and Related Employees	*into*	New Zealand Performance and Entertainment Union
Association of University Teachers *and* Association of University Library Staff	*to form*	Association of University Staff
Reserve Bank Officers	*into*	APEX
Taranaki Natural Gas Processing Union	*into*	APEX
New Zealand Dietetic Association	*into*	APEX
New Zealand Association of X-Ray Workers	*into*	APEX
Society of Hospital Linen Service Workers	*into*	APEX
Forest Industries Staff Union	*into*	APEX
Ice Cream Workers and Related Trades	*into*	New Zealand Dairy Workers Union
North Island Chemical Fertiliser Workers	*into*	United Food and Chemical Workers
Northern Journalists Union *and* New Zealand (except Northern) Journalist and Related Trades Union *and* New Zealand Photo Litho, Art Design and Platemaking Union	*to form*	New Zealand Journalists and Graphic Process
Auckland Saddlers, Collarmakers,	*into*	New Zealand Meat Workers and Re-

etc.

		lated Trades Union
Canterbury Wholesale Oyster Workers IUOW	*into*	New Zealand Meat Workers and Related Trades Union
Association of Clinical Biochemists	*into*	New Zealand Public Services Association
New Zealand Hospital Physicists Association	*into*	New Zealand Public Service Association
New Zealand Orthotics and Prosthetics Association	*into*	New Zealand Public Service Association
New Zealand Society of Biomedical Technology	*into*	New Zealand Public Service Association
Hospitals Scientific Officers Association	*into*	New Zealand Public Service Association
Association of Polytechnic Teachers *and* New Zealand Teachers Colleges Association	*to form*	Association of Staff in Tertiary Education
Auckland District Boilermakers, etc.	*into*	New Zealand Shipwrights, Boatbuilders

1990

NZ Bank Officers *and* NZ Insurance, Trust and Life Agents Union	*to form*	FinSec (Financial Sector Union)
Otago and Southland Cleaners, Caretakers, Liftmen and Watchmens	*into*	Southern Laundry Workers Union
Auckland Society of International Flight Planners	*into*	Electrical Workers Union
Southern Hotel, Hospital, Restaurant & Related Trades Employees	*into*	Otago/Southland Cleaners and Caretakers
Hospital Workers Superintendents Association	*into*	APEX
New Zealand Insurance, Trust and Life Agents	*into*	FinSec (Financial Sector Union)
Auckland and Suburban Local Bodies Labourers and Related Trades	*into*	New Zealand Labourers
Northern Laundries, Dyers and Dry Cleaners Employees	*into*	New Zealand Allied Liquor Trades Union
New Zealand Institute of Medical and Scientific Illustration	*into*	APEX
Central Clerical Workers	*into*	New Zealand Clerical Workers Union
New Zealand Engine Drivers, Firemen, Greasers and Associates	*into*	National Distribution Union
Auckland Dental Assistants and Technicians	*into*	Northern Hotel, Hospital Restaurants and Related Trades Union
Canterbury-Westland Clerical Workers Union	*into*	New Zealand Clerical Workers Union

Otago Clerical, Administrative, Local Authority and Related Workers Union	*into*	New Zealand Clerical Workers Union
NZ Early Childhood Workers Union *and* NZ Free Kindergarten Teachers Union	*to form*	Combined Early Childhood Union of Aotearoa
New Zealand Woollen Mills etc. Union	*into*	New Zealand Dairy Food and Textile Workers
Northern Ship, Yacht and Boat Builders	*into*	Northern Furniture and Allied Industries Union
Canterbury and Westland Stores, Packing and Warehouse	*into*	New Zealand Amalgamating Engineering Union
Northern Woodpulp, Paper Union *and* NZ Timber Union	*to form*	New Zealand Timber & Pulp & Paper
Wellington Tramways Inspectors, Dispatchers and Depot Officers	*into*	Electrical Workers
New Zealand Painters and Decorators, Glazers, Signwriters and Stonemasons Union	*into*	TradeSec (Northern Furniture)
Nelson Timber Workers Union *and* Westland Timber Workers Union	*to form*	New Zealand Timber Workers Union

1991

New Zealand Musicians	*into*	Service Workers Union
New Zealand Stock and Station Agents Clerical Workers	*into*	FinSec (Financial Sector Union)
Taranaki Road Transport and Motor and Horse Drivers and Their Assistants	*into*	New Zealand Labourers Union
New Zealand Locomotive Engineers Association *and* New Zealand Railway Tradesmen's Association *and* Railway Officers Institute	*to form*	Combined Unions of Railway Employees
New Zealand Universities Technicians	*into*	Association of University Staff
New Zealand Workers *and* New Zealand Labourers	*to form*	Amalgamated Workers Union
Society of Technicians, Administrators, Managers and Supervisors	*into*	APEX
South Island Bakers Union	*into*	Food and Textile Workers Union
Northern Hotel, Hospital, Restaurant and Related Trades Employees *and* Wellington Hotel, Hospital, Restaurant and Related Trades Employees *and* Northern Caretakers, Cleaners, Lift Attendants and Watchmens	*to form*	Service Workers Union of Aotearroa

IUOW *and* Canterbury, Marlborough and Westland Cleaners, Caretakers, Lift Attendants and Watchmens IUOW *and* Wellington, Taranaki and Nelson Caretakers, Cleaners and Lift Attendants and Watchmens, IUOW *and* Otago, Southland Service Workers Union *and* New Zealand (except Northern) Otago and Southland Cleaners, Caretakers Union *and* Southland Hotel, Hospital, Restaurant and Related Trades Union *and* Otago Service Workers and Southern Laundry Workers Union	*to form*	Otago Southland Service Workers Union

1992

COMPASS (Commercial, Professional Administrative, Secretarial Staff Union of New Zealand)	*into*	Service Workers Union
Southland Clerical Workers Union (private-sector members)	*into*	Service Workers Union
New Zealand Electrical, Electronics and Related Trades *and* Post Office Union	*to form*	Communication and Energy Workers Unions

1993

New Zealand Nurses Association *and* New Zealand Nurses Union	*to form*	New Zealand Nurses Organization
Central and Invercargill City Local Government Officers	*into*	Public Service Association
Northern Local Government Officers Association	*into*	Public Service Association

Source: Estimate based on "pen portraits" and "obituaries" of unions in Harbridge and Hince 1994.

(a) includes only mergers for which dates are available.

Notes

Chapter 1

1. Undy et al. (1981) proposed another way to categorize unions. "Consolidatory mergers" join unions whose objective is to consolidate a shared position in an industry or occupation. "Defensive mergers" are motivated by attempts to forestall extinction or another adverse eventuality. "Aggressive mergers" occur when the larger merger partner seeks a basis for further expansion and development, sometimes into new territories. This taxonomy, based on motivation, is quite similar to the one used here; consolidatory mergers are usually amalgamations, and absorptions or affiliations are generally seen as defensive by the smaller union and aggressive by the larger one.

2. In the United States, the term "affiliation" has also been used during merger campaigns to promote absorptions that entail low degrees of integration through the creation of industry or craft divisions. For example, the merger agreement for absorption of the Wood, Wire and Metal Lathers into the United Brotherhood of Carpenters and Joiners of America is called the "Agreement of Affiliation" (United Brotherhood of Carpenters and Joiners of America 1979). This title is intended to relieve the anxiety of members of the absorbed union who fear that their union is being taken over.

3. Employer opposition, however, may occur when a local independent union is negotiating a merger with a large, militant national union. McClendon, Kriesky, and Eaton (1995) reported on such a merger attempt. The employer conducted a "vote no" campaign similar to that used to counter a union's organizing drive. The employer's campaign had a significant negative impact on the members' willingness to vote for affiliation. (For a review of the determinants of employee voting behavior in merger elections, see Cornfield 1991.)

Employer opposition to affiliation can also be indirect. In June 1995, the United

Steelworkers of America abandoned an affiliation campaign with the local independent union representing workers at A. K. Steel Holding Corporation in Middleton, Ohio. Workers voted against changing their union's by-laws to allow a majority to approve a merger rather than the present 75 percent. Officers of both the Steelworkers and the local independent union claimed that the employer interfered with the election and bused employees from work to the union hall during working hours to vote against the change in by-laws (Norton 1995).

Chapter 2

1. Membership figures for 1994 are not entirely comparable to those of earlier years because of several changes in the Current Population Survey. They do not, however, differ significantly from those of the preceding year; in 1994 there were 150,000 more union members (mostly in public employment) and aggregate and private sector density fell by 0.3 percent (United States Department of Labor 1995).

2. I should add that unions now often seek to gain bargaining status by demonstrating to employers their majority support through membership cards signed by workers. This avoids the delays, expenses, and protracted employer opposition common to NLRB certification elections. The aggregate number of members gained by recognition through such card counts is unavailable; while it may be important for a few major organizing unions such as the SEIU and UFCW, it has not had a major impact on aggregate union membership (Chaison and Rose 1991b; Bureau of National Affairs 1995b).

3. For a review and evaluation of the causes of union decline in the United States see Chaison and Rose 1991b.

4. See the descriptions of these unions in Finder 1990; Shostak 1991; Grabelsky and Hurd 1994; Rachleff 1994; and Hurd 1995.

5. For a contrary view see McDonald 1992.

6. For details about the merger forming UNITE see Bureau of National Affairs 1995b,i,j; Cooper 1995a,b; Sloane 1995; and Greenhouse 1996b.

7. Despite the revived negotiations, it will still be difficult to reach an agreement because of the complexity of the issues to be resolved in any amalgamation, and the numerous structural and ideological barriers to merger.

There are differences in the unions' general orientations (the AFT is more liberal, the NEA more conservative), federation affiliation (the AFT is in the AFL-CIO, the NEA is not), policies regarding strikes (the AFT is more amenable to striking), and involvement in collective bargaining (many NEA members, but not those in AFT, are represented outside of collective bargaining relationships) (Celis 1993; Lieberman 1993; "Teachers' Unions" 1994; Hodges 1995). "In brief, the N.E.A. is a professional association that gradually became more involved in union activities. The A.F.T. . . . is a union that gradually became more interested in professional development for its members" (Cage 1994, A26).

Moreover, both the NEA and AFT have decentralized structures and the relations between them have varied at the state level. In Minnesota, for example, the state branches of the NEA and AFT are negotiating a merger to form a single 80,000-

member representative of teachers. In New York State, the two unions' branches merged in 1972 but this was dissolved in 1976, primarily in disagreement over antidiscrimination policies. And in New Jersey, the NEA's branch is so strong that officers see little need for a merger (Cage 1994).

If an NEA–AFT amalgamation is eventually agreed to, state branches would each have to believe that they have more to gain than lose. This may be difficult because of the years of bitter rivalry between many of the two unions' locals (Cage 1995).

8. For reviews of affiliation doctrines see Dannin 1981; Hale 1983; Coleman 1986; Kleeman 1986; Service Employees International Union 1990; Bureau of National Affairs 1990a,d; and Schlossberg and Scott 1991. For a discussion of the employer's obligation to negotiate with a union after affiliation, see *United Electrical Radio and Machine Workers* 1993.

9. Since many AFL-CIO affiliates count numerous industries and occupations within their jurisdictions, the community of interest was broadly defined. To have a presumptive community of interest with another union, an affiliate should have at least 20 percent of its members employed in that union's primary industry category, or its members in that industry category should constitute at least 20 percent of the total AFL-CIO membership in that category. A union that cannot meet this requirement would have to demonstrate to the federation that there is nonetheless a sufficient community of interest for the merger to be "rational and appropriate" (AFL-CIO 1983, 33–34).

10. For an analysis of the merger talks between the ITU and the Guild, see L. Walsh 1985. The proposed merger agreement is described in Bureau of National Affairs 1982.

11. Details of the attempted mergers between the ITU and the Teamsters and GCIU are found in Bureau of National Affairs 1983a–d; Apcar 1984a,b; Bureau of National Affairs 1984a–i; "ITU's Leader Appears Defeated in Voting" 1984; "Judge Bars Teamster, ITU Merger until U.S. Rules on Election" 1984; "Labor Letter" 1984; List 1984; "Printers to Pick Union President" 1984; "Talks Advance on Merger of Printers into Teamsters Union" 1984; Bureau of National Affairs 1985a–f; "Graphic Union Board Sets Vote on Merger with ITU" 1985; "ITU Leader Urges Members to Support Merger Accord" 1985; "ITU Rejects Link with Teamsters, Still Seeks Merger" 1985; "Kirkland Lauds ITU Efforts to Repel Teamster Takeover" 1985; List 1985; "Printers Union Rejects a Teamster Merger" 1985; "Printing Trades Unions Draft Plan for Merger" 1985; "Printing Unions Cancel Merger Vote" 1985; Stricharchuk 1985; Tedesco 1985; Chaison 1986; Kopeck 1986; and Stratton 1989.

12. For details on the ITU–CWA merger see Boarman 1986; "CWA–ITU Merger Proposed to Meet Technology Challenge" 1986; "CWA Welcomes Members of ITU" 1986; Eisen 1986; Heritage 1986a,b; "ITU Council Agrees to Merger Plan" 1986; "ITU Delegates Back Merger Plan" 1986; "ITU Will Finally Merge" 1986; McMichen, Austin, and Boarman 1986; McMichen 1986; "Printers to Join with Communications Union" 1986; "ITU Merger into CWA is Finalized" 1987; "ITU Schedules Referendum on Plan to Merge with CWA" 1986; Kopeck 1986; and "Teamsters Score Major Victories Among Former ITU Locals" 1987. The merger agreement is "Agreement for Merger/Affiliation between the International Typographical Union, AFL-CIO, CLC and the Communications Workers of America, AFL-CIO" 1986.

13. The split within the RWDSU is described in "Hospital Division Dispute Re-

solved'' 1984; ''Money and Power Divide a Union'' 1984; and ''The 1199 Fight'' 1984.

14. Details of the merger of the NUHHCE into SEIU and AFSCME are found in ''Health Care Union Explores Merger'' 1987; ''Health Care Union Explores Plan on SEIU Affiliation'' 1988; Abernathy 1989; and Bureau of National Affairs 1988a; Abernathy 1989; and Bureau of National Affairs 1988a, 1989a–e, 1989g–m, 1990b.

15. In 1995, Service Employees Local 8000, the California Interns and Residents Association, voted to merge into the 35,000-member Local 250 representing a variety of health care workers (Bureau of National Affairs 1995m).

Chapter 3

1. For reviews of the reasons that union membership and density in Canada differ from membership and density in the United States, see Kumar 1993; Riddell 1993; Rose and Chaison 1994; Gilson and Wagar 1995; and Lipset 1995.

2. For a review of the impact of free trade on industrial relations see Gunderson and Verma 1994.

3. The Conservative government's threat to cut costs and reduce services by laying-off about one-sixth of Ontario's public workforce was met by demonstrations on February 24 and 25, 1996, in the city of Hamilton. These demonstrations, with over 100,000 participants, were among the largest in Canadian history. Union members were joined by members of church groups and social justice coalitions as well as unemployed persons. After the 2-day demonstration, provincial employees went on a five-week strike which resulted in some concessions from the government. But the government has not withdrawn its plan to lay-off 13,000 workers (Farnsworth 1996; Lakey 1996; Rusk 1996).

4. Descriptions of the autonomy movement within the UFCW and the UFCW–CAW dispute are found in Bagnall 1987; Deverell 1987; ''Fishermen Vote to Abandon International Union'' 1987; Slotnick 1987a–i; ''Union Lifts Trusteeship of B.C. Local'' 1987; Estok 1988; Slotnick 1988b; Sullivan 1991; and Armstrong 1992.

5. For a discussion of the formation of UFCW Local 1252, see Armstrong 1992, 44–47.

6. The prohibitions against raiding and the standards of self-governance are, respectively, sections IV and IX of the CLC Constitution (Canadian Labour Congress 1992b).

7. The evidence needed to determine the status of successor unions after mergers varies among the Canadian jurisdictions. For example, the labor board in Ontario may require proof of membership support of merger, while the Saskatchewan board usually treats mergers as little more than name changes. In most jurisdictions, however, boards inquire as to whether mergers were negotiated and approved in accordance with the relevant sections of participating unions' constitutions. See Carrothers, Palmer and Raynor 1986, 415–418, and Labour Law Casebook Group 1991, 910–911. For an example of the labor-board scrutiny of a union merger, see *Brian Bolt and Airtex Industries Ltd.* 1990.

8. Descriptions of the merger of the postal unions are found in Brunt 1988;

DeMont 1988; "Giant Postal Union" 1988; Slotnick 1988a,c–h; Arnott 1989; "Atlantic Carriers Urged to Resist" 1989; "CUPW Declares LCUC a Rival" 1989; Foley and Heinrich 1989; "LCUC Power Base Losses" 1989; "LCUC 'Power Base' Undermines Negotiations" 1989; Loney 1989; "Merged Postal Workers Union Takes Action" 1989; "Parrot Accuses Union" 1989; Slotnick 1989a,b; "Two Unions at Post Office Arrive at Pact" 1989; "Parrot Calls on CUPW" 1990; Tingley 1990; Papp 1991; Ray 1991. The decision of the Canada Labour Relations Board that consolidated the postal bargaining units is *Canada Post Corporation* 1988. A discussion of the rivalry between the postal unions is found in *Letter Carriers Union of Canada et al.* 1990.

9. For the board's review of CUPW's bargaining status, see *Letter Carriers Union of Canada et al.* 1990.

10. For descriptions of the bargaining unit consolidation in the railroads, see "Rail Labor Leaders" 1989; "Rail Unions Aim for Merger" 1990; "Seven Railway Unions" 1992. The Canada Labour Relations Board's decision combining units is *Canadian National Railway Company et al.* 1992. The order certifying the CAW as the bargaining agent and rescinding the certification of the international unions is *Canada Labour Code et al.* 1994.

11. For a discussion of the bargaining unit consolidation at CBC, see Weinberg 1991 and Moses 1993. The Canada Labour Relations Board's decision combining bargaining units is *Canadian Union of Public Employees et al.* 1993.

12. The concept of union jurisdiction is now largely irrelevant to the selection of organizing targets and the categorization of unions (Chaison 1995). The CLC Task Force on Union Structure recognized this trend in its 1992 report: "The Task Force . . . believes that rigid jurisdictional limits are no longer applicable when it comes to organizing workers still outside the labour movement." Affiliates, however, were encouraged "to organize in the jurisdictions they have historically occupied, where they have acquired the skills and resources needed to provide good standards of servicing" (Canadian Labour Congress 1992a, 9).

13. An additional element of political and economic uncertainty was introduced into Canadian industrial relations in fall 1995 when the possibility of the secession of the province of Quebec was raised. On October 30, voters in Quebec rejected by a margin of only 1 percent (53,000 of the 4.65 million votes cast) a proposal for the province to become sovereign after making a formal offer to Canada for a new economic and political partnership. There was a 94 percent voter turnout. The close outcome is a sign of Quebecois's growing frustration with Canadian federal and provincial governments that had too often refused their demands for greater autonomy to protect their province's culture and use of the French language. In a similar referendum conducted 15 years earlier, 60 percent of those casting ballots voted "no" (Farnsworth 1995a,b; Wren 1995).

Obviously, the conclusion to a chapter, much less a footnote, is not the appropriate place to review why Quebec's concerns have not been met and the impact of the resurgent sovereigntists' movement on Canadian society. With respect to the issues of industrial relations and union mergers, we are left to speculate about the aftermath of the referendum.

Presently, it is unclear what arrangements will be needed to address Quebec's concerns or, for that matter, the probable economic ties between a sovereign Quebec and the remainder of Canada. Negotiations are expected to continue for years; after the recent inconclusive vote, there will be neither a sudden and complete break nor a return to the status quo. The impact on union mergers depends on the changes in union membership and structure.

We might ask, for example, if there will be great uncertainty in world financial markets because of the close referendum, the possibility of a repeat referendum, or a breakdown in negotiations over constitutional changes recognizing Quebec's special status as a "distinct society"? Could this uncertainty lead to declining foreign investment, higher employment, union membership losses, and an increased motivation for unions to merge? If Canadian national unions continue to represent their members in a sovereign Quebec, will they then become international unions and face the same challenges and pressures for sectional autonomy as do the U.S.-based international unions? Will this create new pressures and opportunities for mergers? The answers to these questions must wait until the future relationship between Canada and Quebec becomes clearer. Of course, such questions become irrelevant if, as some antiseparatists argue, Quebec independence means the eventual disintegration of Canada with some provinces seeking an attachment to neighboring American regions (e.g., the Atlantic Provinces and New England) and the more populous, wealthier ones (e.g., Ontario) going it alone.

Chapter 4

1. The recorded figures may actually underestimate the fall in membership and density in the 1980s. Blanchflower and Freeman 1992 suggest that many unions exaggerate their membership to maintain high representation on the Trades Union Congress's Executive Committee and the Labour Party.

2. See Corcoran 1995 and Bird 1995 for discussions of the differences in the membership data collected by the certification officer and the Labor Force Survey.

3. For discussions of the determinants of union growth and decline in Britain see Towers 1989; Kelly 1990; Dibden and Millward 1991; Metcalf 1991; F. Green 1992; Mason and Bain 1993; Andrews and Maylor 1994; Waddington and Whitston 1994; Beaumont and Harris 1995; and Disney, Gosling and Machin 1995. Most studies find that compositional changes (i.e., changes in the labor force or product markets) play only a minor role in the decline in union membership and density. Far more important are labor laws, economic factors, and rising employer opposition at nonunion facilities.

4. For reviews of derecognition trends and causes see Claydon 1989; Swabe 1990; Storey and Sisson 1993; Gall and McKay 1994; "Union Derecognition and Personal Contracts" 1994; and Geroski, Gregg, and Desjonqueres 1995.

5. Decentralization did not increase strike frequency, which probably indicates the unions' concern about the possibility of job losses. In 1994, the number of major strikes was the lowest since records began in 1891 and about one-tenth the figure during the heavy strike activity near the end of the 1970s (Bird and Davies 1995).

6. For the rationale behind the Conservative's industrial relations reforms, see the Green Paper submitted as the proposal for the Trade Union Reform and Employment

Rights Act (*Industrial Relations in the 1990s* 1991). Also see Marsh's 1992 discussion of the evolution of this perspective.

7. For discussions of this legislation see Brown and Wadhwani 1990; Kelly 1990; Hunter 1991; Martin 1992; Edwards et al. 1992; Evans, Ewing and Nolan 1992; Smith and Morton 1992; Simpson 1993; and "United Kingdom" 1993. A review of the ideological foundations of the legislative attacks on unions is provided by Miller and Steele 1993.

It is noteworthy that although laws directed at undermining union power provide opportunities for employers to take legal actions against unions, not many have done so (Hyman 1994). (Martin 1992, 165) has commented on the apparent hesitancy to seek legal remedies: "Employers recognize that they will have to coexist with unions in perhaps very different political and economic circumstances in the future; unsuccessful attempts to undermine union power are counter-productive."

8. The merger procedures are specified in the Trade Union Reform and Employment Rights Act of 1993, the Trade Union and Labour Relations (Consolidation) Act of 1992, and the Trade Unions and Employers' Associations (Amalgamations, etc.) Regulations of 1975. An instructional booklet describing merger procedures was prepared for union officers (Certification Office for Trade Unions and Employers Associations 1994). The 1993 amendments require that merger approval be carried out through postal ballots with full independent scrutiny. They also prohibited union officers from inserting notices recommending the merger or expressing an opinion about it in the written notification of merger sent to the members.

A brief case study illustrating the role of the certification office and the procedure for transfers of engagements is found in "The Road to Recognition" (1994). In this merger of the North of England Building Society into the Banking, Insurance and Finance Union, the employer refused to continue recognition, created a rival union, and granted recognition to the merged union only after it won in an employee vote between the two. In Britain, employer recognition is voluntary and the merger procedures do not carry an obligation to continue a bargaining relationship.

9. Among those who may be excluded from the balloting are retired members, members in arrears, student or trainee members, and others whose interests may be remote from the normal representative functions of the union, its finances and policy making, and its activities in general ("Retired Members Not Entitled" 1991). Approval by more than a simple majority may be required if this is specified by the union's rules (Certification Office for Trade Unions and Employers' Association 1994).

10. For example, a member of the National and Local Government Officers Association complained that he had not received ballot papers for his union's amalgamation into Unison in 1993. The certification officer conducted a hearing and dismissed the complaint, finding that the union had given every member a fair opportunity to vote. The union's arrangements included free phone help lines, the late issuance of ballots for new union members or to replace lost ballots, and a reminder from officers asking members to cast ballots before the close of voting ("Unison Ballot Complaint Fails" 1993).

11. For descriptions of British labor laws' impact on merger form and frequency, see Simpson 1972; Elias 1973; and Buchanan 1981.

12. Although the government has officially maintained a neutral position regarding mergers, the prohibition of officers' endorsements with merger ballots could be construed as a slight move toward greater regulation. It is highly unlikely, however, that the present or next government, Conservative or Labour, would oppose specific mergers. Conservatives have expressed some concerns, though, about the size and power of unions created by mergers if they restrict the choices available to workers who may want to join or switch unions. In a committee debate over the Employment Bill, Conservative member of Parliament Spencer Batiste observed that mergers were continuing apace and this is "thoroughly desirable" (House of Commons 1990, 444). Although he did not oppose the move toward larger unions, he was concerned about their relative power:

> At present, the merger process is not unhealthy and it is desirable that it should continue. However, there will be a time when union members must ask themselves how many different unions can be allowed if healthy competition and choice of membership is to continue. If it is concluded that the whole of the union movement is dominated by two or three single mammoth unions on the one hand, and that a large multiplicity of fragmented small unions is breaking away on the other, hard decisions may be necessary. . . . It is easier to consider directing and controlling mergers in terms of the public interest at a time when it is not controversial than when it is. . . At some point, if not now, we shall have to apply a public interest criterion assessment to the continued uncontrolled merger of trade unions. (House of Commons 1990, 444)

The committee members discussed possible upper limits on the size of unions created by merger but recognized that it was treading on new ground and making arbitrary judgements about union size in terms of the public interest and representational effectiveness. It was concluded that "the philosophy of Department of Employment [is] that mergers are a good thing" (House of Commons 1990, 448), but that someday the public interest in union mergers might have to be reexamined.

13. Autonomy is not usually complete. Waddington and Whitston 1994 found that sectional representation commonly entails autonomy in bargaining, but the larger union usually controls financial matters.

14. An alternative to merger for some smaller unions might be alliances or federations. In September 1994, two regional finance unions, a national finance union and the finance section of MSF, joined to form the Finance Sector Unions. This federation is built on the principle of sharing resources but maintaining autonomy ("Finance Sector Unions" 1994). Other alliances are possible among small, highly specialized unions if the benefits of alliance appear to be greater than those of absorption into national unions which allow the same or a greater degree of autonomy.

15. Because amalgamations create new unions, the AEU had to reapply for affiliation with the TUC as the AEEU.

16. Discussions of super-unions are found in "British Unions Divided" 1989; "Divide and Rule" 1992; Wheal 1992; "Where Are the Super-Unions?" 1992; and Willman and Cave 1994. For an early discussion of the potential impact of super-unions on the TUC and structural reform, see Turner 1964.

17. The Unison Rule Book states in section 3.1.4 that each service group is autonomous in such areas as determining general policy, negotiating pay and conditions of work, participating in joint negotiating committees and settling bargaining disputes (Unison 1993).

18. For example, see "Unions Rush to Merge" 1989; "Unions: Merger Mania" 1996; and "Trade Unions: Big Brothers" 1993.

Chapter 5

1. For reviews of the reasons for union growth and decline, see Deery and DeCieri 1989; Peetz 1990; Frenkel 1993; Kenyon and Lewis 1993; Wooden and Balchin 1993; and Cooper and Walton 1996.

2. For discussions of the Accords, see Dabscheck 1989; Kyloh 1989; Niland and Spooner 1991; and Davis and Lansbury 1993.

3. In 1994, Australian states passed legislation to bring themselves in line with the Industrial Relations Reform Act. To varying degrees, enterprise bargaining and enterprise agreements were encouraged and facilitated. The state laws are reviewed in Reitano 1995.

4. For the description of an important instance when workers chose the nonunion stream—an enterprise-flexibility agreement—see Kelly 1995, 136–37. The introduction of a nonunion stream of representation has been used by some employers to displace unions, but the extent of this practice is presently unknown (Cooper and Walton 1996).

5. The government initially proposed a 20,000-member threshold but withdrew it after unions and employers objected (Hamilton 1991; Parliamentary Research Service 1993).

6. The legislation also provides for the creation of federations as first steps toward merger. Unions contemplating merger within three years may form federations and combine resources and coordinate activities while maintaining their separate identities. Federations cannot be parties to awards. This alternative is used to ease the transition to merger by providing "a useful balance between useful implementation of an amalgamation and the uncertainty of a loose collective which does not enjoy formal recognition" (Andrades 1991, 604).

7. The ACTU claimed that restructuring was "not necessarily designed to establish single-union coverage in every industry or workplace. The process is clearly designed to build a stronger more effective trade union movement in Australia" ("Union Rationalisation" 1990, 22). This would be achieved through the combination of mergers, transfers of members, the creation of bargaining committees at the enterprise or industry level, and the greater unionization of the workforce ("Union Rationalisation" 1992).

Chapter 6

1. Reviews of the labor legislation passed between 1894 and 1987 are found in Hince 1993 and Boxall 1990.

2. For a brief review of the relations between the labor movement and the Labour Party prior to the passage of the Labour Relations Act, see Haworth 1993.

3. This "inflexibility thesis," the premise that there are widespread labor market rigidities, is refuted by Harbridge and Rea 1992.

4. For a discussion of the evolution, philosophy, provisions, and early impact of the Employment Contracts Act, see Hince and Vranken 1991; Harbridge and Hince 1992a; McAndrew 1992; Harbridge 1993b; Harbridge and Moulder 1993; Walsh and Ryan 1993; and Grills 1994.

5. For a case study of the transition from coverage under an industry award to employment contracts at a manufacturing facility, see Lord 1994. See Uren 1993 for a general discussion of the introduction of the employment contract system.

There is some anecdotal evidence that employers have presented workers with non-negotiable individual contracts and have told workers that they could either sign or resign (Oxenbridge 1996).

6. The Employment Contracts Act, however, does constrain freedom of contract. For example, the act requires personal-grievance procedures in all employment contracts, not just those collectively negotiated. These cover unjust dismissal, discrimination, sexual harassment, and the use of duress. Particularly significant is the imposition of a "just dismissal rule" as a starting point for all employment contracts (Cowen 1993).

7. For descriptions of recent economic restructuring and recovery in New Zealand see Barber 1993; Dickson 1993; Field 1993; James 1994; "New Zealand" 1994; A. Smith 1994; and Statistics New Zealand 1994, 1995.

8. For a case study of the organizing efforts of the National Distribution Union and the Service Workers Union after the passage of the Employment Contracts Act, see Oxenbridge 1996.

9. The Amalgamated Engineers has a merger policy under which an absorbed or affiliating union is offered one of three options: (a) forming a semi-autonomous division; (b) having its own officers for two or three years before being fully integrated into the Engineers; or (c) selecting an "umbrella" arrangement under which a smaller union, but one with over 1,000 members, could receive help with services and policy development in return for an agency fee (Amalgamated Engineering Union 1987).

10. Unions could be granted provisional registration if they did not meet the minimum size requirement but were likely to within two years. A union formed by a merger, however, could not receive provisional registration (*The New Zealand System* 1989).

The unions protested the minimum-size threshold to the International Labour Organization but the New Zealand government ignored the subsequent recommendation that it be rescinded, quite a different outcome than the reversal in Australia, discussed in chapter 5.

11. Harbridge and Hince (1993b) found that in 1992, 57 percent of the New Zealand unions belonged to the NZCTU (down from 65 percent the preceding year) and these unions accounted for 80 percent of total union membership (down from 87 percent). Although some unions left because they could no longer afford the per capita fees, a more important reason was dissatisfaction with the federation's policies and leadership. In May 1992, delegates representing 14 unions with 35,000 members in

blue-collar occupations formed a new federation—the New Zealand Trade Union Federation. Most were previously members of the Federation of Labour and had not joined the NZCTU when it was formed in 1987 by merger of the New Zealand Federation of Labour, composed of private-sector unions, and the Combined State Unions, composed of public-sector unions.

The NZCTU was critical of the Employment Contracts Act as well as the government's general economic policies. It proposed that legislation be replaced by a national minimum code of rights and protections for workers, enforceable rights to organize and bargain, tripartite decision-making over key economic issues, and multi-employer bargaining to deal with issues of training, technological change, and industrial policy (New Zealand Council of Trade Unions 1992b).

12. The legislation also provided for contestability of union coverage under which one union could challenge the coverage of another and win its members. This requires the balloting of the members of the acquiring union and the members of the union that is being taken over. For example, see Amalgamated Engineering Union 1987, 60.

13. For example, Harbridge and Honeybone (1995) reported that only about half of the employees covered by collective agreements during the 1994/1995 bargaining round were under agreements that automatically extended their terms to new employees.

14. For example, legislation proposed by the Labour Party in 1993 would simplify the union registration procedure and require that registered unions have at least 20 members (Clark 1993).

Chapter 7

1. For a review of the state of the research on union mergers, see Chaison 1986, 1992.

2. There have been numerous union affiliations in the United States. For example, since 1980, there were more affiliations involving the Service Employees than there were other forms of mergers among all national unions (57 affiliations vs. 48 national-union mergers).

3. The case for and against small unions is reviewed in Chaison 1995. For an analysis of the impressions of small unions' officers regarding the value of mergers, see Chaison 1985.

4. It should be recalled from the discussion of merger trends in Britain, Australia, and New Zealand, that the strongest, most encompassing union merger laws are built on the foundations of union registration. When merger is not approved in a prescribed manner, usually a supervised, secret ballot of the membership, merged unions can be denied registration and full participation in the industrial relations system. But attempts to force unions to merge by threatening the loss of registration can be an infringement on workers' freedom of association, which was how the International Labour Organization viewed the minimum-size thresholds in Australia and New Zealand.

I think that it would be worthwhile to introduce British-style merger legislation in the United States to simplify and expedite union mergers, and to channel opposition to mergers which would avoid costly and disruptive disputes. I understand, however, that if such legislation were enacted in the United States, the resulting system would still lack union registration by a certification officer—the element of compulsion in Britain. During legislative hearings, lawmakers will have to ask: Should there be a certification officer similar to Britain's with the authority to register unions? (This is something quite different from the National Labor Relation Board's certification of bargaining agents.) Can the present union affiliation doctrines and procedures (due process, continuity of bargaining agents) somehow be extended to national union mergers? Can the same legislation deal with mergers of unions of public- (federal, state, and municipal) as well as private-sector employees? Might the best alternative be legislation that imposes minimum standards for merger approval by members, incorporates these standards into union constitutions, and enforces them through the Department of Labor? Finally, if violations of a prescribed merger process can result in the loss of bargaining status, will employers be enticed to challenge mergers and will unions then be discouraged from merging?

References

Abernathy, Roy. 1989. "SEIU Gains 50,000+ Members." *SEIU Local 509 News* 22 (May/June): 12.

"ACTU/TDC Mission to Western Europe." 1987. In Bill Ford and David Plowman, eds., *Australian Unions: An Industrial Relations Perspective,* pp. 288–308. Melbourne: Macmillan.

Adams, Larry T. 1984. "Labor Union Mergers, 1979–84: Adapting to Change." *Monthly Labor Review* 107 (September): 21–27.

Adams, Roy. 1989a. "Industrial Relations Systems: Canada in Comparative Perspective." In John C. Anderson, Morley Gunderson and Allen Ponak, eds., *Union Management Relations in Canada.* 2d ed., pp. 437–64. Toronto: Addison-Wesley.

——. 1989b. "North American Industrial Relations: Divergent Trends in Canada and the United States." *International Labour Review* 128 (April): 47–64.

Advisory Conciliations and Arbitration Service. 1994. *Annual Report, 1993.* London: ACAS.

AFL-CIO. 1985. *The Changing Situation of Workers and Their Unions: Report of the AFL-CIO Committee on the Evolution of Work.* Washington, D.C.: AFL-CIO.

——. 1989. *Report of the AFL-CIO Executive Council.* Washington, D.C.: AFL-CIO.

AFL-CIO Merger Committee. 1981. "Merger Committee Report." Washington, D.C.: AFL-CIO. Mimeo.

——. 1983. "Merger Committee Report." Washington, D.C.: AFL-CIO. Mimeo.

"Agreement for Merger/Affiliation between the International Typographical Union, AFL-CIO, CLC and the Communications Workers of America, AFL-CIO." 1986. *Typographical Journal* (August): 18–24.

Amalgamated Engineering and Electrical Union. 1994. *Annual Report and Accounts, 1993.* London: AEEU.

Amalgamated Engineering Union (New Zealand Amalgamated Engineering and Related Trades Industrial Union of Workers). 1987. *Strategies for Change: Representing Workers in a New Environment.* Wellington, N.Z.: AEU.

Amalgamated Textile Workers Union. 1985. *Eleventh and Final Annual Report of the Amalgamated Textile Workers Union* Rochdale, U.K.: ATWU.

Andrades, Carol. 1991. "Union Amalgamations: Lowering the Hurdles and Raising the Stakes." *Law Institute Journal* 65 July, 602–05.

Andrews, Martyn, and Robin Maylor. 1994. "Declining Union Density in the 1980s: What Do Panel Data Tell Us?" *British Journal of Industrial Relations* 32 (September): 413–31.

Apcar, Leonard M. 1984a. "ITU Agrees to Hold Rerun of Election, Supervised by U.S." *Wall Street Journal,* May 7, 10.

——. 1984b. "Labor Letter." *Wall Street Journal,* April 17, 1.

Armstrong, Enid Carolyn. 1992. "The Legal Relationship Between Parent Unions and Their Locals: A Study of Industrial Unionism in Canada." Unpublished LLM thesis, Montreal: McGill University, Institute for Comparative Law.

Arnott, Sheila. 1989. "Battle of Postal Unions Hanging in the Balance." *Financial Post,* January 13, 4.

Aston, A. B. 1987. "Trade Union Mergers in Britain 1950–1982." Ph.D. diss. London: London School of Economics.

"Atlantic Carriers Urged to Resist Union Merger." 1989. *Calgary Herald,* January 30, C7.

Australian Council of Trade Unions. 1987. *Future Strategies for the Trade Union Movement.* Melbourne: ACTU.

——. 1992. *National Directory and Officials' Manual 1992.* Melbourne: ACTU.

——. 1993. *Union Amalgamations (Federally Registered Unions).* Melbourne: ACTU.

——. 1995. *The Future of Unions in Australia.* Melbourne: ACTU.

Australian Council of Trade Unions and the Trade Development Council. 1987. *Australia Reconstructed.* Canberra, Australia: Australian Government Publishing Service.

Bagnall, James. 1987. "Union Fight May Crack CLC Foundation." *Financial Post,* April 6, 6.

Bailey, Rachel. 1994. "Annual Review Article 1993: British Public Sector Industrial Relations." *British Journal of Industrial Relations* 32 (March): 113–36.

Barber, David. 1993. "Recovery Becomes Political Football." *BRW International* 3 (8): 56–59.

Bassett, Philip. 1993a. "How Long Will Unison Prevail in the Age of the Super-Unions?" *The Times* (London), June 29, 27.

——. 1993b. "Unions Must Find New Strokes to Deliver Employees' Rights." *The Times* (London), September 6, 38.

Beaumont, Phillip B., and Richard I. D. Harris. 1995. "Union De-Recognition and Declining Union Density in Britain." *Industrial and Labor Relations Review* 48 (April): 389–402.

Behrmann, Susan L. 1994. "Union Members in 1993." *Compensation and Working Conditions* 46 (February): 9–14.

Bell, Linda A. 1989. "Union Concessions in the 1980s." *Federal Reserve Bank of New York Quarterly Review* 14 (Summer): 44–48.

Bennett, Laura. 1994. *Making Labour Law in Australia: Industrial Relations, Politics and Law.* Sydney: The Law Book Company.

Bird, Derek. 1995. "Membership of Trade Unions Based on Information from the Certification Officer." *Employment Gazette,* May, 205–9.

Bird, Derek, and Louise Corcoran. 1994. "Trade Union Membership and Density, 1992–93." *Employment Gazette,* June, 189–97.

Bird, Derek, and Jackie Davies. 1995. "Labour Disputes in 1994." *Employment Gazette,* July, 279–89.

Blanchflower, David G., and Richard B. Freeman. 1992. "Unionism in the United States and Other Advanced OECD Countries." *Industrial Relations* 31(Winter, 56–79.

Boarman, Wilham J. 1986. "Some Facts and Figures." *Typographical Journal* 189 (December): 7, 19.

Boxall, Peter. 1990. "Towards the Wagner Framework: Change in New Zealand Industrial Relations." *Journal of Industrial Relations* 32 (December): 523–43.

——. 1993. "Management Strategy and the Employment Contracts Act 1991." In Raymond Harbridge, ed., *Employment Contracts: New Zealand Experiences,* pp. 148–164. Wellington, N.Z.: Victoria University Press.

Boxall, Peter, and John Deeks. 1993. "New Zealand." In Miriam Rothman, Dennis Briscoe, and Raoul C.D. Nacamulli, eds., *Industrial Relations Around the World: Labor Relations for Multi-National Companies,* pp. 297–311. New York: deGruyter.

Boxall, Peter, and Peter Haynes. 1992. "Unions and Non-Union Bargaining Agents Under the Employment Contracts Act 1991: An Assessment After 12 Months." *New Zealand Journal of Industrial Relations* 17 (2): 223–32.

Bray, Mark, and Pat Walsh. 1993. "Unions and Economic Restructuring in Australia and New Zealand." In Mark Bray and Nigel Haworth, eds., *Economic Restructuring and Industrial Relations in Australia and New Zealand: A Comparative Analysis,* pp. 16–37. Sydney: University of Sydney, Australian Centre for Industrial Relations Research and Teaching.

Brereton, Laurie. 1993. "Balanced Initiative on Industrial Reforms." *Telegraph* (New South Wales), December 19, 53.

Brian Bolt and Airtex Industries Ltd. (Engineering Division) et al. 1990. Alberta Labor Relations Board. 8 Canada Labour Relations Board Reports (2nd) 251 (June 7).

"British Unions Divided on Mergers." 1989. *The Worklife Report* 6 (6): 17.

Brooks, George W., and Sara Gamm. 1976. "The Causes and Effects of Union Mergers with Special Reference to Selected Cases in the '60s and '70s." Washington, D.C.: U.S. Department of Labor, Labor-Management Series Administration. Mimeo.

Brown, William, and Sushil Wadhwani. 1990. "The Economic Effects of Industrial Relations Legislation Since 1979." *National Institute Economic Review* (February): 57–69.

Brown, William, and Janet Walsh. 1991. "Pay Determination in Britain in the 1980s; the Anatomy of Decentralization." *Oxford Review of Economic Policy* 7 (Spring): 44–59.

Bruce, Peter G. 1989. "Political Parties and Labor Legislation in Canada and the U.S." *Industrial Relations* 28 (Spring): 115–41.

Brunt, Carol. 1988. "Canada Labour Board: Postal Union Merger." *Our Times,* July, 8–9

Buchanan, R. T. 1974. "Merger Waves in British Unionism." *Industrial Relations Journal* 5 (2): 37–44.

——. 1981. "Mergers in British Trade Unions, 1949–1979." *Industrial Relations Journal* 12 (3): 40–49.

Bureau of International Labor Affairs, United States Department of Labor. 1994. *Foreign Labor Trends: Australia, 1992/1993.* Washington D.C.: U.S. Government Printing Office.

Bureau of Labour Information. 1993. *Collective Bargaining Climate.* Ottawa: Labour Canada.

Bureau of National Affairs. 1982. "Terms for Merger of Newspaper Unions." *Labor Relations Reporter,* September 20, 52–53.

——. 1983a. "Printing Industry Union Officials Meet to Discuss Possible Merger." *Daily Labor Report,* October 26, A5.

——. 1983b. "Printing Unions Planned Merger." *Labor Relations Reporter,* April 11, 287–88.

——. 1983c. "Typographical Union Chief Complains to Kirkland: Urges Teamster Reaffiliation." *Daily Labor Report,* October 12, A10–A11.

——. 1983d. "Typographical Union to Open Merger Talks With Teamsters." *Daily Labor Report,* September 28, A9.

——. 1984a. "Battle Over Proposed Teamster-ITU Merger." *Labor Relations Reporter,* April 16, 313–14.

——. 1984b. "Committee Formed to Battle Proposed ITU–Teamsters Merger." *Daily Labor Report,* April 9, A8–A9.

——. 1984c. "Election of ITU President." *Labor Relations Reporter,* August 6, 271–72.

——. 1984d. "Merger Agreement between International Typographical Union and the International Brotherhood of Teamsters." *Daily Labor Report,* April 11, E1–E4.

——. 1984e. "Protest Over ITU Presidential Election." *Labor Relations Reporter,* August 13, 288–89.

——. 1984f. "Talks Advance Merger of Printers into Teamsters Union." *New York Times,* February 21, A19.

——. 1984g. "Teamsters Merger Plans with ITU Presenting Challenge to AFL-CIO." *Daily Labor Report,* April 11, A7.

——. 1984h. "Typographical Union Officer Election." *Labor Relations Reporter,* September 10, 25.

——. 1984i. "Typographical Union Officer Installation." *Labor Relations Reporter,* September 10, 25–26.

——. 1985a. "CWA's Victory in New York." *Labor Relations Reporter,* June 24, 146–47.

——. 1985b. "Graphic Union Board Rejects Merger with Typographical Union." *Daily Labor Report,* March 15, A14–A15.

——. 1985c. "Merger Terms Worked Out by Leaders of Typographical, Graphic Workers Unions." *Daily Labor Report,* January 10, A10.

——. 1985d. "Single Union in Printing Industry." *Labour Relations Reporter,* October 17, 127.

——. 1985e. "Typographical Union Members Seek Injunction to Block Merger." *Daily Labor Report,* February 6, A11–A13.

——. 1985f. "Typographical Workers Union to Vote March 27 on Merger with Graphic Union." *Daily Labor Report,* January 23, A6–A10.

——. 1988a. "Health Care Workers Announce SEIU Affiliation, Over Health Care Union Presidents' Objections." *Daily Labor Report,* November 18, A10–A11.

——. 1988b. "Marine and Shipbuilding Workers Vote to Merge with Machinists." *Daily Labor Report,* October 19, A12–A13.

——. 1989a. "Court Fight Over Union Merger Jeopardizes Major Organizing Drive." *Daily Labor Report,* February 13, A1–A2.

——. 1989b. "Health Care Union Tentatively Agrees to Hold Referendum on Merger Issues." *Daily Labor Report,* February 23, A9–A10.

——. 1989c. "Hospital Union Affiliations." *What's New in Collective Bargaining Contracts and Negotiations* (June 15): 3.

——. 1989d. "Hospital Workers Bitter Merger Suit Hinges on Disputed Membership Figures." *Daily Labor Report,* January 27, A7–A8.

——. 1989e. "Hospital Workers' President Says Merger With SEIU Would Reduce Him to 'Figurehead.' " *Daily Labor Report,* February 15, A1–A2.

——. 1989f. "Independent Packinghouse Unions Votes to Affiliate with UFCW." *Daily Labor Report,* July 24, A5–A6.

——. 1989g. "Judge Blocks NUHHCE Meeting on Merger with SEIU or AFSCME." *Daily Labor Report,* January 31, A3–A4.

——. 1989h. "Judge Prevents Hospital Union Board from Taking Further Actions on Merger." *Daily Labor Report,* January 5, A6–A7.

——. 1989i. "Judge Postpones Ruling in Court Fight Over NUHHCE Affiliation with AFSCME or SEIU." *Daily Labor Report,* January 9, A4–A5.

——. 1989j. "Majority of Hospital Unions' Members Vote to Affiliate With SEIU." *Daily Labor Report,* May 31, A8–A9.

——. 1989k. "NUHHCE Secretary-Treasurer Defends Merger Agreement with SEIU." *Daily Labor Report,* February 22, A3–A4.

——. 1989l. "President of Hospital Workers Says SEIU Is Trying to 'Steal' His Union." *Daily Labor Report,* January 28, A3–A4.

——. 1989m. "Settlement of Affiliation Dispute Could Permanently Split Hospital Union." *Daily Labor Report,* March 1, A14–A15.

——. 1990a. "Court Affirms Union Voting Procedure, Does Not Invalidate Merger with UFCW." *Daily Labor Report,* March 12, A9–A11.

——. 1990b. "Delegates Vote to Dissolve SEIU Portion of National Hospital Union March 31." *Daily Labor Report,* December 4, A9.

——. 1990c. "Interns and Residents in California Are Chartered as SEIU Local 8000." *Labor Relations Week,* October 10, 934–35.

——. 1990d. "Supreme Court Declines to Review Employer's Challenge to Union Merger." *Daily Labor Report,* October 10, A1–A2.

——. 1992. "Independent Health Care Union Merges with Operating Engineers." *Daily Labor Report,* July 20, A6–A7.

——. 1993a. "AFL-CIO Statistics on Paid Membership of Union Affiliates from AFL-CIO Executive Council Report to 20th Constitutional Convention." *Daily Labor Report,* September 29, D1–D3.

——. 1993b. "Canadian Members to Hold Referendum to Determine Whether to Continue with Union." *Daily Labor Report,* July 27, A3–A4.

——. 1993c. "RWDSU Canadian Locals Reject Merger Plan with UFCW, Opt for Steelworkers Instead." *Daily Labor Report,* July 14, A5–A6.

——. 1993d. "RWDSU, UFCW Reach Tentative Agreement to Merge Unions Effective Oct. 1, 1993." *Daily Labor Report,* April 13, A6–A7.

——. 1993e. "Unionization: Climate Said Right for Union Organizing But Labor May Not Capitalize on It." *Employee Relations Weekly,* March 15, 283–84.

——. 1994a. "Boston Globe Editorial Workers Vote to Join Newspaper Guild." *Daily Labor Report,* March 14, A3–A4.

——. 1994b. "Independent Paperworkers to Vote An Affiliation with Carpenters Union." *Daily Labor Report,* April 1, A8–A9.

——. 1994c. "Newspaper Local Leaders in Toronto Recommend Canadian Union to Join." *Daily Labor Report,* September 30, A9–A10.

——. 1994d. "Proposed Woodworkers, Machinists Merger Sparks Conflict with Carpenters' Affiliate." *Daily Labor Report,* January 6, A2–A4.

——. 1994e. "Western Pulp and Paper Workers Approve Affiliation with Carpenters Union." *Daily Labor Report,* May 10, A3.

——. 1995a. "Academic Observers See Obstacles Ahead for Three-Way Union Merger." *Employee Relations Weekly,* August 7, 861.

——. 1995b. "ACTWU, ILGWU Plan to Merge into New Union Called UNITE." *Daily Labor Report,* February 22, AA3–AA4.

——. 1995c. "AFL-CIO to Move Forward on Creation of Multi-Million Dollar Organizing Fund." *Daily Labor Report,* August 3, A8–A10.

——. 1995d. "Agreement Regarding Merger of UAW, USW and IAM." *Daily Labor Report,* July 28, E1.

——. 1995e. "Auto, Steel and Machinists Unions Announce Accord to Merge by 2000." *Daily Labor Report,* July 28, AA1–AA2.

——. 1995f. "Collective Bargaining Briefs." *Employee Relations Weekly,* July 24, 794.

——. 1995g. "Federation Election Seen as Signal for Broader Change in Labor Movement." *Daily Labor Report,* September 5, C1–C3.

——. 1995h. "Grass Roots Majority at National Education Association Convention Approves Resuming Merger Talks with American Federation of Teachers." *Government Employee Relations Report,* July 17, 924.

——. 1995i. "ILGWU Merger with ACTWU to Form Fourth Largest Manufacturing Union." *Employee Relations Weekly,* July 24, 794.

——. 1995j. "ILGWU to Merge with ACTWU: Form Fourth Largest Manufacturing Union." *Daily Labor Report,* June 28, A1.

——. 1995k. "NEA, AFT End Merger Discussions, Vow to Find New Ways to Cooperate." *Government Employee Relations Report,* January 2, 18.

——. 1995l. "Rubber Workers Convention Approves Merger Pact with United Steelworkers." *Daily Labor Report,* July 5, AA1–AA2.

——. 1995m. "Special Report: Labor Outlook in 1995." *Daily Labor Report,* January 30, S1–S60.

——. 1995n. "Steelworkers Begin Organizing Program with Blitz at 20 Companies in St. Paul." *Daily Labor Report,* March 24, A13–A14.

Byrne, Michael. 1993. "Union Mergers Seen Strengthening Movement." *AFL-CIO News,* August 23, 8.

Cage, Mary Crystal. 1994. "Teachers' Unions See Strength in Mergers." *The Chronicle of Higher Education,* November 16, A25–A26.

——. 1995. "A Merger Misfires." *The Chronicle of Higher Education,* February 17, A17.

Cameron, R. J. 1980. *Labour Statistics 1980: Australia.* Canberra, Australia: Australian Bureau of Statistics.

Canada Bureau of Labour Information. 1995. *Directory of Labour Organizations in Canada, 1994–1995.* Ottawa: Supply and Services Canada.

Canada Labour Code et al. 1994. Canada Labour Relations Board Order 53-1850 (June 29).

Canada Post Corporation and Canadian Union of Postal Workers et al. 1988. Canada Labour Relations Board Decision No. 675 (February 10).

Canadian Labour Congress. 1992a. *Building the Congress of Tomorrow: Report of the Task Force on the Role and Structure of the CLC.* Ottawa: Canadian Labour Congress.

——. 1992b. *Constitution.* Ottawa: Canadian Labour Congress.

Canadian National Railway Company et al. 1992. Canada Labour Relations Board Decision No. 945 (July 10).

Canadian Union of Public Employees et al. 1993. Canada Labour Relations Board Decision No. 1007 (May 3).

Carrothers, A. W. R., E. E. Palmer, and W. B. Raynor. 1986. *Collective Bargaining Law in Canada.* 2nd ed. Toronto: Butterworths.

Castle, Robert, and Nigel Haworth. 1993. "The Economic Imperative for Restructuring in Australia and New Zealand." In Mark Bray and Nigel Haworth, eds., *Economic Restructuring and Industrial Relations in Australia and New Zealand: A Comparative Analysis,* pp. 16–37. Sydney, Australia: University of Sydney, Australian Centre for Industrial Relations Research.

Celis, William, III. 1993. "Teacher Unions, Though Far Apart, Discuss a Merger." *New York Times,* June 23, B7.

Certification Office for Trade Unions and Employers' Associations. Various years. *Annual Report of the Certification Officer.* London: Certification Office.

——. 1994. *Mergers: A Guide to Statutory Requirements or Transfers of Engagements and Amalgamations of Trade Unions.* London: Certification Office.

Chaison, Gary N. 1973. "Federation Expulsions and Union Mergers in the United States." *Relations Industrielles-Industrial Relations* 28 (2): 343–61.

——. 1978. "Criticism and Comment: Union Mergers and Industrial Environment." *Industrial Relations* 17 (February): 119–23.

——. 1979. "Union Mergers and International Unionism in Canada." *Relations Industrielles-Industrial Relations* 34 (4): 768–77.

——. 1980. "A Note on Union Merger Trends, 1900–1978." *Industrial and Labor Relations Review* 34 (October): 114–20.

——. 1981a. "Union Growth and Union Mergers." *Industrial Relations* 20 (Winter): 98–108.

——. 1981b. "Union Mergers, Union Fragmentation and International Unions in Canada." Paper presented at the seventeenth annual meeting of the Canada Industrial Relations Association, Montreal. Mimeo.

——. 1982a. "A Note on the Critical Dimensions of the Union Merger Process." *Relations Industrielles-Industrial Relations* 37 (1): 198–206.

——. 1982b. "Union Mergers and the Integration of Union Governing Structures." *Journal of Labor Research* 3 (Spring): 139–52.

——. 1985. "Union Merger Outcomes: The View from the Smaller Unions." Working Paper No. 85–103, Clark University Graduate School of Management, Worcester, Mass.

——. 1986. *When Unions Merge.* Lexington, Mass: Lexington Books.

——. 1992. "Union Mergers in the United States: Recent Trends and Questions for Research." Paper presented at Symposium on Emerging Union Structures: An International Comparison. Clark University, Worcester, Mass. Mimeo.

——. 1995. "Reforming and Rationalizing Union Structure: New Directions and Unanswered Questions." Keynote address prepared for the Second International Conference on Emerging Union Structures. Stockholm.

Chaison, Gary N., and Dileep G. Dhavale. 1990. "A Note on the Severity of the Decline in Union Organizing." *Industrial and Labor Relations Review* 43 (April): 366–73.

——. 1991. "The Changing Scope of Union Organizing." *Journal of Labor Research* 11 (Summer): 307–22.

Chaison, Gary N., and Joseph B. Rose. 1989. "Unions: Growth, Structure and Internal Dynamics." In John C. Anderson, Morley Gunderson and Allen Ponak, eds., *Union-Management Relations in Canada*, 2d ed., pp. 125–54. Toronto: Addison-Wesley.

——. 1991a. "Continental Divide: The Direction and Fate of North American Unions." In Donna Sockell, David Lewin and David B. Lipsky, eds., *Advances in Industrial and Labor Relations*, pp. 169–205. Greenwich, Conn.: JAI Press.

——. 1991b. "Macro-Determinants of Union Growth and Decline." In George Strauss, Daniel Gallagher and Jack Fiorito, eds., *The State of the Unions*, pp. 3–45. Madison, Wis.: Industrial Relations Research Association.

——. 1993. "The Canadian Perspective of Workers' Rights to Form a Union and Bargain Collectively." Paper presented that the AFL-CIO/Cornell University Conference on Labor Law Reform, October 24 Baltimore, Md.

"Changes to the Industrial Relations Act, 1988." 1991. *The Employers Review* 63 (February 15): 1–2.

Chaykowski, Richard P., and Anil Verma. 1992a. "Adjustments and Restructuring in Canadian Industrial Relations: Challenges to the Traditional System." In Richard P. Chaykowski and Anil Verma, eds., *Industrial Relations in Canadian Industry*, pp. 1–38. Toronto: Dryden.

——. 1992b. "Canadian Industrial Relations in Transition." In Richard P. Chaykowski and Anil Verma, eds., *Industrial Relations in Canadian Industry,* pp. 448–49. Toronto: Dryden.

"Check-off Renewals." 1994. *European Industrial Relations Review* 251 (December): 11.

Chitayat, Gideon. 1979. *Trade Union Mergers and Labor Conglomerates.* New York: Praeger.

Clark, Helen. 1993. "Employment Relations—The New Direction Under Labour." *New Zealand Journal of Industrial Relations* 18 (2): 153–62.

Clarke, Oliver, and John Niland. 1991. "Can Industrial Relations Change? An International Perspective." In Oliver Clarke and John Niland, eds., *Agenda for Change: An International Analysis of Industrial Relations in Transition,* pp. 1–18. London: Allen and Unwin.

Claydon, Tim. 1989. "Union Derecognition in Britain in the 1980s." *British Journal of Industrial Relations* 27 (July): 214–24.

Cohen, Phil. 1994. "Stately Union." *Nursing Times,* March 2, 43.

COHSE-NALGO-NUPE [Confederation of Health Service Employees-National and Local Government Officers Association-National Union of Public Employees]. 1991. *A Framework for a New Union: Report of the COHSE, NALGO and NUPE National Executives to the 1991 Annual Conferences.* London: COHSE, NALGO, NUPE.

———. 1992. *The Final Report of the COHSE, NALGO and NUPE National Executives to the 1992 Annual Conferences.* London: COHSE, NALGO, NUPE.

Coleman, Jerome P. 1986. "Problems Arising from Union Changes in Affiliation." In Richard Edelman, ed., *Proceedings of the New York University Thirty-ninth Annual National Conference on Labor,* pp. 7.1–7.16. New York: Bender.

Colley, Peter. 1996. "National Elections in Australia See Landslide Win to Conservatives." E-mail message, March 6.

Communications, Energy and Paperworkers Union of Canada. 1992a. *Final Merger Report.* Ottawa: CEP.

———. 1992b. *Proceeding of the Founding Convention,* Montreal, November 27–28. Ottawa: CEP.

———. 1992c. *A Profile of Three Great Unions.* Ottawa: CEP.

Conant, John L. 1984. "The Economics of Labor Union Mergers." Ph.D. diss., Knoxville: University of Tennessee.

———. 1993. "The Role of Managerial Discretion in Union Mergers." *Journal of Economic Behavior and Organization* 20 (January): 49–62.

Conant, John L., and David L. Kaserman. 1989. "Union Merger Incentives and Pecuniary Externalities." *Journal of Labor Research* 9 (Summer): 243–53.

Cooper, Muriel H. 1995a. "Needle Trades Unions UNITE for Common Good." *AFL-CIO News,* July 13, 7.

———. 1995b. "The Time to UNITE." *AFL-CIO News,* July 19, 6–7.

Cooper, Rae and Chris Walton. 1996. "Organizing and Recruitment in Australia: The Response of Unions to the 'Membership Crisis.' " Paper presented at the AFL-CIO/ Cornell University Research Conference on Organizing. Washington, D.C. Mimeo.

Corcoran, Louise. 1995. "Trade Union Membership and Recognition: 1994 Labour Force Survey Data." *Employment Gazette,* May, 191–203.

Cornfield, Daniel B. 1991. "The Attitude of Employee Association Members Toward Union Mergers: The Effect of Socioeconomic Status." *Industrial and Labor Relations Review* 44 (January): 334–48.

Cowen, Penelope J. 1993. "Labor Relations Reform in New Zealand: The Employment Contracts Act and Contractual Freedom." *Journal of Labor Research* 14 (Winter): 69–83.

Crawley, Mike. 1994. "Small Unions Vanish as Mega-Unions Provide Safety in Numbers." *Vancouver Sun,* March 7, D9.

Creighton, W. B., W. J. Ford, and R. J. Mitchell. 1993. *Labour Law: Text and Materials,* 2d ed. Sydney: The Law Book Company.

Crocombe, Graham T., Michael J. Enright, and Michael E. Porter. 1991. *Upgrading New Zealand's Competitive Advantage.* Auckland, N.Z.: Oxford University Press.

"CUPW Declares LCUC a Rival Organization." 1989. *CUPW Perspective* 18 (September): 1, 4.

"CWA–ITU Merger Proposed to Meet Technology Challenge." 1986. *AFL-CIO News,* July 12, 5.

"CWA Welcomes Members of ITU." 1986. *CWA News,* December, 6, 8.

Dabscheck, Braham. 1989. *Australian Industrial Relations in the 1980s.* Melbourne: Oxford University Press.

——. 1993. "Regulation Down Under: The Case of Australian Industrial Relations." *Journal of Economic Issues* 28 (March): 41–68.

Dannin, Ellen Jean. 1981. "Union Mergers and Affiliations: Discontinuing the Continuity of Representation Test." *Labor Law Journal* 32 (March): 170–79.

Davis, Edward M. 1988. "The 1987 ACTU Congress: Reconstructing Australia?" *Journal of Industrial Relations* 30 (March): 118–29.

——. 1990. "The 1989 ACTU Congress: Seeking Change Within." *Journal of Industrial Relations* 32 (March): 100–110.

——. 1992. "The 1991 ACTU Congress: Together for Tomorrow." *Journal of Industrial Relations* 34 (March): 87–101.

Davis, Edward M., and Russell D. Lansbury. 1993. "Industrial Relations in Australia." In Greg J. Bamber and Russell D. Lansbury, eds., *International and Comparative Industrial Relations,* pp. 100–125. London: Routledge.

Dawes, Colin Jonathan. 1987. *The Relative Decline of International Unionism in Canada Since 1970.* Kingston, Ont.: Queen's University Industrial Relations Centre.

"A Decade of Radical Change in Industrial Relations." 1993. *European Industrial Relations Review* 229 (February): 21–25.

DeCenzo, David D. 1981. "Union Merger Negotiations." Ph.D. diss. Morgantown: University of West Virginia.

Deeks, John. 1990. "New Tracks, Old Maps: Continuity and Change in New Zealand Labor Relations, 1984–1990." *New Zealand Journal of Industrial Relations* 15 (August): 99–116.

Deery, Stephen. 1983. "Trade Union Amalgamations and Government Policy in Australia." *Australian Bulletin of Labour* 9 (June): 190–207.

——. 1989. "Union Aims and Methods." In Bill Ford and David Plowman, eds., *Australian Unions: An Industrial Relations Perspective,* pp. 74–103. Melbourne: Macmillan.

Deery, Stephen, and Helen DeCieri. 1989. "Determinants of Trade Union Membership in Australia." Working Paper No. 50, Center for Industrial Relations and Labour Studies, University of Melbourne, Parkville, Vic.

DeMont, John. 1988. "Postal Unions Pledge a Peaceful Merger." *Financial Post,* February 23, 6.

Deverell, John. 1987. "Bob White Stands Ground as Labour War Looms." *Toronto Star,* March 29, A14.

Dewey, Lucretia M. 1971. "Union Merger Pace Quickens." *Monthly Labor Review* 94 (June): 63–70.

Dibden, Jennifer, and Neil Millward. 1991. "Trade Union Membership: Developments and Projects." *Policy Studies* 12 (Winter): 4–19.

Dickson, Ian. 1993. "New Zealand: From Chumps to Champs." *Euromoney,* January, 85.

Disney, Richard, Amanda Gosling, and Stephen Machin. 1995. "British Unions in Decline: Determinants of the 1980s Fall in Union Recognition." *Industrial and Labor Relations Review* 48 (April): 403–19.

"Divide and Rule." 1992. *The Times* (London), March 5, 15.

Donaldson, Lisa. 1992. "Women Can Find a Powerful Voice through Britain's Biggest Union." *The Times* (London), March 4, 1.

Donoughue, Bernard, Alan Oakley, and Janet Alker. 1963. "Structure and Organization of British Trade Unions." *Political and Economic Planning* 29: 433–84.

Douglas, Ken. 1993. "Organizing Workers: The Effects of the Act on the Council of Trade Unions and its Membership." In Raymond Harbridge, ed., *Employment Contracts: New Zealand Experiences,* pp. 197–209. Wellington, N.Z.: Victoria University Press.

Druker, Janet. 1988. "Unions in the 90s—Fewer But Fitter?" *Personnel Management* 20 (August): 24–29.

"A Dying Craft." 1986. *New York Times,* November 27, A26.

Eaton, Jonathan. 1995. "Canadian Auto Workers Chose Different Path Ten Years Ago." *Labor Notes* 200 (November): 7.

Edwards, Paul. 1995. "From Industrial Relations to the Employment Relationship: The Development of Research in Britain." *Relations Industrielles-Industrial Relations* 50 (1): 39–65.

Edwards, Paul, et al. 1992. "Great Britain: Still Muddling Through." In Anthony Ferner and Richard Hyman, eds., *Industrial Relations in the New Europe,* pp. 1–67. Oxford: Blackwell.

Edwards, Richard, and Michael Podgursky. 1986. "The Unraveling Accord: American Unions in Crisis." In Richard Edwards, Paolo Garonna and Frenz Todtling, eds., *Unions in Crisis and Beyond,* pp. 14–60. Dover, Mass: Auburn House.

Eisen, David J. 1986. "Union Response to Changes in Printing Technology: Another View." *Monthly Labor Review* 109 (May): 37–38.

"Electricians and AEU in Strong Vote to Merge." 1992. *Labour Research* 81 (April): 3.

"The 1199 Fight." 1984. *Labor Today* 22 (January): 1.

Elias, Patrick. 1973. "Trade Union Amalgamations: Patterns and Procedures." *Industrial Law Journal* 2 (September): 125–36.

Enderwick, Peter. 1992. "Workplace Reform and International Competitiveness: The Case of New Zealand." *New Zealand Journal of Industrial Relations* 17 (2): 185–206.

"Enterprise Bargaining: A National Framework for Change." 1992. *Work and People* 14 (June): 2–6.

Estok, David. 1988. "Unions Agree on New Regulations about Raiding in Stormy Session." *The Spectator* (Hamilton, Ont.), May 10, A8.

Evans, Steve, Keith Ewing, and Peter Nolan. 1992. "Industrial Relations and the British Economy in the 1990s: Mrs. Thatcher's Legacy." *Journal of Management Studies* 29 (September): 571–89.

Ewer, Peter, and Charlotte Yates. 1995. "Changing Strategic Capacities: Union Amalgamations in Canada and Australia." Paper presented at the Second International Conference on Emerging Union Structures, June 14, Stockholm.

Farber, Henry S. 1990. "The Decline of Unionization in the United States: What Can Be Learned from Recent Experience?" *Journal of Labor Economics* 8 (January): S75–S105.

Farnsworth, Clyde H. 1995a. "Ottawa Quickly Moves in Effort to Mollify Quebec." *New York Times,* November 2, A3.

———. 1995b. "Quebec, by Razor-Thin Margin, Votes 'No' on Leaving Canada." *New York Times,* October 31, A1.

———. 1995c. "Quebec's Premier Quits After Loss on Independence." *New York Times,* November 11, A1.

———. 1996. "With Layoffs Coming, Ontario Workers Strike Over Security." *New York Times,* March 5, A11.

Feder, Barnaby J. 1995. "To Union Rank and File, a Merger Means Power." *New York Times,* July 28, A14.

Field, Graham. 1993. "Recovery Spreads to the Domestic Sector." *Asiamoney* 15 (April): 107–08.

Final Merger Report. 1992. Ottawa: Merger Committee of the Communications Workers of Canada, Canadian Paperworkers Unions, and the Energy and Chemical Workers Union.

"Finance Sector Unions Move Closer Together." 1994. *European Industrial Relations Review* 250 (November): 13.

Finder, Alan. 1991. "Unions Court Immigrant Areas, and the Unorganized." *New York Times,* September 16, B1.

Fink, Gary M. 1987. "Review of *When Unions Merge* by Gary N. Chaison." *Labor History* 28 (Winter): 114–15.

"Fishermen Vote to Abandon International Union." 1987. *Calgary Herald,* May 5, A3.

Foley, Dennis, and Jeff Heinrich. 1989. "Postal Workers Choose CUPW." *The Citizen* (Ottawa), January 18, A1.

Fortin, Bernard. 1973. "Preliminary Study on Union Mergers." Mimeo.

Franks, Peter. 1994. "The Employment Contracts Act and the Demise of the New Zealand Clerical Workers Union." *New Zealand Journal of History* 28 (October): 194–210.

Fraser, Robert, and Michael Wilson. 1988. *Privatization: The UK Experience and International Trends.* Essex, U.K.: Longman.

Freeman, Richard B. 1992. "Is Declining Unionization of the U.S. Good, Bad, or Irrelevant?" In Lawrence Mischel and Paula B. Voos, eds., *Unions and Economic Competitiveness,* pp. 143–69. Armonk, N.Y.: M.E. Sharpe.

Freeman, Richard B., and Marcus E. Rebick. 1989. "Crumbling Pillar? Declining Union Density in Japan." Working Paper No. 2963, National Bureau of Economic Research, Cambridge, Mass.

Freeman, Richard B., and Joel Rogers. 1993. "Who Speaks for US? Employee Representation in a Nonunion Labor Market." In Bruce E. Kaufman and Morris M. Kleiner, eds., *Employee Representation: Alternative and Future Directions,* pp. 13–79. Madison, Wis: Industrial Relations Research Association.

Frenkel, Stephen. 1993. "Australian Trade Unionism and the New Social Structure of Accumulation." In Stephen Frenkel, ed., *Organized Labor in the Asia-Pacific Region,* pp. 249–305. Ithaca, N.Y.: ILR Press.

Fuller, Carol. 1989. "The Functioning of the Labour Relations Act 1987—Unions." In Raymond Harbridge, ed., *Evaluating the Labour Relations Act 1987: Proceedings of a Seminar Held at Victoria University of Wellington,* pp. 14–21. Wellington, N.Z.: Industrial Relations Centre, Victoria University.

Gall, Gregor. 1993. "What Happened to Single Union Deals?—A Research Note." *Industrial Relations Journal* 24 (March): 71–75.

Gall, Gregor, and Sonia McKay. 1994. "Trade Union Derecognition in Britain, 1988–1994." *British Journal of Industrial Relations* 32 (September): 433–48.

Galt, Virginia. 1992. "Unions Merge for Survival." *Globe and Mail* (Toronto), November 28, A15.

——. 1994. "CAW's Hardline Stand Grates on Rivals." *Globe and Mail* (Toronto), May 16, A4.

Geare, Alan. 1993. "The Proposed Employment Relations Act." *New Zealand Journal of Industrial Relations* 18 (2): 194–204.

General, Municipal, Boilermakers. 1992. *The Best Way Forward For Better Services and a Stronger Union* London: GMB.

——. 1993. "The Future of Trade Unions: GMB Submission to the House of Commons Employment Committee: October 1993." London: GMB. Mimeo.

Geroski, Paul, Paul Gregg, and Thibaut Desjonqueres. 1995. "Did the Retreat of UK Trade Unionism Accelerate During the 1990–1993 Recession?" *British Journal of Industrial Relations* 33 (March): 35–54.

"Giant Postal Union Vows Hard Bargaining." 1988. *Toronto Star,* March 29, A4.

Gibbens, Robert. 1983. "CPU Executive Feels Merger Possible." *The Globe and Mail* (Toronto), January 4, B8.

Gifford, Courtney. 1982. *Directory of U.S. Labor Organizations, 1982–1983.* Washington, D.C.: Bureau of National Affairs.

Gill, Howard, and Vivien Griffin. 1981. "The Fetish of Order: Reform in Australian Union Structure." *Journal of Industrial Relations* 23 (September): 362–82.

Gilpin, Kenneth N. 1995. "Rubber Workers' Union Acts to Merge with Steelworkers." *New York Times,* May 13, 37.

Gilson, Olive H. J., and Terry Wagar. 1995. "The U.S./Canada Convergence Thesis:

Contrary Evidence from Nova Scotia." *Industrial Relations-Relations Industrielles* 50 (1): 66–83.

"GMB to Avoid 'Beauty Contests.' " 1992. *European Industrial Relations Review* 222 (July): 13.

Goldberg, Arthur J. 1956. *AFL-CIO: Labor United.* New York: McGraw-Hill.

Gouldson, Tim. 1993. "Can. RWDSU Head Says No to Merger." *Labour Times,* July, 1–2.

Grabelsky, Jeffrey, and Richard Hurd. 1994. "Reinventing an Organizing Union: Strategies for Change." In *Proceedings of the Forty-Sixth Annual Meeting of the Industrial Relations Research Association,* pp. 95–104. Madison, Wis.: Industrial Relations Research Association.

"Graphic Union Board Sets Vote on Merger with ITU." 1985. *AFL-CIO News,* February 16, 4.

Green, Francis. 1992. "Recent Trends in British Trade Union Density: How Much of a Compositional Effect?" *British Journal of Industrial Relations* 30 (September): 445–58.

Green, Roy. 1993. "Wage Policy and Wage Determination in 1992." *Journal of Industrial Relation* 35 (March): 142–55.

Greenhouse, Steven. 1995. "A Big Job for Labor." *New York Times,* October 27, A28.

———. 1996a. "Labor Leader Plans Little Steps to Big Economic-Political Goal." *New York Times,* February 16, 18.

———. 1996b. "One Union Label for Old Rivals." *New York Times,* January 3, 49, 54.

Griffin, Gerard. 1992. "Changing Trade Union Structure." In Braham Dabscheck, Gerard Griffin and Julian Teicher, eds., *Contemporary Australian Industrial Relations,* pp. 211–222. Melbourne: Longman Cheshire.

———. 1994. "Re: Extent of Enterprise Bargaining." E-mail message, November 9.

Griffin, Gerard, and Victor Scarcebrook. 1989. "Trends in Mergers of Federally Registered Unions, 1904–1986." *Journal of Industrial Relations* 31 (June): 257–62.

Griffin, Larry J., Holly J. McCammon, and Christopher Botsko. 1990. "The Unmasking of a Movement? The Crisis of U.S. Trade Unions in Comparative Perspective." In Maureen T. Hallinan, David M. Klein, and Jennifer Glass, eds., *Change in Societal Institutions,* pp. 169–94. New York: Plenum Press.

Grills, Walter. 1994. "The Impact of the Employment Contracts Act on Labour Law: Implications for Unions." *New Zealand Journal of Industrial Relations* 19 (1): 85–101.

Gunderson, Morley, and Anil Verma. 1994. "Free Trade and Its Implications for Industrial Relations and Human Resource Management." In M.L. Cook and H.C. Katz, eds., *Regional Integration and Industrial Relations in North America,* pp. 167–79. Ithaca, N.Y.: New York State School of Industrial and Labor Relations, Cornell University.

Hagan, Jim. 1989. "The Australian Union Movement: Context and Perspective, 1850–1987." In Bill Ford and David Plowman, eds., *Australian Unions: An Industrial Relations Perspective,* pp. 18–48. Melbourne: Macmillan.

Hale, Robert M. 1983. "Union Affiliations: Examination of the Governing NLRA Standards." *Detroit College of Law Review* 83 (Summer): 709–42.

Hall, Mark. 1988. "An Uncertain Future for the Unions." *Personnel Management* (September): 33–37.

Hamilton, Reg. 1991. "Promoting Larger Unions: New Amendments to the Federal Industrial Relations Act." *Law Society Journal* 71 (February): 76–79.

Hancke, Bob. 1993. "Trade Union Membership in Europe, 1960–1990: Rediscovering Local Unions." *British Journal of Industrial Relations* 31 (December): 593–613.

Hancock, Keith, and Don Rawson. 1993. "The Metamorphosis of Australian Industrial Relations." *British Journal of Industrial Relations* 31 (December): 489–513.

Harbridge, Raymond. 1993a. "Bargaining and the Employment Contracts Act: An Overview." In Raymond Harbridge, ed., *Employment Contracts: New Zealand Experiences,* pp. 31–52. Wellington, N.Z.: Victoria University Press.

———. 1993b. "Collective Employment Contracts: A Content Analysis." In Raymond Harbridge, ed., *Employment Contracts: New Zealand Experiences,* pp. 70–88. Wellington, N.Z.: Victoria University Press.

———. 1993c. "The Employment Contracts Act: An Assessment of the Impact of the Legislation on Bargaining Arrangements." In Nigel Haworth, Marianne Hill, and Nick Wailes, eds., *Divergent Paths? Industrial Relations in Australia, New Zealand, and the Asia-Pacific Region: Proceedings of the Seventh AIRAANZ Conference,* pp. 214–25. Auckland, N.Z.: Association of Industrial Relations Academics of Australia and New Zealand.

———. 1993d. "New Zealand's Collective Employment Contracts: Update 1992." *New Zealand Journal of Industrial Relations* 18 (1): 113–24.

———. 1994. E-mail message, October 18.

Harbridge, Raymond, and Kevin Hince. 1992a. "A Shift to the 'Right': Legislative Change and Industrial Relations in New Zealand." *Indian Journal of Industrial Relations* 28 (October): 123–38.

———. 1992b. "The Decollectivisation of Industrial Relations in New Zealand: Issues of Union Membership and Structure." In Thomas Kuttner, ed., *The Industrial Relations System: Future Trends and Developments, Proceedings of the XXIXth Conference of the Canadian Industrial Relations Association,* pp. 197–210. Fredericton, N.B.: CIRA.

———. 1993. "Organizing Workers: The Effects of the Act on Union Membership and Organization." In Raymond Harbridge, ed., *Employment Contracts: New Zealand Experiences,* pp. 224–36. Wellington, N.Z.: Victoria University Press.

———. 1994. *A Sourcebook of New Zealand Trade Unions and Employee Organizations.* Wellington, N.Z.: Industrial Relations Centre, Victoria University of Wellington.

Harbridge, Raymond, and Anthony Honeybone. 1995. "External Legitimacy of Unions: Trends in New Zealand." Paper Presented at the Second International Conference on Emerging Union Structures, June 12, Stockholm.

Harbridge, Raymond, Anthony Honeybone, and Peter Kiely. 1994. *Employment Contracts: Bargaining Trends and Employment Law Update: 1993/94.* Wellington, N.Z.: Industrial Relations Centre, Victoria University of Wellington.

Harbridge, Raymond, and James Moulder. 1993. "Collective Bargaining and New Zealand's Employment Contracts Act: One Year On." *The Journal of Industrial Relations* 35 (1): 62–83.

Harbridge, Raymond, and David Rea. 1992. "Collective Bargaining and the Labour Market Flexibility Debate in New Zealand: A Review." *Economic and Labour Relations Review* 3 (June): 126–52.

Hatfield, James E. 1988. "Address of International President." *GMP Horizons* 36 (May): 3–5.

Haworth, Nigel. 1993. "Unions in Crisis: Deregulation and Reform of the New Zealand Union Movement." In Stephen Frenkel, ed., *Organized Labour in the Asia Pacific Region,* pp. 282–305. Ithaca, N.Y.: ILR Press.

"Health Care Union Explores Merger." 1987. *AFL-CIO News,* December 19, 4.

"Health Care Union Explores Plan on SEIU Affiliation." 1988. *AFL-CIO News,* November 11, 8.

Heckscher, Charles C. 1988. *The New Unionism.* New York: Basic Books.

Heritage, Allan J. 1986a. "Pursuit of Merger Costly, Why Desperation Now?" *Typographical Journal* 189 (August): 5–7.

———. 1986b. "30." *Typographical Journal* 189 (December): 5.

Hilmer, Frederick G., et. al. 1993. *Working Relations: A Fresh Start for Australian Enterprises.* Melbourne: Business Council of Australia.

Hince, Kevin. 1993. "From William Pember Reeves to William Frances Birch: From Conciliation to Contracts." In Raymond Harbridge, ed., *Employment Contracts: New Zealand Experiences,* pp. 7–12. Wellington, N.Z.: Victoria University Press.

Hince, Kevin, and Martin Vranken. 1991. "A Controversial Reform of New Zealand Labour Law: The Employment Contracts Act 1991." *International Labour Review* 130 (4): 475–93.

Hocking, Joyce. 1990. "Union Amalgamations: A Journey From Mythology to Reality." Masters thesis, University of New South Wales, Melbourne.

Hodges, Lucy. 1995. "Union Merger Postponed." *The Times Literary Supplement* (London), February 3, 14.

Holusha, John. 1984. "Canadians Breaking from United Auto Workers." *New York Times,* December 12, A17.

"Hospital Division Dispute Resolved." 1984. *RWDSU Record,* June–July, 3.

House of Commons. 1990. *Parliamentary Debates: Standing Committee D. Employment Bill,* March 27. London: Her Majesty's Stationery Office.

Hunter, Laurie. 1991. "Britain." In Oliver Clarke and John Niland, eds., *Agenda for Change: An International Analysis of Industrial Relations in Transition,* pp. 115–46. London: Allen & Unwin.

Hurd, Richard W. 1995. "Contesting the Dinosaur Image—The Labor Movement's Search for a Future." Ithaca, N.Y.: New York State School of Industrial and Labor Relations, Cornell University. Mimeo.

Hyman, Richard. 1994. "Industrial Relations in Western Europe: An Era of Ambiguity." *Industrial Relations* 33 (January): 1–24.

"Independent Joins CWA." 1992. *Compensation and Working Conditions* 44 (May): 29.

Industrial Relations in the 1990s: Proposals For Further Reform of Industrial Relations and Trade Union Law. 1991. London: Her Majesty's Stationery Office.

International Brotherhood of Electrical Workers et al. 1991. Canada Labour Relations Board Decision No. 893, September 20.

"Irreversible Decline in Industrial Relations System Linked to Structural Change." 1992. *IRS Employment Trends* 525 (December): 4–13.

"ITU Council Agrees to Merger Plan, Sets Referendum on Joining CWA." 1986. *CWA News,* August, 2.

"ITU Delegates Back Merger Plan." 1986. *AFL-CIO News,* August 23, 5.

"ITU Leader Urges Members to Support Merger Accord." 1985. *AFL-CIO News,* January 19, 4.

"ITU Merger into CWA is Finalized." 1987. *CWA News,* March, 3.

"ITU Rejects Link with Teamsters, Still Seeks Merger." 1985. *Wall Street Journal,* August 29, 12.

"ITU Schedules Referendum on Plan to Merge with CWA." 1986. *AFL-CIO News,* August 2, 2.

"ITU's Leader Appears Defeated in Voting." 1984. *New York Times,* July 27, B11.

"ITU Will Finally Merge." 1986. *Editor and Publisher,* December 6, 16.

James, Colin. 1994. "Growth Spike." *Far Eastern Economic Review* 157 (March 3): 44.

Jamieson, Suzanne. 1992. "Trade Unions in 1991." *Journal of Industrial Relations* 34 (March): 162–69.

——. 1993. "Australian Trade Unions in 1992." *Journal of Industrial Relations* 35 (March): 157–64.

Janus, Charles J. 1978. "Union Mergers in the 1970s: A Look at the Reasons and Results." *Monthly Labor Review* 101 (October): 13–32.

"Judge Bars Teamster, ITU Merger Until U.S. Rules on Election." 1984. *Wall Street Journal,* May 2, 60.

Katz, Harry C. 1993. "The Decentralization of Collective Bargaining: A Literature Review and Comparative Analysis." *Industrial and Labor Relations Review* 47 (October): 3–22.

Keating, Paul J. 1992. "A New Charter for Industrial Relations in Australia: Address of the Prime Minister Hon. Paul J. Keating." Address to the International Industrial Relations Association Ninth World Congress. Sydney, Australia.

Kelly, Diana. 1995. "Trade Unionism in 1994." *Journal of Industrial Relations* 37 (March): 132–47.

Kelly, John. 1990. "British Trade Unionism 1979–89: Change, Continuity and Contradictions." *Work, Employment and Society* 4 (May): 29–65.

Kelly, John, and Ray Richardson. 1989. "Annual Review Article 1988." *British Journal of Industrial Relations* 27 (March): 133–54.

Kenyon, Peter, and Philip E. T. Lewis. 1993. "Union Membership and the Legal and Institutional Environment: Labour Market Policy in Australia and the United Kingdom." *Australian Economic Review* 102 (April–June): 48–60.

Kerslake, David, 1995. Personal correspondence with attachments A–D, January.

Kilborn, Peter T. 1992. "A Disrupting Change Hits Workers after Recession." *New York Times,* December 26, 1.

——. 1995a. "Prospective Labor Leaders Set to Turn to Confrontation." *New York Times,* October 25, A1.

——. 1995b. "Three Big Unions Are Set to Merge, Creating a Giant." *New York Times,* July 28, A1.

"Kirkland Discusses Issues Facing Labor." 1985. *AFL-CIO News,* April 6, 2.

"Kirkland Lauds ITU Efforts to Repel Teamster Takeover." 1985. *AFL-CIO News,* June 29, 5.

Kleeman, Janet. 1986. "Implications of the National Labor Relations Board's New Standard for Union Affiliation Elections." *Labor Law Journal* 37 (February): 75–93.

Kochan, Thomas A. 1989. "Looking at the Year 2000: Challenges for Industrial Relations and Human Resource Management." Working Paper No. 2108–8999-BPS, Sloan School of Management, Massachusetts Institute of Technology, Cambridge, Mass. Mimeo.

Kochan, Thomas A., Harry C. Katz, and Robert B. McKersie. 1986. *The Transformation of American Industrial Relations.* New York: Basic Books.

Kochan, Thomas A., and Anil Verma. 1992. "A Comparative View of United States and Canadian Industrial Relations: A Strategic Choice Perspective." In Alan Gladstone et al., eds., *Labor Relations in a Changing Environment,* pp. 188–201. Berlin: deGruyter.

Kochan, Thomas A. and Marc Weinstein. 1994. "Recent Developments in U.S. Industrial Relations." *British Journal of Industrial Relations* 32 (December): 483–504.

Kochan, Thomas A., and Kirsten R. Wever. 1991. "American Unions and the Future of Worker Representation." In George Strauss, Daniel G. Gallagher and Jack Fiorito, eds., *The State of the Unions,* pp. 363–86. Madison, Wis: Industrial Relations Research Association.

Kollmorgen, Stuart, and Richard Naughton. 1991. "Change from Within: Reforming Trade Union Coverage and Structure." *Journal of Industrial Relations* 33 (September): 369–94.

Kopeck, Thomas W. 1986. "Merger Ball Fumbled Near Goal Line." *Typographical Journal* 189 (August): 4.

Kumar, Pradeep. 1993. *From Uniformity to Divergence: Industrial Relations in Canada and the United States.* Kingston, Ont.: IRC Press, Queen's University.

Kumar, Pradeep, and Mary Lou Coates. 1991. *Industrial Relations in 1991: Trends and Emerging Issues.* Kingston, Ont.: IRC Press, Queen's University.

Kyloh, Robert H. 1989. "Flexibility and Structural Adjustment through Consensus: Some Lessons from Australia." *International Labour Review* 128 (1): 103–23.

Labour Canada. Various years. *Directory of Labour Organizations in Canada.* Ottawa: Supply and Services Canada.

——. 1993. "Social Contracts: An Added Feature to Collective Bargaining." *Collective Bargaining Review* (May): 75–76.

"Labor Letter." 1984. *Wall Street Journal,* November 27, 1.

"Labor Letter." 1991. *Wall Street Journal,* February 26, 1.

"Labor Ousted in Australia after Ruling for 13 Years." *New York Times,* March 3, A4.

Labour Law Casebook Group. 1991. *Labour Law.* Kingston, Ont.: Queen's University Industrial Relations Centre.

Lakey, Jack. 1996. "Day 2: Labor Turns Up Heat." *Toronto Star* February 25, A1.

"LCUC Power Base Losses at CLRB." 1989. *CUPW Perspective,* 19 (October–November): 1.

"LCUC 'Power Base' Undermines Negotiations." 1989. *CUPW Perspective*, November 1989, 1.

"Letter Carriers Union Fails Again." 1995. *Vancouver Sun*, February 16, D3.

Letter Carriers Union of Canada et al. 1990. Canada Labour Relations Board Decision No. 818 (August 7).

Lieberman, Myron. 1993. "Merger of the NEA and AFT, Prospects and Consequences." *Government Union Review* 14 (Summer): 1–39.

Lipset, Seymour Martin. 1995. "Trade Union Exceptionalism: The United States and Canada." *The Annals of the American Academy of Political and Social Science* 538 (March): 115–30.

Lipset, Seymour Martin, Martin Trow, and James Coleman. 1956. *Union Democracy*. New York: Doubleday.

List, Wilfred. 1984. "Typographers New President Fought Merger." *Globe and Mail* (Toronto), August 1, M5.

——. 1985. "Printers Union May Have More Clout after Merger." *Globe and Mail* (Toronto), January 21, B7.

——. 1990. "Free Trade, Privatization Pose Challenges for Labor." *Globe and Mail* (Toronto), January 4, B1.

——. 1992. "Quest for Efficiency Drives Union Mergers." *CL Reports* 56 (2402): 1.

Little, Bruce. 1994. "November Pacts Bring Only 0.1% in Raises." *Globe and Mail* (Toronto), January 20, B1.

Lohr, Steve. 1988. "In Britain, Renewal Labor Unrest." *New York Times*, February 14, F1.

——. 1993. "Big Business in Turmoil." *New York Times*, January 28, A1.

Loney, Bretton. 1989. "Postal Feud Takes New Direction." *Halifax Chronicle*, November 18, A3.

Lord, Beverly. 1994. "Innovative Contracts—Potential Benefits For All." *Chartered Accountants Journal* 73 (June): 63–65.

Lover, John. 1980. "Why Unions Won't Reform." *Management Today* (September): 98.

Ludeke, J. T. 1993. "The Government's New Charter for Industrial Relations in Australia, 1993–1996." *Journal of Industrial Relations* 35 (June): 316–28.

Madden, Richard. 1993. *Trade Union Members, Australia—August 1992*. Canberra: Australian Bureau of Statistics.

Marginson, Paul, and Keith Sisson. 1990. "Single Table Talk." *Personnel Management* (May): 46–49.

Marsh, David. 1992. *The New Politics of Trade Unionism*. Ithaca, N.Y.: ILR Press.

Martin, Roderick. 1992. *Bargaining Power*. Oxford: Clarendon Press.

Martin, Ross. 1989. *Trade Unionism: Purposes and Forms*. Oxford: Clarendon Press.

——. 1992. "The ACTU Congress of 1991." *Labour History* 62 (May): 138–50.

Mason, Bob, and Peter Bain. 1991. "Trade Union Recruitment Strategies: Facing the 1990s." *Industrial Relations Journal* 22 (Spring): 36–45.

——. 1993. "The Determinants of Trade Union Membership in Britain: A Survey of the Literature." *Industrial and Labor Relations Review* 46 (January): 332–51.

Mawhinney, Michele. 1989. "Union Mergers and Small Unions in Canada." Research

Essay Series No. 26, Queen's University Industrial Relations Centre, Kingston, Ontario.

McAndrew, Ian. 1992. "The Structure of Bargaining Under the Employment Contracts Act." *New Zealand Journal of Industrial Relations* 17 (3): 259–83.

McClendon, John A., Jill Kriesky, and Adrienne Eaton. 1995. "Member Support for Union Mergers: An Analysis of an Affiliation Referendum." *Journal of Labor Research* 16 (Winter): 9–23.

McDonald, Charles. 1992. "U.S. Union Membership in Future Decades: A Trade Unionist's Perspective." *Industrial Relations* 31 (Winter): 13–30.

——. 1993. Personal correspondence, June 2.

McIlroy, John. 1992. "Ten Years for the Locust: The TUC in the 1980s." In Derek Cox, ed., *Facing the Future,* pp. 147–94. Nottingham, U.K.: University of Nottingham.

McMichen, Robert S. 1986. "CWA Merger Approved." *Typographical Journal* 189 (December): 3.

McMichen, Robert S., Billy J. Austin, and Bill Boarman. 1986. "Stepping into the Future with CWA." 189 *Typographical Journal* (August): 2–3.

"Meet Australia's Super Unions." 1993. *Industrial Relations and Management Letter* (February): 3–11.

"Membership of Trade Unions in 1980." 1982. *Employment Gazette* (February): 54–56.

"Merged Postal Workers Union Takes Action Against Old Rival." 1989. *Financial Post,* August 11, 5.

Merrick, Neil. 1995. "Unions Press on With Mergers." *People Management* 1 (February): 10.

Metcalf, David. 1991. "British Unions: Dissolution or Resurgence?" *Oxford Review of Economic Policy* 7 (Spring): 18–32.

Meyer, David G., and William M. Cooke. 1993. "U.S. Labor Relations in Transition: Emerging Strategic and Company Performance." *British Journal of Industrial Relations* 31 (December): 531–52.

Miller, Kenneth, and Mairi Steele. 1993. "Employment Legislation: Thatcher and After." *Industrial Relations Journal* 24 (September): 224–35.

Millward, Neil. 1994. *The New Industrial Relations.* London: Policy Studies Institute.

Milne, Seumas. 1990. "Union Urges Service Role on TUC." *Guardian* (London), December 28, 1.

——. 1992. "New Super-Union Faces Challenge." *Guardian* (London), December 17, 3.

Minister for Industrial Relations (Australia). 1993. *1993 Industrial Relations Reforms.* Canberra: Minister for Industrial Relations.

Mitchell, Daniel J. B. 1982. "Recent Union Contract Concessions." *Brookings Papers on Economic Activity* 1: 163–204.

——. 1985. "Shifting Norms in Wage Determination." *Brooking Papers on Economic Activity* 2: 575–609.

——. 1989. "Will Collective Bargaining Outcomes in the 1990s Look Like Those of the 1980s?" *Labor Law Journal* 40 (August): 490–96.

"Money and Power Divide a Union." 1984. *Business Week,* February 20, 33.

Monks, John. 1994. "The Union Response to HRM: Fraud or Opportunity?" *Personnel Management* (September): 42–47.

Moody, Kim. 1995. "Union Merger: Is Bigger Better?" *Labor Notes* 198 (September): 1.

——. 1996. "Activists to Press for Democracy in UAW-IAM-USWA Merger." *Labor Notes* 204 (March): 4, 13–14.

"More Union Mergers." 1991. *European Industrial Relations Review* 205 (February): 10.

Morris, Tim. 1995. "Annual Review Article 1994." *British Journal of Industrial Relations* 33 (March): 117–35.

Moses, Art. 1993. "Three Unions Compete in CBC Vote." *Labour Times,* June, 1–2.

——. 1994. "CAW Follows in CBRT's Nationalist Footsteps." *Labour Times,* April, 3.

"The Mother of All Reformers." 1993. *The Economist,* October 16, 20.

Narisetti, Raju. 1995. "Rubber Workers Approve Merger after USW Agrees to Concessions." *New York Times,* July 5, B2.

National Union of Public Employees. 1993. *NUPE Executive Council Report 1993.* London: NUPE.

"New Moves toward Delegation in Civil Service." 1994. *European Industrial Relations Review* 243 (April): 12.

The Newspaper Guild/Communications Workers of America. 1995. *TNG/CWA: Answers to Your Questions.* Washington, D.C.: TNG/CWA.

"News Union Gets OK to Leave U.S. Union." 1994. *The Spectator* (Hamilton, Ont.), September 30, 1.

"New Zealand." 1994. *OECD Outlook* 55 (June): 102–3.

New Zealand Council of Trade Unions. 1988. *The Need for Change: Challenges for the Trade Union Movement of Today.* Wellington, N.Z.: NZCTU.

——. 1992a. *1992 NZCTU Directory.* Auckland, N.Z.: NZCTU.

——. 1992b. *A Quality Future.* Wellington, N.Z.: NZCTU.

New Zealand Department of Labour. 1981. *Annual Report.* Wellington, N.Z.: Government Printer.

New Zealand Employers' Federation. 1992. *Working Together: Employment Relations in the 1990s.* Wellington, N.Z.: NZEF.

The New Zealand System of Industrial Relations. 1989. Wellington, N.Z.: Industrial Relations Centre, Victoria University of Wellington.

Niland, John R. 1994. "Change and the International Exchange of Ideas." In John R. Niland, Russell D. Lansbury, and Chrissie Verevis, eds., *The Future of Industrial Relations,* pp. 451–71. Thousand Oaks, Calif.: Sage.

Niland, John R., and Keri Spooner. 1991. "Australia." In Oliver Clarke and John Niland, eds., *Agenda for Change: An International Analysis of Industrial Relations in Transition,* pp. 147–63. London: Allen & Irwin.

——. 1992. "Structural Change and Industrial Relations: Australia." In Alan Gladstone et al., eds., *Labour Relations in a Changing Environment,* pp. 215–31. New York: deGruyter.

Nolan, Peter. 1989. "Walking on Water: Performance and Industrial Relations under Thatcher." *Industrial Relations Journal* 20 (Summer): 81–92.

234   REFERENCES

Norton, Erle. 1995. "Steelworkers Union Is Set Back in Bid at AK Steel Plant." *Wall Street Journal,* June 12, B4.

Nulty, Leslie E. 1994. "Retrospective on Collective Bargaining in the 1980s." In *Proceedings of the Forty-Sixth Annual Meeting of the Industrial Relations Research Association,* pp. 541–48. Madison, Wis: Industrial Relations Research Association.

Ogden, Max. 1993. *Towards Best Practice Unionism: The Future of Unions in Australia.* Melbourne: Australian Fabian Society.

"125th TUC Congress." 1993. *European Industrial Relations Review* 237 (October): 12–13.

O'Reilly, David. 1993. "Backroom Rumpies." *The Bulletin,* August 17, 22–23.

Oxenbridge, Sarah. 1996. "New Zealand Unions and the Organization of the Low-Wage Service Sector." Paper presented at the AFL-CIO/Cornell University Research Conference on Organizing. Washington, D.C. Mimeo.

"Packing Union Joins UFCW." 1989. *UFCW Action* 11 (September–October): 5.

"Pact Merging Postal Unions Falls Through." 1988. *Montreal Gazette,* November 14, A5.

Pannick, David. 1994. "End This Affront to Industrial Freedom." *The Times* (London), January 18, 35.

Papp, Leslie. 1991. "Postal Union Backing U.S. Raid." *Toronto Star,* May 27, A20.

——. 1992a. "New Union a Challenge to Established Labor Ranks." *Toronto Star,* November 29, A3.

——. 1992b. "Union Mergers on the Rise." *Calgary Herald,* October 15, F4.

——. 1992c. "Unions Rebuild Clout with a Flurry of Mergers." *Toronto Star,* October 14, A17.

Parks, James B. 1995. "Bridgestone Top Priority for Merged Steelworkers." *AFL-CIO News,* July 17, 6.

Parliamentary Research Service. 1993. *Industrial Relations Reform Bill 1993.* London: Department of the Public Library.

"Parrot Accuses Union of Using Extortion Tactics." 1989. *The Gazette* (Montreal), February 1, B8.

"Parrot Calls on CUPW to End Feud." 1990. *Financial Post,* June 12, 6.

Paul Horsley et al. 1991. Canada Labour Relations Board Decision No. 861 March 26).

Pavy, Gordon R. 1994. "Winning NLRB Elections and Establishing Stable Collective Bargaining Relationships." In Sheldon Friedman, Richard W. Hurd, Rudolph A. Oswald, and Ronald L. Seeber, eds., *Restoring the Promise of American Labor,* pp. 110–21. Ithaca, N.Y.: ILR Press.

"Pay in the Privatized Utilities." 1994. *Bargaining Report* 136 (February): 12–14.

Peetz, David. 1990. "Declining Union Density." *Journal of Industrial Relations* 32 (June): 197–223.

Plowman, David. 1981. *Australian Trade Union Statistics.* Sydney: Industrial Relations Research Center, University of New South Wales.

——. 1992. "Arresting Union Decline: Membership Retention and Recruitment Strategies." In Michael Crosby and Michael Easson, eds., *What Should Unions Do?,* pp. 266–88. Leichhardt, N.S.W., Aus.: Pluto Press.

Plowman, David, and Maryann Street. 1993. "Industrial Relations and Economic Restructuring in Australia and New Zealand: Employers' Agendas.'' In Mark Bray and Nigel Haworth, eds., *Economic Restructuring and Industrial Relations in Australia and New Zealand: A Comparative Analysis,* pp. 91–121. Sydney, Australia: Australian Center for Industrial Relations, University of Sydney.

''Printers to Join with Communications Union.'' 1986. *New York Times,* November 27, A26.

''Printers to Pick Union President.'' 1984. *New York Times,* June 26, A13.

''Printers' Union Rejects a Teamster Merger.'' 1985. *New York Times,* August 29, A21.

''Printing Trades Unions Draft Plan for Merger.'' 1985. *AFL-CIO News,* January 2, 1.

''Printing Unions Cancel Merger Vote.'' 1985. *AFL-CIO News,* March 16, 3.

''Public Sector Pay Bargaining.'' 1994. *European Industrial Relations Review* 249 (October): 12–14.

Rachleff, Peter. 1994. ''A Page from History: Seeds of a Labor Resurgency.'' *The Nation,* February 21, 226–29.

''Rail Labor Leaders Tackle Forced Merger Issues.'' 1989. *BMWE Journal,* March 1, 11.

''Rail Unions Aim for Merger to Thwart Company Pressure.'' 1990. *The Spectator* (Hamilton, Ont.), June 7, A23.

Ray, Randy. 1991. ''Time Running Out for Raiders in their $3-million Campaign to Seize CUPW.'' *Labour Times,* July, 1–2.

———. 1993. ''Trio of Unions Pools Resources to Battle Closures, Deregulation.'' *Labour Times,* January, 5.

''Rebuilding Australia.'' 1992. *Workplace: The ACTU Magazine* 6 (Winter): 24–33.

Rees, Jacqueline. 1993. ''Workplace Revolution.'' *Far Eastern Economic Review,* July 15, 76–77.

Reitano, Robert. 1995. ''Legislative Change in 1994.'' *Journal of Industrial Relations* 37 (March): 84–94.

''Retired Members Not Entitled to Vote in Transfer Ballot.'' 1991. *Industrial Relations Legal Information Bulletin,* April 26, 10–11.

Richardson, Valerie. 1993. ''NEA to Set Merger Talks with Rival Union.'' *Washington Times,* July 3, A6.

Riddell, W. Craig. 1993. ''Unionization in Canada and the United States.'' In David Card and Richard B. Freeman, eds., *Small Differences That Matter: Labor Markets and Income Maintenance in Canada and the United States,* pp. 109–47. Chicago: University of Chicago Press.

''The Road to Recognition: BIFU and the North of England Building Society.'' 1994. *IRS Employment Trends,* January, 13–16.

Robinson, Ian. 1992. *Organizing Labour: The Moral Economy of Canadian American Union Density Divergence, 1963–1986.* Kingston, Ont.: Queen's University Industrial Relations Centre.

———. 1994. ''Social Unionism, and Labour Movement Power in Canada and the United States.'' *Relations Industrielles–Industrial Relations* 49 (4): 657–95.

Roper, Brian. 1993. ''The End of the Golden Weather: New Zealand's Economic Crisis.'' In Brian Roper and Chris Rudd, eds., *State and Economy in New Zealand,* pp. 1–25. Auckland, N.Z.: Oxford University Press.

Rose, Joseph B., and Gary N. Chaison. 1990a. ''Fortune and Misfortune: Union

Growth in Canada and the United States.'' In *Proceedings of the Forty-Second Annual Meeting of the Industrial Relations Research Association,* pp. 585–93. Madison, Wis.:IRRA.

——. 1990b. "New Measures of Union Organizing Effectiveness." *Industrial Relations* 3 (Fall): 457–68.

——. 1992. "Union Density and Union Effectiveness: The North American Experience." Paper presented at the Ninth World Congress of the International Industrial Relations Association, Sydney, Australia.

——. 1996. "Linking Union Density and Union Effectiveness: The North American Experience." *Industrial Relations* 35 (January): 78–105.

Rose, Robert L., Nicole M. Christian, and Asra Q. Nomani. 1995. "Union Merger Sounds Painless, but It Won't Be." *Wall Street Journal,* July 28, B1–B2.

Ross, Jain, and Richard Johnstone. 1991. "Recent Legislation: Industrial Relations Legislation Amendment Acts 1990 (6th)." *Australian Journal of Labour Law* 4 (August): 171–87.

Royal Commission on Trade Unions and Employers' Associations. 1969. *Report: 1969.* London: Her Majesty's Stationery Office.

"Rubber Workers Ends Strike." 1995. *Monthly Labor Review* 118 (August): 73.

Rubenfeld, Steven. 1983. "Today's Contract Concession: Tomorrow's Impact." Working Paper No. 83-6. School of Business and Economics, University of Minnesota/Duluth, Duluth, Minn.

Rusk, James. 1995. "Ontario Unions Target London for Shutdown." *Globe and Mail* (Toronto), November 14, A3.

——. 1996. "Tories Undeterred by Labour Protest." *Globe and Mail* (Toronto), February 26, A4, A14.

Schenk, Christopher, and Elaine Bernard. 1992. "Social Unionism: Labor as a Political Force." *Social Policy* 23 (Summer): 38–46.

Schlossberg, Stephen I. and Judith A. Scott. 1991. *Organizing and the Law.* 4th ed. Washington, D.C.: Bureau of National Affairs.

Scotland, Randall. 1995. "Struggling Unions Cast a Wider Net." *Financial Post,* July 29, 8.

Service Employees International Union. 1990. "Memo Re: SEIU Affiliations and Mergers," May 11. Washington, D.C.: SEIU. Mimeo.

——. 1993. "Service Employees International Union Affiliations Since 1970 (November)." Washington, D.C.: SEIU. Mimeo.

——. n.d. (a). "Resolution 32: Organizing." Washington, D.C.: SEIU. Mimeo.

——. n.d. (b). *SEIU: Putting the Power of Diversity to Work.* Washington, D.C.: SEIU.

——. n.d. (c). *SEIU: Straight Talk About Affiliation—Prepared for the San Francisco Police Officers Association.* Washington, D.C.: SEIU.

"Seven Railway Unions Ordered to Merge." 1992. *Globe and Mail* (Toronto), July 14, B12.

Shabecoff, Philip. 1980. "Big Labor, Little Labor." *New York Times,* May 11, 19.

Sherman, Barrie D. 1986. *The State of the Unions.* Chichester, U.K.: Wiley & Sons.

Shostak, Arthur B. 1991. *Robust Unionism.* Ithaca, N.Y.: ILR Press.

——. 1994. "America's Labor Movement: Sociological Models and Futuristic Scenarios." In *Proceedings of the Spring Meeting of the Industrial Relations Research Association*, pp. 511–517. Madison, Wis.: IRRA.

Silverstone, Brian, and Bridget Daldy. 1993. "Recent Labour Market and Industrial Relations Experience in New Zealand." *Australian Economic Review* 104 (4th Quarter): 17–22.

Simpson, Bob. 1993. "Individualism versus Collectivism: An Evaluation of Section 14 of the Trade Union Reform and Employment Rights Act 1993." *Industrial Law Journal* 22 (September): 181–93.

Simpson, D. H. 1972. "An Analysis of the Size of Trade Unions." *British Journal of Industrial Relations* 10 (November): 382–91.

"Single-Union Deals Examined." 1993. *European Industrial Relations Review* 235 (August): 22–27.

"Single-Union Deals in Perspective." 1992. *IRS Employment Trends* 523 (November): 6–15.

Sleemi, Fehmida. 1995. "Collective Bargaining Outlook for 1995." *Monthly Labor Review* 118 (January): 3–22.

Sloan, Judith. 1992. "Until the End of Time: Labour Market Reform in Australia." *Australian Economic Review* 100 (4th Quarter): 65–77.

Sloane, Leonard. 1995. "The Two Big Apparel Unions to Outline a Merger Today." *New York Times,* February 20, D1.

Slotnick, Lorne. 1987a. "Canadian Attitude Worries Union." *Globe and Mail* (Toronto), January 17, A9.

———. 1987b. "Food Workers' Union Grapples with Autonomy." *Globe and Mail* (Toronto), January 27, A14.

———. 1987c. "Image Problem: White's Reputation Is Taking a Beating As His Union Grows." *Globe and Mail* (Toronto), March 25, A1–A2.

———. 1987d. "Key Leaders of Union Want Full Autonomy for Canadian Section." *Globe and Mail* (Toronto), January 6, A1.

———. 1987e. "Union Takeover Condemned." *Globe and Mail* (Toronto), January 16, A11.

———. 1987f. "Union Vows Fight Over Loss of Fishermen." *Globe and Mail* (Toronto), March 18, A12.

———. 1987g. "U.S.-Based Parent Imposes Trusteeship on Fishermen's Union." *Globe and Mail* (Toronto), April 23, A8.

———. 1987h. "White Reprimanded Over Raiding by CAW." *Globe and Mail* (Toronto), July 23, A1.

———. 1987i. "Won't Move on Autonomy Call, U.S. Based Union Leadership Says." *Globe and Mail* (Toronto), January 29, A15.

———. 1988a. "Biggest Postal Unions Will Bargain as a Unit for 45,000 Workers." *Globe and Mail* (Toronto), February 12, A1.

———. 1988b. "CLC Approves Reforms to Halt Union Raiding." *Globe and Mail* (Toronto), May 10, A1–A2.

———. 1988c. "Huge, Merged Union Would Carry Big Clout, Union Delegates Told." *Globe and Mail* (Toronto), April 20, A14.

———. 1988d. " 'No Holds Barred' As Postal Unions Battle to the Death." *Globe and Mail* (Toronto), November 21, A8.

——. 1988e. "Postal Union Leaders Face Vote." *Globe and Mail* (Toronto), November 8, A15.

——. 1988f. "Postal Unions to Negotiate as Single Unit." *Globe and Mail* (Toronto), February 12, A1–A2.

——. 1988g. "Three Postal Unions Set to Merge as 'Super-union.' " *Globe and Mail* (Toronto), September 26, A1.

——. 1988h. "Two Unions at Post Office Arrive at Pact for Merger." *Globe and Mail* (Toronto), November 11, A1.

——. 1989a. "Both Sides Confident of Victory as Postal Unions Wait for Count." *Globe and Mail* (Toronto), January 14, 1.

——. 1989b. "Parrot's Union is the Winner in Postal Vote." *Globe and Mail* (Toronto), January 18, A1–A2.

"Small Unions Happy to Fight On." 1992. *Labour Research* 81 (May): 15–16.

Smith, Anna. 1994. "Where Have All the Workers Gone?" *Management* 41 (April): 86–87.

Smith, G. R. 1994. "Industrial Relations in Australia: A Break from the Past." Paper presented at the Annual Meeting of the British Universities Industrial Relations Association, Worcester College, Oxford University.

Smith, Paul, and Gary Morton. 1993. "Union Exclusion and the Decollectivization of Industrial Relations in Contemporary Britain." *British Journal of Industrial Relations* 31 (March): 98–114.

——. 1994. "Union Exclusion—Next Steps." *Industrial Relations Journal* 25 (September):3–14.

Snape, Ed. 1994. "Reversing the Decline? The TGWU's Link Up Campaign." *Industrial Relations Journal* 25 (September): 222–31.

Snape, Ed, and Greg Bamber. 1989. "Managerial and Professional Employees: Conceptualizing Union Strategies and Structures." *British Journal of Industrial Relations* 27 (March): 93–107.

Soskice, David. 1984. "Industrial Relations and the British Economy." *Industrial Relations* 23 (Fall): 306–22.

Spencer, Bruce. 1993. "Workplace Union Organization into the 1990s: Experience from the U.K." In Thomas Kuttner, ed., *The Industrial Relations Systems: Future Trends and Developments: Proceedings of the XXIXth Conference of the Canadian Industrial Relations Association,* pp. 519–33. Federicton, N.B.: CIRA.

Statistics Canada. Various years. *Annual Report of the Minister of Industry, Science and Technology under the Corporations and Labour Unions Returns Act, Part II—Labour Unions.* Ottawa: Supply and Services Canada.

Statistics New Zealand. 1994. *Labour Market Statistics, 1993.* Wellington, N.Z.: Statistics New Zealand.

——. 1995. *Key Statistics (January/February).* Wellington, N.Z.: Statistics New Zealand.

Stevenson, Richard W. 1995. "Smitten by Britain, Business Rushes In." *New York Times,* October 15, F1.

Stewart, Andrew. 1989. "The Industrial Relations Act 1988: The More Things Change . . ." *Australian Business Law Review* (April): 103–25.

Storey, John, and Keith Sisson. 1993. *Managing Human Resources and Industrial Relations*. Buckingham, U.K.: Open University Press.

Stratton, Kay. 1989. "Union Democracy in the International Typographical Union: Thirty Years Later." *Journal of Labor Research* 11 (Winter): 119–34.

Stratton-Devine, Kay. 1990. "Inter-organizational Relationships Among U.S. Labor Unions: Mergers and Affiliations." In *Proceedings of the 42nd Annual Meeting of the Industrial Relations* Research Association, pp. 155–68. Madison, Wis.: IRRA.

——. 1992. "Union Merger Benefits: An Empirical Analysis." *Journal of Labor Research* 13 (Winter): 133–43.

Strauss, George. 1993. "Issues in Union Structure." In S. Bacharach, R. Seeber, and D. Walsh, eds., *Research in the Sociology of Organizations*, pp. 1–49. Greenwich, Conn.: JAI Press.

Stricharchuk, Gregory. 1985. "Tying the Knot: With Ranks Thinning, Unions Seek Mergers to Retain Their Clout." *Wall Street Journal*, January 18, 1.

Sullivan, Deana Stokes. 1991. "Richard Cashin: Head of Fishermen's Union Counters the Romantic." *Labour Times*, July, 8.

Swabe, Anthony. 1990. "Recent Developments in Collective Bargaining—Implications for the 1990s." *Federation News*, May, 7–13.

Swoboda, Frank. 1995. "Three Merging Unions Invite Others to Join." *Washington Post*, July 28, C2.

Szekely, Peter. 1995. "Two Major Garment Unions Sew Up Merger Deal." Reuters press release, February 20.

"Talks Advance on Merger of Printers Into Teamsters Union." 1984. *New York Times*, February 21, A19.

"Teachers' Unions Interrupt Merger Talks." 1994. *Washington Post*, December 23, A6.

"Teamsters Score Major Victories Among Former ITU Locals." 1987. *The International Teamster*, January, 28–29.

Tedesco, Theresa. 1985. "Merger Option Unacceptable to ITU Locals." *Globe and Mail* (Toronto), June 26, M6.

Thatcher, Margaret. 1993. *The Downing Street Years*. New York: Harper Collins.

"The Thatcher Record." 1992. *The Economist*, November 24, 17–20.

"Think-Tank Forecasts 2 M Fall in Membership." 1993. *The Times* (London), September 6, 2.

Thompson, Mark. 1991. "Plus ça change? Canadian Industrial Relations in the 1980s." *Bulletin of Comparative Labour Relations* 21: 65–84.

——. 1992. "The Industrial Relations Impact of Privatization and Contracting Out: Evidence from British Columbia." In Thomas Kuttner, ed., *The Industrial Relations System: Future Trends and Developments, Proceedings of the XXIXth Conference of the Canadian Industrial Relations Association*, pp. 633–645. Charlotte, Prince Edward Island: CIRA.

——. 1994. "Current Developments in Canadian Industrial Relations." In M. L. Cook and H. C. Katz, eds., *Regional Integration and Industrial Relations in North America*," pp. 37–51. Ithaca, N.Y.: New York State School of Industrial and Labor Relations, Cornell University.

Thompson, Mark, and Albert A. Blum. 1983. "International Unionism in Canada: The Move to Local Control." *Industrial Relations* 22 (Winter): 71–86.

Tieman, Ross. 1991. "Unions Link to Reshape Industry." *The Times* (London), December 18, 21.

———. 1993a. "Union Merger Brings Concentrated Power." *The Times* (London), March 5, 1.

———. 1993b. "Willis Braces Himself to Address the Perilous State of the Union." *The Times* (London), September 4, 19.

Tingley, Darrell W. 1990. "One Year Later." *CUPW Perspective,* January–February, 2.

"Toward a Public Service Super-union." 1991. *Labour Research* (May): 15–16.

Towers, Brian. 1989. "Running the Gauntlet: British Trade Union Under Thatcher, 1979–1988." *Industrial and Labor Relations Review* 42 (January): 163–88.

Trades Union Congress. 1988. *First Report of the Special Review Body.* London: TUC.

———. 1989. *Organizing for the 1990s: The SRB's Second Report.* London: TUC.

———. 1992. *British Manufacturing Industry and The World Economy: An Assessment of National Performance.* London: TUC.

———. 1993a. "Submission to House of Commons' Employment Committee." London: TUC. Mimeo.

———. 1993b. *TUC Disputes Principles and Procedures.* London: TUC.

———. 1993c. *Report of the 124th Annual Trades Union Congress, 1992.* London: TUC.

"Trade Union Mergers: Uniting for Strength." 1982 *Labour Research* (May): 110–11.

"Trade Unions: Big Brothers." 1993. *The Economist,* July 3, 54.

Troy, Leo, and Neil Sheflin. 1985. *Union Sourcebook: Membership, Structure, Finance, Directory.* West Orange, N.J.: Industrial Relations Data and Information Services.

"TUC Membership Figures." 1992. *European Industrial Relations Review* 222 (July): 13.

Turner, H. A. 1964. "British Union Structure: A New Approach." *British Journal of Industrial Relations* 2: 165–81.

Turner, Lowell. 1991. *Democracy at Work: Changing World Markets and the Future of Labor Unions.* Ithaca, N.Y.: Cornell University Press.

"Two Unions at Post Office Arrive at Pact for Merger." 1989. *Globe and Mail* (Toronto), November 7, A1–A2.

Uchitelle, Louis. 1994. "Job Losses Don't Let Up Even As Hard Times Ease." *New York Times,* January 22, 1.

Undy, Roger, et al. 1981. *Change in Trade Unions.* London: Hutchinsons.

"Union Amalgamations—March 1989 to October 1994." 1994. *Workforce* 1008: 3–6.

"Union Derecognition and Personal Contracts." 1994. *European Industrial Relations Review* 245 (June): 24.

"Union Lifts Trusteeship of B.C. Local." 1987. *Globe and Mail* (Toronto), January 20, A14.

"Union Membership, 1992." 1993. *Compensation and Working Conditions* 45 (February): 21–26.

"Union Merger Moves." 1989. *European Industrial Relations Report* 185 (June): 20–21.

"Union Mergers." 1983. *Industrial Relations Review and Report* 300 (July 26): 2–8.

"Union Mergers." 1992. *European Industrial Relations Review* 219 (April): 11.

"Union Mergers: For Growth or Survival?" 1992. *IRS Employment Trends* 508 (March): 12–15.

"Union Rationalisation." 1990. *ACTU Bulletin,* July, 22–27.

"Unions Agree on New Regulations about Raiding in Stormy Session." 1988. *The Spectator* (Hamilton, Ont.), May 10, A8.

"Unions: Merger Mania?" 1990. *Labour Research* 79 (June): 9–11.

"Unions Race to Merge." 1991. *IRS Employment Trends,* May 10, 2.

"Union Vows to Defend Wages." 1990. *Metal Workers* 11 (August): 1–2.

Unison. 1993. *Unison Rules (As at Vesting Day 1993).* London: Unison.

"Unison Ballot Complaint Fails." 1993. *Industrial Relations Law Bulletin* 477 (July): 12–13.

United Brotherhood of Carpenters and Joiners of America. 1979. *Agreement of Affiliation.* Washington D.C.: UBCJA.

United Electrical, Radio and Machine Workers v. NLRB (Newell Porcelain Co.) 1993. CA4, No. 92–1791 (February 12).

United Food and Commercial Workers. 1993. "Independent Union Affiliations with UFCW, 1985–1993." Washington, D.C.: UFCW. Mimeo.

"United Kingdom: More 'Step-by-Step' Industrial Relations Reform." 1993. *International Labour Review* 132 (5): 559–67.

"United Kingdom: Union Mergers." 1992. *European Industrial Relations Review* 219 (April): 11.

United States Department of Labor. 1981. *Earnings and Other Characteristics of Organized Workers, May 1980.* Bulletin 2105. Washington D.C.: U.S. Government Printing Office.

——. 1995. *News: Union Members in 1994.* Washington, D.C.: U.S. Government Printing Office.

"A United Voice Gains Recognition." 1994. *Workplace: The ACTU Magazine* (Spring): 28–33.

Upham, Martin. 1993. *Trade Unions and Employers Associations of the World, (Release 1).* London: Longman.

Uren, David. 1993. "New Zealand's Act of Faith." *BRW International* 3 (November): 24–27.

Van Alphen, Tony. 1995. "Hargrove Touts New Union for Metal Workers." *Toronto Star,* July 31, A4.

Visser, Jelle. 1989. *European Trade Unions in Figures.* Deventer, Netherlands: Kluwer.

Waddington, Jeremy. 1992. "Trade Union Mergers." In Derek Cox, ed., *Facing the Future,* pp. 105–146. Nottingham, U.K.: University of Nottingham, 1992.

——. 1995. *The Politics of Bargaining: The Merger Process and British Trade Union Structural Development 1892–1987.* London: Mansell.

Waddington, Jeremy, and Colin Whitston. 1994. "The Politics of Restructuring: Trade Unions on the Defensive in Britain Since 1979." *Relations Industrielles–Industrial Relations* 49 (4): 794–819.

Wallace, Michael. 1985. "Responding to Technological Change in the Newspaper Industry: A Comparison of the United States, Great Britain, and the Federal Republic of Germany." In *Proceedings of the Thirty-Seventh Annual Meeting of the Industrial Relations Research Association,* pp. 325–32. Madison, Wis.: Industrial Relations Research Association.

Walsh, Louise D. 1985. "A Study of the Proposed Merger of the International Typographical Union and the Newspaper Guild." Master's thesis, Cornell University, Ithaca, N.Y.

Walsh, Pat. 1993. "The State and Industrial Relations in New Zealand." In Brian Roper and Chris Rudd, eds., *State and Economy in New Zealand,* pp. 172–91. Auckland, N.Z.: Oxford University Press.

Walsh, Pat, and Rose Ryan. 1993. "The Making of the Employment Contracts Act." In Raymond Harbridge, ed., *Employment Contracts: New Zealand Experiences,* pp. 13–30. Wellington, N.Z.: Victoria University Press.

Way, Nicholas. 1993. "State Labor Bodies Past Their Peak." *Business Review Weekly,* June 11, 66–69.

Weinberg, Paul. 1991. "Battle Royal Shaping Up Over CBC Jurisdiction." *Labour Times,* May, 4.

Weinstein, Michael M. 1995. "Can Merger Save the Unions?" *New York Times,* July 31, A12.

Wheal, Chris. 1992. "When Union Officials Get the Urge to Merge." *The Engineer,* September 17, 18.

"Where Are the Super-Unions?" 1992. *Labour Research* 82 (September): 9–10.

Williamson, Lisa. 1993. "Collective Bargaining in 1993: Jobs Are the Issue." *Monthly Labor Review* 116 (January): 3–18.

———. 1995. "Union Mergers: 1985–1994 Update." *Monthly Labor Review* 118 (February): 18–25.

Willman, Paul. 1989. "The Logic of 'Market Share' Trade Unionism: Is Membership Decline Inevitable?" *Industrial Relations Journal* 20 (Winter): 260–70.

Willman, Paul, and Alan Cave. 1994. "The Union of the Future: Super-Unions or Joint Ventures." *British Journal of Industrial Relations* 32 (September): 395–417.

Willman, Paul, Timothy Morris, and Beverly Aston. 1993. *Union Business: Trade Union Organization and Financial Reform in the Thatcher Years.* Cambridge, Eng.: Cambridge University Press.

Windmuller, John P. 1981. "Concentration Trends in Union Structure: An International Comparison." *Industrial and Labor Relations Review* 35 (October): 43–57.

Wooden, Mark, and Jeffrey Balchin. 1993. "Unionization in Australia: Evidence from the AWIRS." *The Economic Record* 69 (September): 305–14.

Wooding, Paul. 1993. "New Zealand and the International Economy." In Brian Roper and Chris Rudd, eds., *State and Economy in New Zealand,* pp. 91–107. Auckland, N.Z.: Oxford University Press.

Wren, Cristopher S. 1995. "Canadian Dollar Buoyed by Quebec Vote." *New York Times,* November 1, A8.

"Writers' Bloc: National Writers Union Votes to Join the UAW." 1991. *Solidarity* 34 (October): 22.

Ybarra, Michael J. 1994. "Waxing Dramatic: Janitors' Union Uses Pressure and Theatrics to Expand Its Ranks." *Wall Street Journal,* March 24, A1.

Zwolinski, Mark. 1993. "TTC Local Mass Meeting to Consider Job Action." *The Star* (Toronto), July 11, A4.

Index